There is no need for the tourist of today to feel embarrassed. What was Marco Polo but a tourist? What are we but men and women driven by that same curiosity—the same urge to see the wonders of the world.

WEST
WITH THE
SUN

By STUART CLOETE

is a brilliantly written and unique journal of a voyage around the world on a freighter which the author and his wife recently completed.

Stopping at Manila, Hong Kong, Thailand, Vietnam, Java, Malaya, Singapore, Ethiopia, and Egypt, the Cloetes not only saw a great slice of the Far East but observed the mores, studied the political situations, and met the people.

No ordinary traveler nor ordinary reporter, Stuart Cloete describes the beauty of the sea and the jungle, the animals and the birds, the temples, the jewels, spices—everything that makes these locales the exotic splendors they are. In addition, there is an appendix listing a breakdown on the cost of such a trip ($5,000 for four and a half months including $500 worth

(continued on back flap)

Books by Stuart Cloete

West with the Sun
The Fiercest Heart
The Mask
African Giant
Congo Song
The Turning Wheels
Watch for the Dawn
Mamba
The Hill of Doves
African Portraits
The Curve and the Tusk
Gazella
The Soldiers' Peaches
Yesterday Is Dead
The Third Way

Stuart Cloete

WEST WITH
THE SUN

DOUBLEDAY & COMPANY, INC.
GARDEN CITY, NEW YORK
1962

Library of Congress Catalog Card Number 62-7614

Copyright © 1962 Stuart Cloete

Printed in the United States of America

To

TINY

We wish to express our thanks to the Fern-Ville Lines, Captain Gunnar K. Bergan, and Mr. Ole Niklegaard for their help, and all the other officers, men, and young ladies of the ship's company for a very pleasant and wonderful voyage around the world.

Also to Jerry and Monica Chiole, Mr. and Mrs. Lim, Mr. Liew, Dr. and Mrs. Duguid, Mrs. Betty Olsen, Mr. Udom, Mr. Liek, Mr. Robert Fasson, Mr. Tommy Teng, Mr. Johnnie Chic, Mr. and Mrs. Frank Chao, and Mr. J. Hegan, and the other passengers with whom we shared this experience.

CONTENTS

10   *Contents*

28,300 Miles by Freighter

from

New Orleans to New York

via

the Panama Canal, San Pedro, Manila, Hong Kong, Saigon,
Bangkok, Singapore, Jacarta, Surabaya, Semarang, Port
Swettenham, Kuala Lumpur, Penang, Galle, Assab, Suez, the
Suez Canal, and Cairo.

INTRODUCTION

This is the story of a journey around the world by freighter, following the sinking sun, never catching up, but facing each night into the sunset and rising each day with the sun astern.

Following ancient sea routes, picking up and dropping cargoes the way they have been picked up and dropped for thousands of years by our predecessors. Picking up fruits, hides, minerals, spices—agricultural products of all kinds in exchange for manufactured goods. Sailing seas that, had they been land, would have been sunken roads worn low by the keels that have traversed them.

Taking sights from the same stars, sailing under the same moon, and seeking the same rewards as the sailors of the past.

There is no need for the tourist of today to feel embarrassed. What was Marco Polo but a tourist? What are we but men and women driven by that same curiosity—the same urge to see the wonders of the world.

THE METROPOLIS

One

THE IDEA—THE TELEPHONE CALL—HEAVY LUG-
GAGE—CHAOS ON BOARD—SCANDINAVIAN BLONDES
—WINE AND WHISKEY—THE APPLE-GREEN STATUE
—HAVANA AND THE CONGO—WHAT IS A TOUR-
IST?—THE MADNESS OF SUN BATHING—HOW TO
WATCH PEOPLE AND ANIMALS—CHRISTMAS PREP-
ARATIONS

At ten o'clock on Tuesday we got a call from the shipping line saying our heavy luggage—two suitcases of clothes
and a box of books—had to be on board the *Pleasantville* by
ten-thirty Wednesday morning. The voice—it was female—
then told us that the *Pleasantville* was at the Barber Line
dock on Pier 19, on Staten Island.

A short era of hysteria and panic ensued, but three
hours later Tiny had everything packed. At nine o'clock on
Wednesday morning when we left the hotel, our trip around
the world had begun, although we had to return to the hotel,
stay in New York for another three weeks, and then go to
New Orleans by rail to pick up the ship. But all this was
nothing. Our minds were projected into the Far East. We
were no longer here. Nor, of course, were we there, but lost
in a kind of imaginative limbo where the memory of other
ships was superimposed on our daily life of getting shots, seeing the dentist, lunching and dining with friends to say
good-by, and all the other activities of this great city that are
so often described as a rat race.

Perhaps in reality the trip began years ago, not only this

one but all the others we have ever made, when, as children, we heard such mystic place names as Hong Kong, Manila, Colombo or Bangkok, Malacca, Zanzibar, and Lagos mentioned by the grownups whose legs and skirts surrounded us like a jungle in those early years. Perhaps all trips anywhere by anyone begin when a child first breaks bounds, opens the door whose handle it can suddenly reach, slips down the garden path through a gap in the fence into the bright new world of something "I have never seen before"—an Alice Through the Looking-Glass world of wonders and excitement.

Perhaps the desire to travel is a natural instinct, for without it men would have stayed put, only moving beyond the narrow valleys where they lived when forced out by hunger, the failure of their hunting, the exhaustion of their hunting grounds, pastures, or tilled fields. There seem always to have been two kinds of people—the many who are prepared to stay at home and the others, those of the itching foot, the men who want to see what things are like on the other side of the river, or over the range of mountains that lies like a blue scarf along the horizon's edge. The fields there may be no greener, the hunting no better, but they may be different. Perhaps it is this difference that we all seek; and begin to find in the smell of the air on the docks, in the wheeling of the screaming gulls. In the forest of masts and booms, the panoply of flags, the colors of smokestacks—all lipstick bright, if one can imagine green, blue, and yellow lipsticks. In the strange new smells of the warehouses on the wharves.

Going on board the *Pleasantville,* we passed bags of cocoa, from Ghana, copra in sacks, bales of rubber. Some, cut open as samples, looked like Swiss cheese. They had the same color and consistency. On our left were ingots of tin from Malaya, on our right bales of sisal. Men swarmed like ants over this accumulation of produce that had reached here from every corner of the globe. Spun out like the web of a spider, sea lanes reach out from every seaport; along them outward bound flow our manufactured goods and back come the raw materials, the basis of so much we use in their finished state, without ever thinking of where they came from or how they were produced.

On board ship the apparent chaos increased. Young blond Norwegian sailors were dragging ropes, carrying cartons, sweeping the decks, engaged in a thousand to us inexplicable tasks that have to be done before a ship can sail.

We found the first mate and he found two seamen who collected our stuff and put it into our cabin, which was still in a state of disorder, the beds unmade, almost warm from the last passengers who had only just left the ship. The stewardess, also blond, was much upset, thinking that we were going to stay on board. Having reassured her, we looked for the chief steward and inquired about the possibility of obtaining drinks. He had the essentials—whiskey, gin, and vermouth. He had no wine, so we said we would send some wine on board at New Orleans.

With that we left our future home, scrambled down the gangway, and returned past the rubber, cocoa, sisal, and copra to our waiting taxi. Our heavy gear was on board and a month later we would join it.

Manhattan looked very beautiful as the ferry approached it. The Statue of Liberty, apple green on her pediment, seemed to smile her welcome to all travelers. Welcome and Godspeed with impartiality. I had seen her many times before but never from quite so close as this, and had no idea she was such a pretty green, a lady as green as an apple. We passed several warships and two flat-tops destined, we found later, for the Caribbean to keep watch in those troubled waters.

It was curious to think that Havana was out now. Another of those places which the swift tempo of our time has crossed off the tourist's list of places he can visit. Not that we regard ourselves as tourists. We always say, with great contempt, "Just look at those tourists," as we watch them getting out of the bus that has followed ours. Of course no one else could possibly know that we are not tourists except for the fact that we carry no cameras, have quite a lot of luggage, and have no time schedule. We can and do stay anywhere we like for as long as we like. That, we feel, makes us travelers. The true traveler is a kind of nomad whose home is his suitcase. But of course since no one knew these fascinating details about our personal lives we were, to them, just tourists,

and rather poor ones at that, since we did not seem to have even one camera between us and bought no souvenirs. We therefore would have no tangible proof of having been anywhere when we got back to wherever we had come from. As we do not like sun bathing we always return from a voyage rather paler than the people who have stayed at home, and much paler than those who have used sun lamps or gone to Florida to cook themselves in a more natural way. Sun bathing has always astonished me. No animal is mad enough to lie in the sun except in the early morning or in a sheltered place on a cold day. Animals lie in the shade. But animals don't have to prove anything to each other. They are not democratic and know that one is stronger or smarter than another. The pecking order of hens is no figment of the imagination. I had a book about it once. But all people are equal and the ones who can afford to get sun-bronzed by taking sea voyages are more equal than the others. Girls with curly hair are more equal than girls with natural straight hair. This applies to tourists too. A tourist with several cameras is more equal than a tourist with one camera, even if it is a very good one.

This is the great charm of travel. It is not just a matter of seeing places but of meeting and watching people. We are great watchers. There are interesting resemblances between watching game at a water hole in Africa and people at a cocktail bar in Manhattan. Some people lower their heads to drink, like zebras. Some throw them back to swallow, like ostriches. They quarrel, they maneuver for position, they roar, they bray, they squeak and squeal. They make love. Sometimes they even fight.

We are also very fond of eavesdropping. A phrase caught on the wing can be much more interesting than a complete anecdote, for one has the pleasure of developing it oneself.

Time, being a variable, now began to go very fast. There

were a great many people to see and things to be done. Final injections, their certification at the Department of Health. Packing the things we were going to take and the things we were going to leave behind. Bills to pay. The horrible and irrevocable sound of checks being torn from the checkbook. The weather remained wonderful. The warmest December since 1916, the papers said, as New York, the wonder city, was being dressed up for Christmas. Truckloads of fir trees tightly corseted in rope girdles were being unloaded. Big trees braced with wires sprang up in Park Avenue. Fairy lights trembled like stars in shop front decorations. The radio blared offers of Christmas loans. The newspapers were filled with advertisements for gifts. The stationers' shops were piled with greeting cards. Everyone was making lists and buying presents. We went through our address book, our hearts a curious mixture of love, hope, and irritation. On top of all we had to do this card sending was the penultimate straw. But how beautiful the city was as we looked out of our window over Gramercy Park at the tall buildings, gold-plated with lights in the early crepuscular dusk.

This was the time of hope. The end of a year, the beginning of a new one. But everyone seemed to be whistling in the dark. A New Year, a new President. The dollar, no longer almighty, omnipotent, seemed in danger. There was Russia on our doorstep in Cuba, and South America with a "Yanqui go home" attitude. The Congo debacle. The Far East unsettled and uncertain of its destination. The Algerian question still a question. Trouble in our own South. The whole world uncertain, driven half crazy by the boredom of prosperity, at a loss with its new-found leisure, the crime rate rising with not only children but whole nations behaving in an utterly delinquent and irresponsible manner. We in the West suffering from a surfeit of goods and services, while the rest of the world starves and the gap between the haves and have-nots increases daily. Tonight there seemed little hope that the deluge would come after us, very little that we should not have, in our time, to face the inconceivable. Not much seemed left but hope and not too much of that. This was the New York we were leaving behind us for a few months to escape not merely the winter but the pressure of events.

THE CITY OF
FOOD AND SIN

Two

At last the day we had been waiting for came. Our train,
the Crescent Limited, was due to leave Pennsylvania Station
at 1:15 P.M. So, being what I am, we got there at 12:30 and
sat around feeding a pigeon that had got into the building
and was walking about quite unconcerned by the people
who practically fell over him. Tiny bought some crackers for
him and we became so entranced that we nearly missed the
train and had to run for it. One of our great dangers is being
too happy. We get somewhere early because I have train
fever, and am very punctual by nature and training. Then
we become interested in something and end up late.

We had lunch on the train and then sat in the parlor car
and watched a romance between a white-haired politician
going to Washington and a well-preserved and well-dressed
woman with jingly bracelets. I always like the term "preserved" with women. As if they were peaches or gherkins
preserved in syrup or vinegar. Sweet or sour . . . By the time
they had had four whiskey sours the politician had told the
jingly lady that she was quite a girl, well stacked, and that

he had six grandchildren—which he proved with photographs. This confidence in photographs is very interesting. She also had three grandchildren. She had pictures too.

"I can't believe that," the solon said. "Why you look like a bride." That must have been the whiskey sours. She bridled and jingled at him as he ordered another round of drinks.

We bought four little bottles of bourbon for the dry states (I never want a drink very much except in these drought areas) and then we went off to read and doze till dinnertime. The trip was not beautiful. The trees, almost bare of leaves, looked ragged and dirty. Here and there were chimneys standing in the scrub, lonely reminders that once there had been a house here. There were miles of cut-over timber, shacks, little towns, occasional herds of cattle—white-faced Herefords, Brahmans, and Black Angus—and then suddenly the following day we reached the real South with its palmetto underbrush and Spanish-moss-draped trees.

We reached New Orleans at seven-thirty in the evening the day after we left, and were met by the friends with whom we were going to stay till we sailed.

According to the Northern papers there should have been a civil war going on here over the desegregation of the schools, but we saw no sign of it. In the dining car we had eaten with Negroes. Everyone, both black and white, seemed calm, and in the days we spent in New Orleans everything seemed normal, though there was a certain amount of discussion, both about segregation and states' rights, among the people we met. There is no doubt that desegregation will take place. There is also very little doubt that this will not improve race relations, and may even set back the clock, for the time being at any rate. I have never liked people because they were white or disliked them because they were black, but, like most people, black or white, I prefer men of my own race, education, and income group. I have no desire to associate with either millionaires or truck drivers, however estimable they may be, possibly because I am never likely to have a million dollars and cannot drive a truck.

There is, I think, a great deal of hypocrisy about segregation. Most of the liberals I know, and that includes most of my friends, do not entertain Negroes or send their children to an integrated school. It is obviously a matter of proportion. There is no problem in Vermont, where there are hardly any Negroes. In a little hamburger joint where we often eat on Third Avenue there are usually a half-dozen Negroes. It seats fifty people. If there were a dozen or more Negroes I should not go back. But equally I should not go back if there were more than a dozen teen-agers or Italians or sailors. It would then have become a Negro joint, a teen-ager hangout, a place for Italians or sailors. Human relations are rather like a cocktail—the mixture has to be just right.

The whole question of color is so highly charged emotionally that rational argument becomes difficult. On the one hand there is the moral, ethical, and Christian view of the brotherhood of man. On the other are deep-rooted atavistic instincts that are incalculable and can only be overcome by education. This may take a long time, since in the final analysis it is based on sex, and white people, particularly in the South, where the contact between the two races is the most intimate, are averse to miscegenation. In spite of every denial it boils down to the old question of "Do you want your daughter to marry a Negro?" Yet where any two races come into permanent contact with each other there are in the end only two solutions: marry them or kill them.

The Indians were killed. The Negroes in the end will probably be married. But this is not the end. This is the period between the Negroes, or Afro-Americans, being regarded as second-class citizens and their absorption by the white race. Once accomplished, this would probably make very little difference to the nation, but such an achievement seems at the moment to be highly improbable (though advocated by some authorities) when we consider the difficulties involved even in the marriage of white people who belong to different faiths or racial groups.

Where soldiers and sailors come in contact if a quarrel

breaks out between two of them no one asks who was right or wrong. Within minutes all the soldiers are fighting all the sailors. And, unfortunately, the dark skin of the Negro is a uniform he can never take off. That a great deal of miscegenation has already taken place is obvious. There are few pure Negroes left in America. Not more than 30 per cent of people classed as Negroes are of pure African descent. Thousands have passed over, probably hundreds of thousands, and a great deal of Negro blood is diffused among white Americans who are entirely unaware of the fact. Sinclair Lewis based a novel, *Kingsblood Royal*, on this thesis. Another vital point, considered constitutionally, has been brought up by a Washington State Supreme Court judge, when he accused the N.A.A.C.P. for compulsory togetherness as an attempt to deprive white people of their right to choose their associates in private life. It is this association that is the key to the question. We tend to associate with the kind of people we marry, and by and large we marry within our class, race, religion, and income group. This would appear to be a natural law, a continuation of tribal custom still existing today, where the stranger is always suspect and the more he differs in appearance the more strange and difficult to absorb he becomes. There is no difficulty in passing a law which says the lion and the lamb must lie down together. The problem is to make them do it.

We think New Orleans is the most beautiful and romantic town in the United States. Perhaps that is because we like trees. Nowhere else have I seen so many or such beautiful trees in the streets. Great live oaks, palms, poinsettias, azaleas, rain trees, gums, crepe myrtles, and bananas clothe the city with a mantle of greenery and flowers, varying with the seasons. They embellish the yards, the houses, and drape themselves over walls in prodigal luxuriance. The streets are not numbered but have colorful names such as St. Charles, Napoleon, Jeannette, Carrolton, Congress, Lopez, Feliciana, Tulane, Spain, Oak, St. Claude. Each tells a story and asks a

question, and it is a relief to get away from numbers for a
while even if it makes it harder to find one's way. There is
even a part of the city called Desire, with a streetcar by that
name that serves it.

Then there is the French Quarter with its lace grillwork,
its art stores, jewelers, hotels, dives, and bars where passing
by at night one gets a glimpse of beautiful near-nude women
exposing their charms on a stage. Strip-teasers, white-skinned
and tinseled in the gloom, go through their acts. But New
Orleans is not as wicked as it used to be and perhaps its
greatest charm is the sense of continuity one gets here. The

feeling of history that makes one wonder. What Spanish dons
have ridden up Royal Street, Calle Royale as they called it,
on their long-tailed horses? What troops have paraded in
Jackson Square, which was once the Place d'Armes? What
expeditions have left the city on the long road that follows
the Gulf of Mexico to California? How many dead of yellow
jack have been picked up by the death carts in the epidemics
that swept the city every few years? How many gamblers
have trodden these ancient cobbles? How many whores have
lived here when every second house was a brothel? How
many fights have there been between the river-boat champions who, wearing a red feather in their hats to show they

were cocks of the walk, challenged all comers? How many fortunes made and lost in these old, unchanged streets?

We now had a setback. Our little eight-dollar ivory white Westclox traveling clock stopped going. It would go for a minute or two if we shook it and then stopped again.

I said, "We'll throw it away and buy a new one." Tiny said, "We can't do that. We've had it so long—nearly ten years—and it has been so far with us. Africa twice—all over Africa, Europe, America. It must have done fifty or sixty thousand miles. We can't just throw it away. We'll bury it at sea."

We went out and bought a new Westclox, a silver $12.00 one this time, and a small flag in which to wrap the old one when we dropped it overboard. The flag was my idea. If we are going to do something we might as well do it properly. So we packed it away, gift-wrapped in stars and stripes, and set the new clock up by the bed.

New Orleans is famous for the strip-tease joints in Bourbon Street. They are highly controversial but we always enjoy them, having perverted tastes, perhaps, in still being old-fashioned enough to think that a beautiful girl's body is the last word in creation, the chef-d'oeuvre of evolution. Of course a woman's body is very old-fashioned and no longer admired by real artists.

I should think there are few virgins among these young ladies and some of their dances and pelvic movements could be described, according to the nature of the describer, as rude, coarse, vulgar, or sexy. But they are all very old, very natural movements whose origins go back to the fertility cults and phallic worship of our ancestors and are, as such, of great anthropological interest. All dancing is in essence sexual and a great deal of everyone's life, as every psychiatrist knows, is governed by sexual instincts, overt or direct, that come out under analysis. The interesting aspect of all this is the fear of sex, and guilt-feeling about it that seems to be an integral part of our culture.

In no other country, so far as I know, are the advertisements more sexually slanted; in no other are there more educational courses in sex, in physiology; more books about sexual satisfaction, more sexy novels, more marriage and premarriage counselors; more, and more varied, laws per state about sexual procedures, ages of consent, of marriage, of methods of intercourse, of prostitution and contraception. No nation is better informed in the theory of sex, from savage to Kinsey, and none appears to make a worse job of it in practice.

And it is here in these New Orleans burlesques that one key lies. We are afraid of naked beauty, particularly if it is a little funny in an earthy, natural manner. We are ashamed of our feelings of natural desire, and somehow feel that to love a woman and make love to her is a kind of insult to our mothers' purity. We tend to separate sex and love, to hate the woman we make love to for degrading us, and to love the woman we don't make love to because she epitomizes some obscure ideal of purity. So we fall between these two stools of love and hate, right onto the analyst's couch.

The whole question is of the greatest moral and ethical interest. It is difficult to see why the emotions aroused by an erotic dance, which if it is not well done are ones of disgust, are worse than the emotions aroused by the bloody brutality of a boxing bout or a bullfight. Why is it better to see a man strike a woman repeatedly on television than to see him begin to make love to her, which of course is never permitted, yet every adult watching the show has made love and every child will do so. Whereas only a small proportion, it is to be hoped, have struck or been struck by a person of the opposite sex.

There is some deep cause here that produces these effects. It is evident that we still fear sex, fear its power and mystery as much as our phallus-worshiping ancestors did, but dare not acknowledge it. It is also apparent that however much we deny it we retain a certain savage love of brutality in our beings to which, given the sanction of public social acceptance, we give full play. Some examples of this are boxing, bullfighting, rodeos, cockfights, dogfights, wrestling, and so on.

The last public execution took place in Europe less than a century ago and was well attended. The last lynching took place in America a year or so ago. The records of the war show that any race of men, given the license to do so, can revert to savagery and sadism. It is impossible to open a paper that does not prove this thesis, and this we tend to condone. The soldier acted under pressure in war. The SS man was under orders to torture. The sadistic criminal is a sick man. But the ordinary man in the street who goes to bed with a pretty girl who is more than willing is a sinner. So is the man who sees a pretty girl and thinks it would be nice to go to bed with her.

"Disgusting!" the woman said in the half-dark as she left the show with the other tourists on the night tour. "Yes, wasn't it?" her friend said.

"Was that what you expected?" the first lady said to Tiny, who was standing beside her. The lady's hair was gray and curly as the wool of a Merino sheep; her hat, a red omelet of red velvet, set flat on the top of her head like a plate, was garnished with a dyed turkey feather.

I heard Tiny say, "Yes, that's what I came to see. We often come."

The turkey feather trembled with her indignation. "Disgusting!" the woman said. "Disgusting!"

THE SPANISH MAIN

Three

We had left our friends' house and were waiting for the ship at the Royal Orleans Hotel. At nine-thirty the phone rang. It was Bheil and Company, the agent, telling us we could go on board at any time. The ship was sailing at midday. She was at the Press Street dock. Everything except our night clothes, washing kit, and Tiny's toiletries and beauty preparations was packed. This quite small bag takes longer to pack than all the others put together. To start with, it has to be packed last because when a woman has done packing she feels so awful that she has to put on a new face. A new face means Kleenex, astringent, face cream, powder, lipstick, eyebrow pencil, eye shadow, comb, brush, hair spray. All these things and many others besides arrived in this bag, but will never go back into it. Which is why I do not close my brief case till Tiny's face bag is packed. There are always some things that I have to find room for if we are ever to get away.

Ten pieces in all. One large blue suitcase, one soft leather Nigerian bag made of camel skin containing medicines and reserve beauty preparations, one soft leather goatskin zippered bag from Seville with night clothes and washing kit, two brief cases fastened together with a strap, one blue canvas Scandinavian Airlines bag given to us in Nairobi containing a bottle of Bucchu brandy, an African remedy for stomach-aches, and some books, one small basket from Tobago with our transistor radio and some magazines, one rubberized-canvas bag from Windhoek in South-West Africa, filled with painting materials, sketchbooks, illustration boards, etc., one dressing case, also from South-West Africa, with toilet preparations—this is the one there's always so much trouble about. Then there is one large lady's handbag —it is so large that I generally have to carry it—and a big Christmas-wrapped box with our tree in it. This luggage, set in a curious-looking heap on the pavement by the bellboy, was finally loaded into the taxi by an outside porter who was dressed like a French policeman except that everything he wore, including his cloak, was old gold in color.

We drove through the streets of the old French Quarter up Esplanade, one of the world's loveliest streets, to the docks. We passed warehouses filled with produce that had just arrived or was being loaded to go. Bales of compressed cotton, drums of oil earmarked for Monrovia and Dakar. Tree trunks with great knobby roots that looked like giant's clubs, almost three feet in diameter, destined, we found later, to be made into pipes.

Bheil's was the next warehouse and we drove in. Our luggage was picked up by a couple of longshoremen and taken aboard. The ship was gray, the smokestack black with a wide red band on which the letter K was painted in white. Owing to the levees which protect the city from the river the ship lay very low and the gangplank would have been hard to negotiate in high heels.

The cabin was newly painted in white. All the draperies were crisp and fresh, printed in a cottage design of red roses on a white and green ground. The two beds, separated by a dressing table, could be closed off by curtains. In the sitting-room part there were a sofa and two armchairs and a chair for the writing desk. There were two cupboards with plenty of hangers and enough drawers. A bathroom with a real bath completed the accommodations. It was as large as a small apartment, and we had just about got our things stowed away when our friends, the Stephenses, turned up. Luckily we had whiskey, some small bottles left over from the train trip, as no ship's bar can be opened in port, as the customs officers always seal up the liquor and the slop chest.

We did not sail till two, so we all had lunch together. The food was good and there was plenty of it. But it was not *too* good—not so good that we would overeat out of sheer gastronomic delight. Once, coming back from Africa on the Farrell Line, a three-week trip, none of the women could do up their dresses when they went ashore. Good food in this sense, food that you want to eat whether you are hungry or not, is a mistake at sea except for a short three- or four-day trip.

Leaving New Orleans, the ship went down river. Civilization was behind us. This was bush country, scrub land with low, eroded gray banks littered with stumps and fallen trees. There were still leaves on the bushes, yellowed by autumn. Among them the white-barked trunks of bigger trees stood out like bones. Here and there a stone-banked levee followed the river, like a snake. In the distance there were chimneys of brick and silver aluminum, each with its ribbon of smoke floating like a dark banner over a near-wilderness, where once the cotton and sugar fields must have come to the water's edge. At intervals we saw the roofs and white walls of the old proud houses that had once sustained a specialized Creole culture. Masked by great live oaks, the windows look out at the river that has seen so much and such varied traffic —one of the longest rivers in the world, sister to the Amazon and Congo. French, British, and Spanish battleships have sailed between these low shores. Jean Laffitte and his pirates, Indians, trappers, escaped slaves, and criminals, all knew these swamps.

We passed villages and small towns, some newborn of the oil industry that has brought prosperity to the coastal flats. Beyond each enclave, each clearing or settlement, the trees closed in again, creeping down to the river's edge. This could have been West Africa. We could have been on the Cross River or the Calabar. The West African slaves who worked the plantations must have felt it too, a deep nostalgia for their swamps and forests across the sea, for lands that looked so much the same but were so different.

This is an area of paradox. Oil rigs pumping the black gold, on which our civilization moves, out of muskrat swamps. White herons fish in the shallows and a fish hawk, its white wing tips flashing in the sun, sails in endless circles overhead.

The ships of all nations pass on this waterway. We saw two other Norwegians, a United States Line freighter, a British ship, a ship flying the Liberian lone star and stripes, and an Argentinian vessel. In harbor before we sailed we saw the French training ship that had just come in, flying an immense tricolor at her stern, the largest I have ever seen.

From now on there will be little news, and the last we have had is bad. Two air crashes with great loss of life and a *coup d'état* in Ethiopia. While the Lion of Judah was in Brazil talking of African unity and the glories of freedom, his son appears to have taken over. The African pattern seems to remain unchanged. William L. Shirer's remark that "we cannot make even an intelligent guess about the future of a people unless we understand at least a little of their past"* has particular application in the Dark Continent where most history is myth.

We are now in the Caribbean, the seas are running big and blue-white spume topped in a strong wind from the east, the spray of each a scattered rainbow prism of green, red, mauve, and violet on the dark blue trough that divides crest from crest.

This is the Spanish Main. These waters and those to the south and east of us have seen more blood and death than most. This must be one of Davy Jones's largest lockers. Men-

---

* William L. Shirer. *Midcentury Journey*, p. 117.

of-war of half a dozen nations, Spanish treasure ships, slavers, pirates, privateers, have all passed this way, fought and gone down half hidden in the smoke of battle. These bright blue, green, and purple seas with their palm-fringed islands and white-gold sands are all stained with blood and still echo with the roar of cannon.

This was the gateway to the West Indies, the sugar islands, to the gold of Mexico. The entrance to California by the land route along the gulf. A soft, perfumed sea that grew barnacles on the keels of ships and rotted the hearts of men.

Floating in the waves like a child's boat is a spar. At first it looked like a small tree with the stub of a broken branch sticking up out of the water. The stub turns out to be a young bird, at least it looks young, largish, brown, desperately alone, riding the waves, appearing, disappearing, and finally lost to sight. Another little tragedy of the sea. We have seen so many of them now. Yet they never cease to move us.

These are the waters—from Florida to Haiti and Mexico—that were once famous for their mermaids. First reported by Columbus and thus confirming all the classic myths that sailors were only too ready to accept—a wish-fulfillment dream, a rumor now proved true. After months at sea, anything with breasts looked like a woman and to these starved seamen anything that looked like a woman was beautiful. Of course her hair might not be quite so long or as golden as that of the Mediterranean sirens, nor her skin so white, nor her tail so sleek and shining silver. But such men were in no mood to be fussy. Nor, even when disillusioned themselves, were they going to tell the truth to their wide-eyed and open-mouthed listeners back home. "Mermaids? Of course we saw them, sitting on the rocks combing their long golden hair. We even caught one once . . ." They did not say they ate her and that the meat resembled veal or pork.

The mermaid of those days is the manatee of today, a big gray sluglike animal that may weigh almost a ton, with a girth of seven feet. They are often seen by fishermen in Florida, even by bridge fishermen in downtown Miami.

We saw no manatees, but it was fascinating to speculate about them and the sailors who first saw them and came home to tell the tale. Another variety, the dugong, a smaller cousin, as it were, lives in other waters we shall pass through —the tropical West Pacific, the Indian Ocean, and Red Sea.

It is difficult to realize the life that is in the sea—the wild life. The great sea mammals: whales, porpoises, sea elephants, seals, sea otters, polar bears, leopard seals. The great fish: sharks, manta rays, swordfish, sailfish, marlin, tarpon. They are the big game of the sea. And the terrible monsters, myths that are neither proved nor fully disproved: giant squids, octopuses, sea serpents, and the rest of the teeming life that inhabits these vast hidden plains, valleys, high mountains, cliffs, caves, and deep crevasses.

A fishing bank corresponds to a grassy hilltop on land—a grazing area for herbivores and a hunting ground for the predators that prey upon them. Only in the fishing world almost all fish are predators, preying on anything small enough to swallow, all swallowing and being in turn swallowed till they end up in something so big as to be invulnerable. So from the giant whales, the leviathans of the Bible, life in the sea is scaled down to plankton, to tiny mollusks and the single-celled pinpoints of protoplasm that may be our ancestors.

This is part of the fascination of the sea, part of what is in our minds as we sail over its surface and look at the charts on the table. What lies below us? What wild fishy beasts? What marine forest? What coral garden? What sunken ships? What treasures? What bones?

It is the same curiosity that makes us search the rocks at low tide or peer over the edge of a volcano. We want to see more of the world, more of its hidden parts, its secrets. This is the curiosity of the geologist and mining engineer, of the archaeologist, anthropologist, and zoologist—to know more,

to seek out, to search for both knowledge and beauty, to
grasp for a deeper understanding of something that may be
found under a big stone or in the heart of a little flower. To
realize, as one looks, the mystery of a raised beach, a petri-
fied tree, a flock of migrating birds, and to feel oneself to be
a part of all this, an integral part of life—not of a machine
or an organization, not even as a man or woman, but of
something that includes men, lions, fishes, and geraniums—
part of the great vibration, of the pulse that we call life.
And maybe another name for God.

The canal was not at all what I thought it would be. At
about nine-thirty we sighted land, a long, low hill on the
horizon. I had expected the isthmus to be flat, invisible till
we came within a close distance of it. The visibility was
poor. We were enveloped in a warm blanket of mist. Then
there was a squall. The rain was like a warm shower bath.
Big mountains now appeared to the south rising out of a
green, pewter-colored sea that undulated with slow ground-
swell rolls as if the Atlantic was flexing its muscles, threaten-
ing the little strip of land that kept it from joining the great
ocean of the west.

The arms of two long black breakwaters of random blocks
came out into the sea. The green rollers were torn into frills
of white lace as they smashed against them. Inside, the water
was as smooth as silk. The harbor enclosed by this artificial
reef reminded us of Monrovia, where the same thing had
been done.

A snow-white lighthouse surrounded by windswept palms
marked the entrance on one side. A steel skeleton at the end
of the breakwater marked the other. This was the entrance
to the Pacific, the man-made passage to the ocean that no
Western man had seen till the conquistadores came upon it
less than five hundred years ago. A passage that cost thousands of lives and took ten years to build. In order to reach
the Far East it is no longer necessary to brave the Horn
or go around the Cape of Good Hope. The Americas,

North and South, have been split by a knife thrust a hundred or so yards wide that has become one of the great arteries of commerce—a ditch through which fifty great ships pass each day.

The green hills of the shore were lined with installations—large barrackslike buildings of what looked like apartment houses. Separate houses, bungalows, two-story houses, all neat, trim, and American. Docks, wharves, storehouses, and business establishments crept down upon and appeared to overwhelm the old town of Colón. All that could be seen of it from the deck were the two spires of the cathedral dark with age and typically Iberian, held up like two grubby ancient fingers. They accented the stunning white cleanliness of the rest of the shore line.

There we lay idling with three other ships, waiting our turn. Various launches with officials came alongside and men with brief cases climbed the rope ladder that had been dropped over the side for their convenience. Gulls, some of them dark brown, that I took to be skuas, flew around the ship mewing like kittens in distress. There is something exciting about the crying of all gulls, something wild and wonderful. Certain other birds' calls have the same effect on me. Wild geese, whimbrel, curlew, peacock, cock pheasants, all have this quality of evoking some atavistic emotion of excitement, of striking some special chord in my nature, and I assume in the nature of many other men who feel this curious bond with living things, a sharing of something with them, so that these wild cries of the birds are really sounds that we would make ourselves if we could—are indeed cries of our own hearts.

At last we moved into the narrow channel of the canal. A couple of hundred feet above us, or so it seemed, a big ship was silhouetted on the sky line of the hill. Between it and us were the locks that would raise us in three steps to her level. Three lines on each side of our ship were made fast to small engines known locally as *mulas eléctricas,* or electric mules, that look as if they were running on very large roller coasters.

Each of them had a kind of enormous fishing reel set horizontally on its back. Working from either side, they pulled us into the lock. The enormous gates closed behind us and the water gurgled in in great swirls below us, raising us visibly. It was like being in a toy boat at the bottom of a giant's bath that was being filled by pressure from below. We were in forty-two feet of water and were raised to seventy-four, level with the concrete bank, or edge of the bath. The gates in front of us now opened. We were at the same level as the second ship. Our roller coasters started climbing like beetles up the steep ramp till they were high above us but leading and guiding us till we had advanced far enough for the gate to close behind us. And again we were floated upward out of the dark, dripping canyons of the lock into the bright sunshine above.

It was very curious to see all this modern machinery, the great locks and the electric engines, the workers, all American and most of them Negroes, neatly dressed with shining aluminum helmets against a backdrop of primeval jungle only a few hundred yards away. This seems typical of so much of South America. The magnificent road that leads from Santos to São Paulo in Brazil plunges upward through impenetrable rain forest. I doubt if many of these hills and mountains of Panama have been fully explored or even prospected. It would be fascinating to explore an area like this and collect mammals, birds, reptiles, insects, and plants, to see what actually inhabits this heavy bush. There should be jaguar, ocelots, peccaries, boa constrictors, and many wonderful butterflies and moths.

Once again the floating process was repeated and then, by the Gatun lock house, which bore in large letters the words "SEASONS GREETINGS," our lines were cast off and we were on Lake Gatun.

It was now about midday and the following few hours were among the most wonderful we have experienced. The day was a beautiful blue day. Everything was washed with blue like a kind of tropical Maxfield Parrish picture if one could imagine him painting the tropics instead of snow scenes.

Gatun is a lake of a thousand little round, jungle-covered islands. Some may be a few hundred yards in diameter, others are smaller than a billiard table, but all are rounded little breastlike hills, and each covered with a glorious mantle of variegated foliage. Ten or fifteen different kinds of leaves were distinguishable from the ship. Big trees, trees weeping into the water, tall palms like floor mops, low palms, lianas, bushes with yellow flowers and pink flowers, dark trees with almost black foliage, trees that were almost apple green, and all, archipelago after archipelago, spread over the vast expanse of blue water, their own green color fading with the perspective of distance till they merged into the blue mountains of the interior which were blurred soft-edged into the sky.

The whole afternoon had a dreamlike quality. There we were, perched, floating like a cork on a high lake midway between two continents and the world's two greatest oceans. We were actually on the Great Divide, as much so as if we were in the Western Rockies (as we have been) on the apex of the watershed. For here, had the locks been opened, the lake would have been drained into the two oceans.

Ships eastward bound passed us. Two British ships flying the red ensign astern, two Japanese with their red ball on a white ground, a Dane, two Norwegians, and a ship flying the Liberian flag with an enormous deck cargo of sawn timber. The channel was well buoyed. Between many of the islands dead trees, white as bones with age, stood in the water. Hardwoods that had died when the lock had raised the level of the water. We saw one heron, a number of gulls, and a few of the same white-rumped martins that we had seen flying in the same way, low over the water, in Surinam. High in the air were the usual vultures—turkey buzzards—endlessly circling in search of death. We had been very lucky in our timing, because very often the trip is done by night and, dramatic as this may be, all the beauty of scenery would have been missed.

In the distance we saw a train moving like a toy along the lake bank. It takes one and a half hours to do the trip from Colón to Panama City, as opposed to seven by ship. We did not see anywhere any signs of agriculture except a small plantation of papaya and some others of bananas. There was one row of biggish, dark-foliaged trees that might have been mangoes.

It has always surprised me that a greater variety of tropical fruits and vegetables are not cultivated in areas where they do well. Breadfruit, oil palm, alligator pear, grapefruit, pine-apples, mangoes, pistachios, guavas, yams, taro, custard apple could all be grown from Central and South America and the West Indies right across Africa to the Indian Ocean.

It might take time to accustom the natives to eating fruits and vegetables that are strange to them, but, considering the monotony of their diet and the general scarcity of food in such countries, fruit crops would seem to be an easily grown addition, just as, where there is ample water, fish farming, such as the Belgians practiced in the Congo, would give a supply of protein to natives who are always short of it. The return of talapia in the Congo was nine tons to the hectare in twelve months, or approximately four and one half tons to the acre of water.

These thoughts may have entered my mind because Lake Gatun resembled Lake Kivu, Central Africa, in many ways. I thought it even prettier than Kivu though it is smaller and not surrounded by high mountains. It is extraordinary to think that the beautiful houses, plantations, hospitals, and experimental stations we visited in the Congo are now aban-doned and our hosts of five years ago are ruined men.

We now passed a large service settlement, neat as a garden, where there was the largest floating crane I ever saw, and the prettiest and cleanest dredge. We entered the Gaillard Cut, a channel cut through the hills a hundred yards wide and nine miles long. Because of its narrowness, we moved at about a walking speed, three or four miles an hour, so as to create no wash. The water on both sides had neon lights every few yards, only three feet or so above the surface, to illuminate it at night. On the hills there were innumerable traffic markers and lights. Green lights, red lights, white arrows, big white markers that had to be aligned, checkerboard markers of black and white and numbers everywhere. At intervals there were waterfalls pouring into the cut. Their courses had been lined with concrete to avoid erosion, but erosion and rockfalls are a great problem in the canal, which is still being widened at danger points. We passed two tugs pushing barges of waste rock up to the lake where they would dump it. The high cliffs are cut with a water gun, a kind of immense hose operated by compressed air that washes the mud into solution and sends the rocks rolling down to a level prepared to receive them, where they are scooped up and loaded for disposal. Where they were working there was a memorial to the men who had died or were killed building the canal. It consisted of a bronze plaque showing two men digging with spades, set into a square of white marble some fifty feet above water level. There were no inscription and no figures. That this work could be done by hand in a tropical climate without refrigeration, air-conditioning, proper housing, or hospitals is difficult to believe today. Like Suez, it was a French concept, but, abandoned by them, was completed by the United States, who, appalled at the loss of life from yellow fever, discovered its cause in these swamps. It was easy to imagine the swarms of mosquitoes that would breed here if uncontrolled. All along the canal there were patches of yellow-and-blue strelitzia—some people call them bird-of-paradise flowers—and other wide-leaved marsh plants. The great leaves of wild bananas stood out like bright green flags. Feather-topped reeds drooped over the water, and as the evening closed in the birds began to call. There would be a loud, raucous cry that was answered. Then a musical, chimelike trill that sounded like a Mexican clarino.

It all had a dreamlike quality as we drifted, our engines hardly turning, in silence through the cut.

Mosquitoes, ticks, ants, fleas, microbes, and bacteria are now man's greatest enemies. We have destroyed all the great predators—lions, tigers, wolves, leopards, bears, and so on— that menaced our ancestors and their flocks, and these are the residue, as it were, the rear guard, of wild nature's resistance to man's encroachment. Killers, too, in a more subtle but no less dangerous form. But still, perhaps, ecologically necessary as we may one day discover. With diseases such as malaria, yellow fever, plague, and bilharzia gone, with no checks on population growth, the world may yet face starvation.

Panama and Central America, which never interested us very much before, have now become real, invested with romance—countries whose history we must study.

Tiny and I never read about or even look at pictures of places we want to go to if we can help it. This is because we, like all true explorers, wish to be astonished. If Livingstone had seen pictures of the Victoria Falls he would not have experienced the emotion he did at his discovery of them, though of course he had heard about "the smoke that thunders." Movies are bad. They show too much. So are snapshots. Drawings and engravings are the best way to get an idea of strange places and things. For instance, I shall never forget the first time I saw a giraffe. My reaction was not one of wonder but of saying to myself, "It's just like the ones I saw in the films." It has taken years to cure myself of this reaction.

This principle might even apply in what is described as human relations. If little boys and girls knew less about each other, knew less physiology and indulged in less sexual experimentation, in their tender years, they might find more mystery and pleasure in adult explorations. The aim of education should be to inculcate an insatiable curiosity about the unknown, and not to satisfy it with facts and figures. The length and depth of the Panama Canal are supremely unimportant and can be found in any encyclopedia. The romance is in the drive, the aspiration, the courage, pain, danger, and horror, and final glory of this immense achievement.

The grand total excavation of the canal is estimated at 240,000,000 cubic yards, and 5,000,000 cubic yards of concrete was used. The French excavated 78,000,000 cubic yards. Of this amount only 29,000,000 cubic yards has proved useful in the present canal, so 49,000,000 cubic yards of soil and rock was excavated by the French to no purpose. How many men died doing this? What was the ratio of death to cubic yards? What is the equation in terms of mothers, wives, or sweethearts who lost their men? This is the kind of arithmetic that interests us. What did these men who died hope? What did they write home? How many could even write? Who recruited them? What were they promised? What did the survivors get?

Today we ride through in air-conditioned comfort. But that past is very near. The first ship went through the canal in 1915, only forty-five years ago.

We went out of the canal through the last lock in darkness and a blaze of light. We did not even wait for the end of it, but went to bed exhausted by the emotion we had felt, the beauty we had seen, the memories of our time in the Congo, and thoughts of how this tremendous undertaking had been conceived and carried out.

THE GREATEST OCEAN

Four

THE PACIFIC—COMMUNISTS AND PARLOR PINKS—
AN EXAMPLE OF MODERN ART—THE HOUSEMAIDS
OF THE SEA—FOUR PRETTY GIRLS—THE TEACHING
OF HISTORY—FREIGHTER PASSENGERS—THE PEOPLE
ONE MEETS—GULLS AND CLOUDS—SAFARI—ENGI-
NEERS HATE AIR—CHRISTMAS AT SEA

In the morning we woke in the Pacific. It was living up to its name—a calm sea of navy-blue moiré silk. We passed ships bound east to the canal. We sailed along the coast of Costa Rica, passing mountains and one large island. If all goes well we should reach San Pedro, which means Los Angeles and Hollywood for us, in seven more days.

It is strange to us to have America to the east of us and the sun to rise there instead of setting. Strange to be in this great ocean that seems, though it is probably only imagination, to have a feel and color of its own. It covers one third of the world's surface, and here where we are now is its widest point. Singapore lies 12,500 miles away to the west, with a scattering of islands that reach from the shores of Asia to Hawaii, submerged mountaintops, coral islands, atolls, volcanic islands, great continental islands like New Zealand, and tiny pocket-handkerchief-sized islands that scarcely break through the sea. All this is before us as we join the long line of those who have come to look, each of us in our little niche of time and history. From Marco Polo to Mac-Arthur, from Captain Cook to Eisenhower, there have been great names and great adventures in this ocean and the

Eastern seas that adjoin it. Captain Bligh of the *Bounty* with his cargo of breadfruit. The French Admiral Bougainville, after whom the island and the flower were named. There have been pirates and blackbirders and shiploads of criminals bound for Botany Bay. Great sea, land, and air battles, from Pearl Harbor to Hiroshima, have been mounted here.

The Portuguese, Dutch, French, and British have all sailed these seas, beating round the Cape, fighting each other, and imposing the stamp of their colonial culture on the people of the East who were civilized thousands of years before ourselves. Gunpowder and paper were Chinese inventions. They invented printing long before we discovered it. There were elaborate cultures in China and India before Athens flourished. Before Christ was born ancient religions here had run their roots of custom and taboo into the very heart stuff of humanity, creating a psyche which we are incapable of understanding, so different are our basic values. Here, too, in China the new religion of communism, that terrifying phenomenon of inspired materialism, is growing in power daily. This is something we cannot or dare not recognize. We refuse to see that many communists are inspired and devoted men, capable of immense self-sacrifice to achieve their ends. The fellow travelers, fifth columnists, and spies in our midst are not all bought men. They are believers. The sums they receive are too small to tempt them to take the risks they run. In many ways they resemble the early Christians in pagan Rome, who shocked the orthodox conservatives of their day as much as the communists shock us now. The real danger of communism seems to lie in the fact that we seem to have no positive philosophy to set up against it. Capitalism and free enterprise are not philosophies. Our Christianity could hardly be taken seriously by an objective observer, say, a man from Mars. Our stand is purely negative. We are merely anticommunist and seem to hope that by refusing to recognize Communist China its six hundred million people and immense industrial potential will just disappear.

Never in the history of the world have things been quite so bad, with so many people enslaved, so many hungry, with a war that would end all civilization, should it take place, hanging like the sword of Damocles over our heads. Never have there been so many broken homes, juvenile delinquents, alcoholics, suicides, homicides, drug addicts, and mentally deranged people. And all the while we talk of progress, as if change and progress were synonymous and that everything new must be good. People as such have no virtue. A hundred people are not better than ten people. They merely consume more. And we are thinking of consumers today, not realizing that tomorrow we may have consumed ourselves off the face of the earth.

We are off the coast of Mexico now, out of sight of land, but have seen some small gulls. At first I thought they were flying fish, but they seem to be tiny terns. No other sign of life, though the sea here is one of the great game fishing areas of the world.

The iron deck astern has just been painted black, with great splotches of red oxide in a really modern abstract design. It is evident that artists must use very large paint brushes to get such wide strokes of color and cover such large surfaces.

The deck we use has been oiled and all over the ship sailors are engaged in what are almost housemaid or housewifely tasks—washing, sweeping, painting, scraping, polishing—with rags, pails, mops, or brushes in their hands. A ship, like a house, is never finished, a sailor is a housemaid of the sea whose work is never done. By the time the end of the ship is reached and everything clean, painted up, and shipshape, the whole thing has to be done again, so great are the wear and tear and the deterioration of sun, wind, and salt water on the wood and paint work.

The wide, empty horizon stretches out, not endlessly in all directions but ends in a hard line, serrated by the wave tips on the horizon. It has an apparent edge that moves with the ship, the ship being in the middle of a dark blue saucer, for the horizon has perspective and bends away in an arc from any point one stares at.

There is certainly no reason at sea to believe the world is round. It quite obviously is flat. If it were not flat how could the water remain upon it? The reasoning of the first seamen is easy to understand. The appearance of a mast on the horizon when a ship was coming toward them or the disappearance of a hull when it was going away was no doubt accepted as fact—just one of those things—as a phenomenon like so many others that had no logical explanation, for it seems likely that in those days men could live happily by faith and without logic. They lived largely by rule of thumb, empirically, without inquiring too deeply into causes.

We have four blond stewardesses on board—a plump one, a thin one, a pretty one, and a small one. These are wide definitions. None of them are ugly but one is prettier than the other three; one is plumper than the other three; and one is taller than the other three, and one is smaller than the other three, and all are very nice girls. The plump one is married to an engineer on the ship and speaks fairly good English. The other three would, I think, like to be married to someone and no doubt will be before long. None of them speak more than a few words of English, which presents certain problems, as the same word has different meanings in English and Norwegian. "Envelope" in English means "cheese sandwich" in Norwegian. At least that is what Tiny got when she asked for some envelopes.

It seems a good custom for officers to be able to take their wives to sea with them as stewardesses. The girls see the world with their husbands and the couple can save a little nest egg with which to start their home. The Norwegian merchant marine is the third largest in the world and sailing is in their blood. Most of the officers we have sailed with are the sons and grandsons of sea captains. Many of them first went to sea as boys, sailing under their own fathers.

The psychology of the Norwegian and perhaps all real sailors is rather special. They appear to have a sense of vocation, a call to the sea. This may be hereditary. The sea has been in their blood since the days of the Vikings, or they may be conditioned by their environment as children—sons and grandsons of sailors—and the talk they have heard of adventure and danger. Also, they may be influenced by the limited opportunities in Norway. Forestry, fishing, the merchant marine, and hard subsistence farming are the most usual careers, other than business in the towns or being artisans. But a Norwegian sailor gets home only every eighteen months or two years, so it is no calling for a uxorious or even a moderately sensual man, as the French say. The sailor is cut off from everything but the sea. He has, in principle, no telephone, no mail, no newspapers, no films, no TV, no dissipation, no exercise, no recreation, no music, no theaters, no conversation. Of course he has all these things but only occasionally, when he is in port, if he is not too busy to take advantage of the amenities that are on hand.

He cannot drink at sea, he cannot make love. He can read, play records, watch the few mediocre films they have on board. He must be able to get on with the same men for months at a time and to live without news of those he loves. It is the sea itself, the fickle, cruel sea that becomes his mistress, the sea's face he must watch, the sea's moods he must interpret. The sailor is at once unbelievably naïve in a material, worldly sense, but very sophisticated, very advanced indeed in his relation to reality. Very close to the infinite, to what, if we are not afraid of being considered corny, we call God. It is impossible for a man, day after day, year after year, to take shots at the stars, to go on watch in the night, to experience the fearful terror of great storms at sea, to see men killed in accidents or fights, without being changed, without being different from the run-of-the-mill banker, clerk, or shopkeeper whose life, wound up like a clock at puberty, runs down, ticking less loudly every day in the rut of habit that leads him from his cradle to his grave. The man who goes out with the boys to play poker on Thursday and sleeps with his wife at 10:30 with the lights out on Saturday, who goes to the First Baptist Church on Sunday at 11 A.M. precisely, dines on pot roast at 1 P.M., has a nap from 2 to 3 P.M., and then finishes those sections of the Sunday paper he missed in the morning. These honest citizens may be the backbone of any country, but they are neither its brains nor its guts.

The merchant sailor is not given the credit he should have, for it is to him we owe most of the comforts and luxuries that we use daily without thinking how they got into our homes. The shelves of any supermarket will tell the story. Coffee from Brazil, tea from Ceylon and China, crab and tuna from Japan, sardines from Portugal, wine from France. It is the merchant marine that brings the rubber for our cars, the tin for our cans, the sisal for our string, the hides for our leather, the wool for our clothes.

It was the early mariner who opened up the world, who traded for tin in Britain and exchanged it among other things for dogs from Assyria. Dogs—mastiffs that were later imported by the Romans to fight in their games. It was mariners seeking the Indies who discovered America and rounded the Cape of Storms.

World history should be taught in these terms. In the terms of exploration and trade routes, of raw materials and finished products rather than by memorizing a series of dates and the names of kings or of battles, which would never have taken place had there been no material motive. The wars of Canada were about the fur trade, those of the West Indies were based on rum and sugar, the conquest of Mexico on gold and silver. The battles of the East were for spices, silks, rare curios, and perfumes.

These are the thoughts we think, the reasons we like to travel by freighter, for the romance is still with us. World trade continues becoming daily more complex as each part of the world becomes more dependent on imports from some other part and less self-sufficient.

Going to South America last year, we took tractors and farm machinery, fertilizer and tin plate, ingots of aluminum, and telegraph poles. Homeward bound, we carried 1200 tons of bones for fertilizer from the stockyards of Rosario, coffee from the interior, and bales of sisal from Bahía.

Every ship we sight is carrying a cargo of some kind. Moving things from where they are plentiful to where they are scarce. This is the basic principle of trade—a free movement of supply toward demand. The values are high or low, according to the scarcity of the product and the world's need for it.

The passengers on a freighter are of a special type, usually middle-aged or older, usually retired or they would not have the time to travel in such a dilatory manner. Not rich, because the rich are accustomed to greater luxury. Not poor, because fares are not cheap, and there are always the additional expenses of side trips. There would be no point in traveling if one never got off the ship.

We have had some interesting fellow passengers. On one trip to Africa we were alone with ten missionaries. On another trip we made we had a charming colored undertaker and his wife who were going to a morticians' convention in Miami. I should like to have attended it. As I told him, he was in a very good business because everyone he looked at was a potential customer. He was a keen fisherman and had a great sense of humor. On another trip we sailed with a thick-set man from Chicago who we were convinced was a gangster. We have sailed with a photographer who had spent months in Tahiti taking films, who disillusioned me completely by telling us that none of the girls there have any teeth, that you may follow a beautiful girl with long black hair down to the small of her back, and when she turns her head she has no teeth. It seemed to me, however, that if she were pretty enough the solution would be to buy her pretty store teeth and say, "You be a good girl or I'll take my teeth back." She would have to sign a receipt for them and of course I should have to be much younger and not married.

It is true, however, that women everywhere seem to look better from behind and are often disappointing when faced. This back view attraction is one of nature's devices. Our primitive ancestors who saw a girl modestly running slowly away with her hair waving like a flag behind her, her little behind wobbling in a dainty and seductive manner, could not help pursuing her and catching her by her pony-tail. Then he was stuck with her and in all these thousands of years the pattern has changed very little. There is not a man in the world worthy of the name who has not followed some girl whose face he has never seen.

In a way freighter passengers resemble the people who travel in Greyhound busses, except that they are much better off. But there are plenty of people who seem to spend most of their time cruising about the United States in busses, spending the winter in California or Florida, and the summer in New England. People who know to the last nickel the value of each hot dog or glass of milk, who never buy a paper but read those that are abandoned. They are real travelers, solvent hobos with small pensions or savings who like to see new places and new faces.

When we visited the Winthrop Rockefellers in Arkansas we went by bus. There are no trains from New Orleans to Little Rock. We never fly if we can help it and our car is in Africa. It took us three days, as we spent one night in Jackson and one in Memphis en route. We not only saw America first but met some very interesting people and overheard some remarkable snatches of conversation. One well-dressed woman who looked like a fashion consultant sat next to a young farmer in very clean khaki clothes and a white cowboy hat. Evidently she had been brought up on a farm, because they began talking cow, horse, and mule. One sentence ran like this. The smart-looking lady said, "And, oh boy, if you didn't get that head collar over her left ear first you never got it on." That was about a mule.

An old man beside us next day was a great talker. When he had talked nonstop for forty-five minutes he told us so. "You know," he said, "I like to talk. Well, one day I got into a bus and looked around for someone who looked as if they would like talking to sit next to. I saw a nice-looking lady and sat beside her. 'Ma-am,' I said, 'do you like to talk?' 'I sure do,' she said, and started. She never stopped for a hundred and fifty-two miles. No, sir," he said, "for a hundred and fifty-two miles I never got a word in edgewise."

The South is a great place for femininity. They have more "queens" to the square mile than anywhere else in the world. There was the Cotton Carnival, which we struck in Memphis. It was full of queens, ladies-in-waiting, little pages and pagesses, complete with male boll weevils waiting in the wings. But the girls were certainly lovely. In pale bouffant dresses, with shoulder-length hair, they really looked like girls. I had almost forgotten what a girl looked like. They really look very nice, and we should have more of them around in the North. They exert a softening influence. They are the flowers in the rather somber garden of life, decorating it, as they wait to be picked by some rich old man.

Today the sea was rough. Great combers rolled by, in enormous vomit-making arcs, from the northwest, striking us diagonal blows below the belt. The ship rises, falls, reels, staggers, rolls, and pitches. There is the crash of broken crockery, and storm soup—a kind of very liquid Irish stew— for supper.

By next morning the big seas are behind us and we see the mountains of Mexico rising out of a blue satin sea. There are sea gulls, some large ones, and more little terns. Over the land, as always seems to be the case in these latitudes (we noticed it in the West Indies and South America, too), are long, low banks of ostrich-plume-shaped clouds with horizontal bottoms, as flat as tables.

We respect doctors, and surgeons in particular, because they have our lives in their hands. But so has the captain of a ship at sea. Each has the lives of his crew and his passengers, say some fifty-odd souls on a ship like this, to perhaps two or three thousand on one of the *Queens*, in his keeping. There is the ship as well, and the cargo, and more lives on other ships that might be lost in collision. The captain can pass no buck. He has no assistants in disaster, no excuses. By one mistake the work of a lifetime, his whole career, is wrecked and he is on the beach, a ruined man.

There is, too, the isolation of his position, the loneliness of his responsibility. For the gap between the captain and the first mate is far greater than that between the first mate and the fourth. There can be no democracy on a ship. Nothing can be decided by a committee. There are only the captain, the ship, and the sea.

Perhaps the charm of a slow sea voyage on a freighter is the opportunity it gives one to think without the usual interruptions of telephone calls, wires, and letters, newspapers and the radio.

We are no longer lashed by the copper wires of the telephone company to every person we have ever met. There are no outside impacts, no worries, because, since nothing can be done about anything, worry is useless. In this way a sea trip has much the same charm as a safari except that in the bush one is occupied by watching game and exploring the country. At sea there is nothing much to explore but one's own mind.

In the monotony of the sea little things assume a great importance. Like the bird we saw afloat on a piece of timber. As we watched it people were being run over by motorcars, murdered and raped, babies by the dozen were being born, but they were, by the mystery of being at sea, quite irrelevant. Only the little bird drifting to its death on a bit of 4 x 2 was important.

A flight of flying fish like silver finches, like skipped stones, skims out of the sea and flicks into it again a hundred yards away. A school of small porpoises passes us, leaping out of the water like black hoops. The porpoise, they say, is the most intelligent mammal after man. It might be very nice to be a porpoise. Certain animals and birds appear to get great pleasure out of movement. Porpoises, seals, and otters, in water. Fewer things on land. Some gazelles such as the Tommy in East Africa, impala, and spring buck all seem to run and jump just for the hell of it. And many birds like to fly. Hawks, eagles, gulls, storks, swifts, swallows, nightjars, all big or medium-sized birds. The only little bird that likes to fly seems to be the hummingbird. But the birds that do not enjoy flying have other pleasures. Many of them like to sing.

Engineers are very interesting. They seldom know where they are or even pop out to look, and always seem to carry a flashlight in one hand and a piece of cotton waste in the other. They also seem to be allergic to air unflavored by Diesel oil. They always know the temperature of the water, the revolutions of the propeller, the amount of fuel consumed in the last twenty-four hours, the number of knots per hour the ship is making, and all the detailed and manifold perfections of the splendid engines that they serve. This is their life, moving about, up and down in the innards of the ship, watching the round clock faces of a hundred gauges for symptoms of mechanical illness—ready at any moment, like surgeons, with the tools of their trade, and supported by their assistant nurses, to operate upon any part of the engine's body.

Of all the ship's officers, the engineers are the best off because at any time in almost any place an engineer can get a job ashore, whereas an executive officer's skill can be applied only at sea.

The engine room, running vertically up the center of the ship, is its most vulnerable point. A collision or a shell burst here will sink it in a matter of minutes. There is no cargo to slow up the inflow of water, no safety door to close.

This was our first Christmas at sea. The Norwegians have their Christmas on Christmas Eve. Fortunately the big rollers of yesterday had disappeared and the sea is smooth. There are twisted paper streamers across the dining saloon, folding red paper bells hung in the corners. On a small table the ship's Christmas tree stands braced by wires to the bulkhead and illuminated with colored lights. We brought out our little tinseled tree and put it on the radio, lashing it fast with colored ribbons.

The evening began with the captain's cocktail party, where we had old-fashioneds and nuts. The *pièce de résistance* of dinner was a kind of salt cod à la king. This is a Norwegian national dish and is made by soaking the cod for some days in water and then cooking it with cream. All the officers turned up for the party in full dress, and the stewardesses had made a good job of their appearance and looked wonderful. After dinner everyone danced on deck. It was all very gay and rather sad. For these men were so far from their homes and those they loved. Christmas is, after all, a time for children, and their children were four thousand miles away in distance and months away in time—for it would be months before they went home on leave again.

CHRISTMAS DAY

Very calm again, blue, blue water, and we go quite close to the coast of Mexico. Close enough to see Acapulco in the distance and to think of some of our friends who are spending the winter there. During the morning we saw seven enormous turtles, all swimming singly. They each dived as we went past them, popping up later in the froth of our wake.

THE CITY OF ANGELS

Five

HANGOVER DAY—TURTLES AND CONDORS—A SEA
OTTER—SAN PEDRO—A GIANT CRANE—A FEELING
OF GUILT—OIL WELLS—BEL AIR—A LOST DOG—
INDIANS—A QUIET NIGHT—THE BEST FOOD—SWANS
IN A GARDEN

December 26 is Boxing Day in England and hangover
day in most parts of the Christian world.

We are now off the long peninsula of Baja California,
a wild and dangerous coast, I'm told. We pass two light-
houses close together—one on the cliffs and one, a new one
striped like a wasp, higher up in the beginning of the foothills. There is range upon range of mountains here, five thousand to six thousand feet high, according to the chart, which
have drifts of sand that look like snow on their tops and in
the sheltered ledges where they have been protected from the
wind.

Far above the mountains, with the captain's 7 x 50 glasses,
I watch a very large bird sailing in great circles on the air
currents of the upper air. It must have been a condor from
its size at that range, particularly as this is one of the few
breeding areas left to these splendid birds. A little later we
disturbed a marlin that must have been sleeping. It leaped
out of the water sail up, sharp beak fully visible, and dived
with a splash not fifty feet away.

More turtles—two big ones swimming with their bodies
hidden under the surface of the water. Their heads, green
and shining in the sun, looked like the big glass demijohns
that people have made into lamps.

A solitary brown pelican flies by us circling the ship very low, its wing tips almost touching the water, and settles down near our wake. We are some fifty miles from the shore, the mountains now are just a haze in the distance.

It will be interesting to see the news. We have had none since we left, but much of our trip seems to consist of passing through one troubled area or another. We sailed from New Orleans, where the legal battle of desegregation of the schools is being fought. We passed Cuba, the spearhead of communism stuck into the soft warm belly of the Caribbean. We went through the Panama Canal, where there is flag trouble. Flag trouble is always a symptom of some deeper sickness. The Panamanian flag must fly everywhere. It must fly at the same level. Now, when we have left the West Coast we shall proceed westward to the Far East, all of it in the news, all seething, bubbling, simmering like a pot. We shall see Hong Kong, the tiny doorway into Red China. Bangkok, filled with refugees from Laos. We are on the way to the edge of the Bamboo Curtain. Out of our own Western world into another that will be strange in every way—as different in its own way as Africa. It is easy to talk about one world and write of it as if it were an accomplished fact. But it is not one world. In fact, while we talk of it and hope for it the world seems to become more fragmented day by day.

DECEMBER 27

The weather is much colder and there is some fog. We pass large patches of floating seaweed about room size, with gulls walking about on them as if on a carpet. On one of them there was a small dark brown animal that popped up to look at us like a prairie dog out of its hole, and then popped back again. Then it peeped out from under the water, showing only a bullet head. Not having our glasses with us, we couldn't check carefully. But if sea otters were not almost extinct and if they were coming back into California waters

I should have said this was a sea otter. In fact I do not see what else it could have been. It was not adrift in the sense of being marooned on its island of weed. It seemed happy and at home there. Not so long ago there were thousands of sea otters in the Pacific.

We have been followed by quite a lot of gulls. They seem more used to ships than most, for several have perched on the masts and rails. About lunchtime there were high mountains rising out of the mist and in the early afternoon we passed an island to the west.

DECEMBER 28

We pass other islands and a gray battleship that was highly lit in the sunshine. Mottled with dark shadows, it looked like some venomous insect, a scorpion armed with prickles, stings, and claws. Another reminder of the times in which we live.

We are back in American waters now, having left them ten days ago. We have been down the Mississippi, crossed the Gulf of Mexico within sight of Cuba, crossed Panama through the canal and sailed up the western coast of Costa Rica, Nicaragua, Honduras, El Salvador, Guatemala, and Mexico, and now we are back again in almost the same latitude as New Orleans on the other side of the continent.

It is amazing to think that in 1847, before the discovery of gold, this coast was all but uninhabited. San Francisco was a sleepy little Mexican trading station, composed of a cluster of fifty adobe dwellings, mud-, skin-, or hide-covered huts, that was occasionally visited by a New Bedford or Nantucket whaling ship that came to pick up its only exports—the hides, tallow, and horns of the cattle ranches. Between April 1, 1847, and April 1, 1848, only one barque and one brig arrived in San Francisco from Atlantic ports. And nine whalers called in for water, meat, and wood. In 1849, after the discovery of gold, 775 vessels left Atlantic ports for San Francisco and 91,000 passengers in ships from all parts of the world landed in California.

San Diego, the Harbor of the Sun, as it has been called, was discovered by Cabrillo, who sailed into the bay in 1542 and claimed it for the King of Spain. Nothing much seems to have taken place there, though, till the eighteenth century, when the Russians, hunting seals and whales, threatened to settle on the coast, and Fra Junípero Serra in 1769 established a chain of twenty missions along the Camino Real to thwart their designs.

The mission in Los Angeles, Our Lady of the Angels, which still exists, was built in 1781. The whole area at that time seems to have consisted of immense ranches, some of them a million or more acres in extent, that were grants from the Spanish Crown.

But what happened between the eighteenth and twentieth centuries I have still to discover. Everyone I have asked remains very vague about it.

San Pedro is a pretty little harbor. Above it is a hill surmounted by a round silver water tower. There are a number of smart fishing craft tied up. A small nylon-sailed yacht passes us going out to sea. Following us in was the lovely turquoise-blue ship, also Scandinavian, that we saw in Lake

Gatun. How beautiful some freighters can be. Seeing ships day after day, one can easily see why they are considered feminine. There are fine, strong, buxom ships, gay flirtatious ships, old whores of the sea, queens like the *Mary* and *Elizabeth*, and the old dead *Normandie*, and saucy little yachts flashing their white undies. There are bold ships, capricious ships, unlucky ships. Each ship, even the new steel motor-driven ship of today, has a personality, each a quality of life, a kind of soul that has grown with her from her creation on the drawing board to the laying of her keel and on up to the day she does her trials. All this time men have thought of her as they worked to build her. Hundreds of men have had her in their minds. Building a ship is not the same as assembling a motorcar. And a vessel that has been in the minds of hundreds of men for months becomes imbued with some special quality, a quality that houses once had, and that most churches still have. For if there is one thing a ship cannot be it is jerry-built, though some of those mass-produced during the war may have approached it.

Immigration and health officers come on board to look at our papers, our passports and health books with their manifold entries of paratyphoid, tetanus, cholera, smallpox, and yellow fever. It is extraordinary how guilty one feels in the presence of any uniformed official when one of them says, "Where did you sail from? When did you sail? Why did you sail? Where are you going?" Everyone who does not have a criminal training becomes unbelievably embarrassed. This is not the moment when the meek, the pure, and the innocent can feel any comfort. In spite of possessing no narcotics, having paid our fares, and having every necessary visa, every kind of fear sweeps over one. This of course is apparent to the officers in question, who pay no further attention to those who are embarrassed and concentrate on those who are at ease. It is curious that thumbprints are not used on such vital documents as passports. A man does not have to be highly trained to see that two prints do not coincide, and every official should be entitled to ask anyone for a print. These test prints could be made with a clean grease and returned to the maker where there was no question of error. As it is, the ordinary respectable citizen is worried more than he should be, and the criminal with forged papers travels with relative impunity.

The agent had a message for us. We are to call up the Twentieth Century-Fox studio. Which we did. And an hour later a car arrived to pick us up. The drive to Hollywood took more than an hour and was fascinating. We were docked at Pier 232 on Terminal Island. This island is joined to the mainland by two drawbridges and a ferry. We drove past Long Beach Naval Installation, past one of the world's largest cranes (the Russians and the Japanese have the other two). Built in Germany, stretching 200 feet into the air, they are capable of lifting 580 tons. The cables that looked like bits of string as we drove past are five inches in diameter.

On both sides of us were shallow oil wells. The oil here is only a few hundred feet below the surface but is of low quality, having been damaged by the seepage of salt water from the sea, and since there is no pressure from natural gas, which has all escaped, it has to be pumped mechanically. I had no idea before that oil was like wine, some good, some so poor that it was hardly worth the expense of putting it into barrels. But here they were, these well heads, like black hammerheaded birds, pulling out the black worm of the rods. That is what they looked like—hundreds of black birds pecking at the holes and dragging up the thin, worm-like rods in their beaks. Next we came to an area where the oil lay deeper and a steel forest of tall derricks pointed their skeleton fingers to the sky. And after the forest we came to houses, hundreds of thousands of new little lingerie-colored houses—pink, blue, mauve, cream, green—crowded together in housing projects that were prevented from being semi-rural slums only by the brilliance of the paint and that would, as it faded, degenerate into them. Now suddenly there were palms, tall, naked, with feather-duster heads and these only in one smallish residential, and small shop area.

All the time we were driving toward the mountains that cup Los Angeles. It was a clear day without smog. In the distance there was snow. This is the fantastic feature of California. Skiing in the mountains, sun bathing in the desert, and surfing in the ocean—all within easy reach.

Much of the town was just like any other town except the houses were lower, the feeling was flatter, and the papyrus and poinsettias showed that we were in a subtropical area. There were more shops, more cars, more people as we left the freeway. And then I said, seeing the skeletons of some buildings by the roadside, "That must have been a hell of a fire." Three or four large houses or small loft factories stood, gutted, with sagging roofs and windows like empty eye sockets. "Fire?" was the reply. "That's a forty-acre lot. Belongs to Sam Goldwyn. There's everything in there: New York streets, Western streets, ranch houses, saloons." This was Hollywood all right.

At last we reached Bel Air, passing the homes of some of the richest people in America (mostly retired men from the East) and drew up at the hotel. There a porter took our luggage, looking at it with some disdain, and, bidding farewell to Mr. Foster, who had fetched us, we went over a small bridge into the lobby of one of the world's most famous and fascinating hotels. The Bel Air Hotel is a converted riding academy situated in a cup in the hills that surround it on three sides. After registering we were taken to our room —No. 131—a large room with twin beds. Leaving our gear, we returned to the lounge for a drink that turned into two drinks. When we went back up an open alley lined with flowering camellias in attractive concrete pots, rightly called "Camellia Lane," we found that only one bed had been turned down. This we felt was really the Hollywood psychological red carpet treatment. "Dale Carnegie has been here," Tiny said, giving me one of her long low looks to which I responded with one of my long low looks.

From our dinner table we looked out onto a floodlit garden of bananas, traveler's palms, tree ferns, giant papyrus and bougainvillaea. There were some nice pictures on the walls. A fire was burning brightly and the place was full.

Our excellent dinner was somewhat spoiled by a lost dog, a sort of golden cocker with a long tail, that was searching desperately for its owner. We are always profoundly affected by lost dogs, partly by the seeking look in their eyes, and partly for the feelings of their owner. There is also a feeling of horror at the knowledge that many people deliberately abandon their dogs.

Many years ago we picked up a small white bitch pup that was lost. We named her Susan and kept her until she died of old age. But we found then that in Florida hundreds of puppies and kittens are given to children as presents and abandoned when the holidays are over. This is a strange way to bring up a child. The whole idea of a pet is to teach a child the idea of love and responsibility, the idea of respect for other living things.

An animal is not a toy. It shares the world with us, shares the vital quality of life with us, and is a kind of very distant relative if we accept the term in its widest sense. We refuse to think of meat as part of an animal. Wrapped in cellophane in a supermarket, it certainly bears no relation to its source. We do not think of eggs coming out of hens or milk coming out of cows. This is due, I think, to our refusal to think anything unpleasant through. We even refuse to face the realities of juvenile delinquency or organized crime.

We have done a lot of odd things that we refuse to recognize. The manner in which we solved our colonial problem with the Indians was extremely simple and effective, but scarcely one of which we can be proud. What were our territories anyway but colonies? And how neatly we took them over. In some ways our economic and dollar imperialism must appear to other nations as somewhat hypocritical, since we reap benefits without accepting the responsibility of administration or the moral obliquity now leveled at the ex-colonial powers.

Our room was charming and we had one of the quietest nights I have ever spent anywhere, so quiet that I could hear our new Westclox ticking for the first time since we bought it in New Orleans. I had objected to its soundlessness, as I like to hear a clock tick. How else do you know it is still going? But this silence at Bel Air was audible. That is to say, you heard the absence of sound and listened for your own heartbeat. Not a bird chirped, not a cock crowed to greet the dawn. Even in the desert in Africa there are sounds. The sound of the wind, of a calling bird or a crawling insect. In the wilds there is no real silence. There are multiple little sounds that add up to what we think is silence. Real silence is something a man cannot stand. One of the problems of space travel is going to be how to supply sounds to fill this vacuum.

On the other hand, man can be made ill and even sent mad by too much sound. Sound, like everything else, has to be just right. To be happy, a man, at least a man like me, should be awakened by the crowing of cocks—I'll never forget them in Nassau twenty years ago—or the singing of birds. The shock of being awakened day after day, year after year by the ringing of an alarm clock must do something to the soul of a man, and this is what we live by today. By bells, like Pavlov dogs—alarms, telephones, doorbells, each producing a shock, each causing a rush of adrenalin into the blood as we wonder, What now? Who now?

After breakfast—coffee, toast, and the best orange juice I have had since we were in Zebediela in the Transvaal—I sat down to watch Tiny pack. Tiny is the best packer in the world. Nothing ever has to be pressed.

Thinking of the orange juice, we talked about where we had had the best things, because certain things have always stuck in our memory as quite outstanding. For instance, we have never had a cauliflower equal to one we bought in Gulf-port, Florida, when we were living there. Just one. We never got another. The best watermelon we have ever eaten was in Puerto Rico, the best grapefruit in Nigeria, the best rice in Liberia, the best alligator pear in the Northern Transvaal, the best plums in Somerset West at the Cape. The best asparagus I grew myself on our farm in South Africa. The best pears were in Northern France, again from my own garden. The best apple, Cox's Orange Pippin, was in England. The best pineapples in Ghana and Puerto Rico. The best salmon in Spain, the best sole in Paris, the best chicken in Paris. No chicken can compare with a *poulet de Bresse*.

I am not a big eater but will try anything. I have eaten frog's legs, snails, octopus, locusts, cat, horse, zebra, goat, lizards, flying ants, lynx brains, tortoise, tortoise eggs, penguin, sea gull, duck's and plover's eggs, iguana, turtles, wild boar, suckling pig, all sorts of venison, eels, snakes, and small birds of many kinds. I do not think there is anything I would not try, except the chunks of raw meat they eat in Ethiopia or the whole sheep's eyes that are considered a delicacy in North Africa. I do not understand people who go to Europe and ask for steak and French-fried potatoes and drink high-balls. A great deal of the pleasure of travel is gastronomic. Why should curiosity end with our eyes? To live fully, we need all our senses, and taste is not the least of them.

The garden at Bel Air is interesting, somewhat formal and obviously under Japanese influence, which is apparent the moment you arrive and cross the bridge. There are bronze cranes. There are little streams, ponds, and waterfalls.

After breakfast I went around the garden. There were some redwoods by the stream and tree ferns that now always make me think of those we saw at Kells in Kerry. The roses were still in flower but almost over. There were strelitzias, giant papyrus, azaleas, yellow pansies, bamboo, orchids, pampas grass, a lot of trimmed ivy instead of grass, and two white swans in a pool, one asleep and drifting on the breeze like a paper boat. I have always admired swans. These are not birds to be trifled with. Before I had finished going around the garden Tiny appeared, having convinced herself that I was lost, run over, or that I had wandered into the wrong patio and been seduced by some exotic blonde. Her packing finished, and I saved from myself, we went to the main lounge together and waited for the car that was to take us to the studio.

FILMLAND

Six

We arrived at the Twentieth Century-Fox lot with our luggage, as if we had come to stay. The soft thing (as we call it) with clothes, Tiny's dressing case with make-up, a parcel of new make-up from the drugstore to get us over the Pacific, and a roll of magazines and newspapers—*McCall's, Vogue, Time, Life, Newsweek*—were all stowed away in Ted Strauss's office, and we were led to a small projection room and waited there in the darkness for my first picture to begin.

It was an amazing experience, for what I saw bore very little resemblance to what I had written. My name was on the screen long after that of every other person, from the director to the make-up man, and the title of the picture was that of the book—*The Fiercest Heart*. The names of some of the characters were mine. It was set theatrically in Africa and there was some African footage showing wild game. The rest I think, judging from the type of vegetation, was done in Mexico. It was an interesting story, a kind of African Western with a nice battle at the end of it. I can imagine people who like Westerns liking it. I should not think it cost too much to produce or that it could fail to make money. There were some sex, sadism, and scenery arranged in palatable proportions. It lacked only emotional quality, humor, and tension.

There was a little boy I had never seen before. The hero and the villain might have been brothers. Juliet Prowse smoldered effectively but never flamed like the Boer Bardot I had seen in my mind. Our friend Raymond Massey, who had wanted for twenty years to play a Boer patriarch, achieved the role, but the dialogue he was given did not match the part.

We left when it was over with a feeling of having killed an hour or so not unpleasantly. I had been surprised to find the Foreign Legion in red jackets at the castle in Cape Town in 1837, and a water buck being cut up for food. The water buck is about the only buck that no one wants to eat. But there the picture was, still to be finished as far as cutting and sound were concerned, but done. A real workmanlike job, out of conferences by expediency. A very practical camel that I had seen as a horse had been born.

As a young author I might have been upset. Now I was relieved that it was not worse. It easily could have been. African stuff is hard to handle, the film of *Something of Value* being a good example. Unless the curious paradoxes of the continent are understood, unless its mystery is felt, nothing can be made of it. *Where No Vultures Fly* was African and made in Africa, but that is the only good film I can think of. The material is there, more drama to the acre than anywhere else, but not the men who can turn reality into credible and artistic pictures.

We had lunch at Dales' in Wilshire Boulevard with Ted Strauss of the story department. I had two Bloody Marys and a broiled white fish which was excellent. Tiny had spaghetti and meat balls. There were three very interesting coincidences which occurred during lunch.

The first was when we got talking about Hollywood and I said I had worked here for Paramount in '43 and had had a wonderful secretary whose first name was Judy and whose last name I had forgotten. We wrote to each other for five or six years and then I lost track of her. She was then in the armed forces in Germany and I had gone to Africa.

"Her last name wasn't Unell, was it?" Ted said.

"It was," I said. "Do you know how I can get in touch with her?"

"She's working for me," he said.

Number Two was when we were talking about cars for camping and he said he had ordered a Volkswagen camper but wasn't sure about it, and I said we had one in Africa and were delighted with it.

This led to the final coincidence. We now got to talking about fishing, game, and so on, and Ted mentioned Roderick Haig-Brown and I said I knew his father. He had taught at Lancing College, Sussex, where I was at school. He commanded the O.T.C.—Officers' Training Corps, was very keen on shooting, and I used to take care of his ferrets, clean his guns, and handle his dogs. His black cocker spaniel bitch had had a golden pup. This was a mutation and one of the first born in England.

The lunch and the conversation had been so good that we had forgotten we were sailing at five, and we had to rush back to the office to pick up our luggage and get a car from the transport pool to take us to the ship. Once again we had been too happy, inexcusably so, since we were sober. We have often been accused of laughing and enjoying ourselves when sober. This is very antisocial. But I am somewhat antisocial by nature. I hate crowds and like only a few people. I have no sense of the team spirit or togetherness. This may account for the fun we have.

Hollywood has changed a great deal since we worked here. The offices and lots that once were alive with people are now empty. Pictures were being made, but the old gray mare ain't what she used to be. We drove out past houses of all types and kinds, past sets, past acres of props, furniture of all kinds, doors, chimneys, shuttered windows, and out through the gate.

My general impression of Los Angeles was that here we had a prototype of the city of the future, a city spread over such an immense area that a man's legs were utterly useless.

In fact, a place where walking was impossible. The city is sixty or more miles in diameter, and is flat. There are hardly any tall buildings. The parking space and road areas must equal the amount of ground covered by houses in terms of acreage. Los Angeles is a metropolitan suburb, a suburb that has grown like an ulcer, uncontrolled and uncontrollable, with seventy thousand people pouring into it every month and some thirty thousand leaving it.

It gives one the impression of a place where anything can happen and most things do. An impression, not of evil, but of a place where crime prevention and control must present almost incredible difficulties, with an area of 455 square miles, with 7,600,000 cars in the state and most of them registered in this county, with a shifting population and a climate that permits almost continuous night-and-day outdoor living and all the temptations that go with it.

Here is a new concept, or new to me at least, of a world where a man is lost, immobilized without a car—as much lost as an Arab in the desert without a camel or a gaucho on the pampas without his horse. The stadium, for example, has parking space for six thousand cars.

This is the land of fairy gold, of thwarted hopes, a Sargasso Sea of brains, brawn, and beauty as far as the film industry is concerned. There are lots of industries—steel, chemicals, fruit processing, wine making, aircraft factories, oil refining—some 10,000 plants that employ 800,000 hands. But though the film industry has declined in importance, its flavor remains. The waitress hopes someone will notice how well she is stacked. The filling-station attendant tries to show his profile because one never knows, does one? The small-town beauty queen is still given her screen test here as promised, and that's about all. But she seldom goes back if she does not make the grade. This is not a gentle place, not a place for the weak.

There is hardly a worker in any industry who does not dream, who does not say in his heart, "If I were in pictures . . ." and spend in his dreams the millions he will never make.

The population is now six million. It is expected to be

eight million by 1970. The city is in the center of the world, halfway between the poles and equidistant from Europe and the coast of Asia. It is a city for the young and the strong, and perhaps the hard of heart. In this town pedestrians are not people.

The driver who took us back to the ship from the Twentieth Century-Fox lot was a local man who had spent much of his time diving for abalone. By the time we got to San Pedro we were very well informed about abalones. There are three kinds, he said—black, pink, and yellow. They are dangerous to get, for if a man got his finger trapped by one he would drown. They are prized off the rocks to which they cling by means of a tire iron that is pushed between the great muscle that is the abalone and the rock to which it clings. None are allowed to be taken that are immature—that is to say, less than a certain diameter. Our friend had perfected a method of cleaning off the top of the shell by an acid bath so that the outside was as pretty as the inside. In South Africa, around the Cape of Good Hope, we have a similar shellfish, the pearlemon, exactly like it in appearance but lacking the abalone's green mother-of-pearl brilliance.

Our driver was a great friend of Vic Tanny, the health expert. I gathered they had been brought up together, and either he had taught Vic Tanny to get abalones or Vic Tanny had taught him. Anyway, the moral of the story was that in those days Vic Tanny had been poor but happy and now he was rich and not so happy. I said we were poor and happy and we all became very sorry for rich people like the Rockefellers, Kennedys, Vanderbilts, Astors, Goulds, and so on.

I would have enjoyed this conversation more if I had not been worried about catching the boat. The traffic was very bad and we were somewhat uncertain of the way to San Pedro and Terminal Island. It was now dusk and as the lights went on everything looked different. The ship was due to sail at five. It was already five.

I have never known a ship to sail exactly on time, but we were getting nervous when at five-fifteen we were lost near the Long Beach Navy Yard. It was then that Tiny saw the giant crane. We had passed it on the right going out so we had to pass it on our left to get back. We asked directions once more and then found the dock. The ship was still there and we sailed at six.

It had been a wonderful experience, but we had cut it rather fine. We had enjoyed our lunch too much.

NEW YEAR'S

Seven

New Year's Eve and another party. We had cocktails
and wine for dinner, and after it most of the officers, with
our lady stewardesses, in evening dresses, joined us in the
lounge to await the arrival of the New Year. We drank "Norwegian Coca-Cola"—that is to say, aquavit with a beer chaser
—we drank brandy, sherry, and Grand Marnier in the *jam-
sing* (which means bottoms up in Chinese) manner.

This is a sad season for the sailors who keep thinking of
what is going on at home, working out the difference in
time and saying they are doing this or that now in Norway.
We had never been at sea at these festive seasons before and
so never thought of the feelings of men who year after year
are away from their families and friends at this time.

We lost one passenger, the Danish-American photographer, in Los Angeles, and picked up three more people. A
charming Chinese couple on their honeymoon, and a lady
missionary, all three bound for Hong Kong, as was Mrs.
Finlay, a Canadian who had come with us all the way from

New Orleans. She was going to visit her married daughter who lived there.

This is the first day of the New Year. We are four hundred or five hundred miles out at sea. All the gulls except two dark-colored albatrosses have left us.

We are well north of the equator, so this knocks the theory about albatrosses' never crossing the line on the head, unless, of course, they are not albatrosses. It is very difficult to get any information about gulls at sea. You say, "What are those birds?" and the answer is, "Gulls."

We have seen lesser albatrosses resembling these in the Atlantic off the Cape of Good Hope and were accompanied by a greater albatross on one voyage from Table Bay to St. Helena. These are enormous birds with a wingspread of up to twelve feet. They have big heads and wicked long yellow beaks that end in a hook. They are more common in the Indian Ocean off the coast of Mozambique, and never, the officers told us, follow a ship beyond St. Helena.

One of their breeding places is the Falkland Islands, and we were told by the mate of the *Nopal Express* when we were off Buenos Aires that they were often seen in these waters. He had been to the Falkland Islands sealing and whaling and said they had found a nestling which was big and fat and excellent eating in the prefeather stage. According to him the parents did not feed it often or protect it.

It is stories like this that make travel so interesting.

More albatrosses have joined us. At one time there were six visible, bent like beautiful bows over the waves, falling back till they were almost out of sight and then effortlessly reappearing at our stern. They seem able to ride the air currents more skillfully than any other birds except the great land predators such as vultures, eagles, and hawks. The difference between them is the altitude at which they fly and the manner of flight. Vultures swing in great circles on the rising thermal currents so high that they cannot be seen by the human eye, yet they are still able to see a dead or dying beast in the vast area spread out below them.

Except to breed, the albatross never goes ashore. It not only sleeps on the water but is able, if the sea is too rough, to doze while in flight. This would be an amazing sight—to see this great bird drifting like a ghost in the moonlit night above a raging sea.

Watching them come down on the water, we could see the way their long wings folded back, hinged like screens in three sections. The wing bones are very strong, light, and hollow. Sailors in the old days when they did scrimshaw work used to use them for pipestems and make pouches with their feet. My brother, who was a sailor, told me all this when I was a small boy, which is one reason I have always found these birds particularly romantic and the *Ancient Mariner* one of my favorite poems.

We have been reading the papers and magazines we bought in Los Angeles. There is no good news from the Congo, Algeria, Ethiopia, Somalia, Belgium, or Venezuela—all are troubled, all in a state of revolution or near revolt.

There is, one hears, a new process which will soon make hydrogen bombs available to small, poor nations. The possession of these dime-store bombs will have a devastating effect upon the nationalistic ego. They will be the equalizers, as the six-guns were in the old West. A little man with a gun or a little nation with a bomb can kill a big one. Someone has come up with the idea that to be able to destroy another nation a hundred times is perhaps no greater deterrent to war than to be able to destroy it once.

If the first bomb does the trick the others are merely surplus. Another question is: What would happen if there were real disarmament, real peace, and the black bear and the bald eagle lay down to rest together? What would happen to our economy? Even our ideals? Whom would we have left to blame? What red herrings, what scapegoats should we find?

Without news for days, without society, without the thousand little impacts that divert and occupy the mind, these items strike harder than they would ashore. The ship, a speck in the infinity of the ocean, frees the mind. There is nothing but the sea and the sky to distract thought, nothing to take one's mind off things—horrors, beauties, possibilities.

In a city it is possible to say, "It is impossible that all this could be destroyed." We can still say that in spite of Hiroshima and Nagasaki. Just as we can pretend that the German concentration camps did not exist. Perhaps to be able to forget past horrors is a good thing, but this attitude, this escape from the past, becomes unbelievably dangerous when it is reversed and used to blind us to the dangers of the future.

At sea the picture changes. There is nothing to destroy here, nothing to prevent our visualizing destruction, no possibility of saying this could not happen here and to me. Curiously, one is often aware of how only a few inches of steel separate one from the sea and death, though few lives are lost at sea today, while ashore death on the roads is always near.

A sea trip on a freighter is less a holiday than an experience. A sensation of being suspended in time, hanging in it, dangling by the thread of one's own personality. There is nothing to do. Not many people to talk to, and they may or may not be congenial. The decks are small, the library limited, the food adequate, even good, but not titillating. The hours of the meals—twelve noon and five-thirty—are strange.

So what is left? The horizon. The line where sky and sea meet, which we sail toward and can never reach—the Holy Grail, the Golden Fleece, the rainbow's end. Everyman's dream of gold and fair women lies beyond it. The horizon is a symbol, something toward which inevitably we lift our eyes, something that those who are used to the sea and open spaces miss in the city. The horizon is the bed of the sun, the bed into which it sinks at night and from which it rises in the morning.

We are about halfway across the Pacific now. The albatrosses are still with us. There are more of them—ten to fourteen. Two pairs with white bodies and black wings. These
I think are adults and the others, brown ones, young birds.
When rubbish is thrown over the side they all land beside
it like chickens, and then when they have done come after
the ship. I have always wondered how sea birds follow a
ship for days. They must rest on the sea at night and then
be able to see an almost invisible wake, a spoor or trail of
disturbed water or water containing ship's refuse that is left
behind. Since we do over a hundred miles in the hours of
darkness, even if they went up very high we should, I imagine, be quite invisible.

This ocean is different from the Alantic. The endless rollers with wide troughs are what make the beaches of California, Hawaii, and Australia famous for surfboarding. The
seas seem to have more pattern and a more regular design.
The color, when it is not just the usual metallic color of all
water, is often a Mediterranean blue or even purple. The
air is much more dead and lacks the bite of the Atlantic. I
have never heard of air being analyzed, but it must have
recognizable medicinal qualities, since sick people are sent
to special places for the air—the sea, the mountains, to
Arizona or Switzerland. Some air is described as strong and
bracing; other places are known to be relaxing. The air of
our great cities is recognized as poisonous and a possible
cause of cancer.

It is the air I first notice when I go to sea. The best air, the
cleanest, the most perfumed, is in the Caribbean or off the
coast of New York City in from the east. Near the land it has
a smell, a smell of spices, of flowers, of fish and seaweed, a
fecund, living smell, and air that a man can drink into his
lungs as he takes wine into his belly, savoring it, being suddenly aware that this is what he has been missing, that this
is his right. I could trade good air for good food any day.
For with good air any food is palatable and in bad air in

most restaurants I find the best food nauseating. Some of the
best air I know is at our home in Hermanus at the Cape of
Good Hope. This is strong air. It is even stronger at Danger
Point and Agulhas, the southwest point of Africa. Here, as
it comes straight from the antarctic, a few lungfuls of it are
enough to put one to sleep. The east coast of England, Mar-
gate and Herne Bay, has this kind of air. So has the north
coast of France in winter.

Not enough has been written about air or its effect on
people. Breath is life. When a man ceases to breathe he dies.
In the latest methods of lifesaving the lungs of the drowned
man are inflated by being breathed into, mouth to mouth.
Lovers share their breath. The basis of yoga is breath control. A newborn baby is slapped to make it breathe. Of all
the things we need air is the first. We can go without air for
only a few minutes. We can do without water for a few hours,
without food for several days or even weeks, without shelter
indefinitely in a warm climate.

We are now entering, and shall remain until we reach
Ceylon, the great battle areas of the last war. At the moment we are not too far from Pearl Harbor. The Japanese
and American fleets must have sailed these seas and their
planes patrolled these skies. To the south and west, below
the horizon, are the myriad islands and atolls of Micronesia,
the South Seas, and the steppingstones to Japan that were
fought over so bitterly. Some of these are the island paradises
to which men disillusioned after the First World War retired
to be out of it all, only to be swept up in a tidal wave of
Japanese invasion. These are ghostly waters, for the dead
here in terms of history are still new.

There is no way for a civilized man to get out of it all
today. Only the savage is secure in his insecurity, the African
bushman, the cannibal head-hunter of New Guinea, the Indians of the Orinoco and Amazon could survive another war,
could live through it, and probably never even hear about it.

It was very interesting to travel with two Westernized Chinese people. I had met students, an ambassador, who wrote some Chinese and explained their system of pictographs to me, and of course waiters in Chinese restaurants, but had never come in close contact with any of them before. My impression was one of great racial antiquity and perfection—something that had taken a long time to bring about. Their ancestors had resembled them culturally when most of ours were running about dressed in skins and blue paint, murdering one another with stone clubs.

Certain physical features are very attractive, the beautiful color and quality of the skin, the lips, almost mauve against the dark cream, the almond eyes, the well-shaped ears. Their straight hair, which is like very fine horsetail.

There was also in this couple a very complete sexual differentiation. Frank Chao was a big, very handsome young man, his wife Elizabeth a beautiful girl. They were unmistakably a man and woman, a quality which is being lost among us of the West. They were going to live in Hong Kong—Mr. Chao's home—and he told us some very interesting things about China and the East. The communists have broken the pattern of Chinese life, of family, love, tradition, respect for age, and even beauty. He also told us that if Western men married Orientals it was generally all right so long as they stayed in the East, but the girls were seldom happy if taken to America. It would appear that men transplant better than women, or that, having more occupation, notice their surroundings less. It must be a great ordeal for a girl to have her first baby, or any baby, alone in a foreign land, and, having had it, to raise it there.

A man's nostalgia for his home is something different. It can be for a house he lived in, a tree he played near, for the food he used to eat. And if, as so often happens now, his old home has gone and the trees have gone—swallowed up in some new development—the whole basis of his homesickness has been destroyed. It is only the past he can regret now, and to do that is un-American. We are a people dedicated to the future.

This is nowhere more apparent than in Los Angeles, the City of Angels, where there are no sidewalks in most of the new developments, so that even to visit a neighbor a hundred yards or so away is impossible without a car. Moreover, if they live on the opposite side of one of the express highways a long detour might be necessary to get there.

We now have new rivers that should be marked on our maps, rivers of four-lane and eight-lane traffic as dangerous to cross as any rapid. A picture of the future is taking shape, one of mobility, of meaningless homes, meaninglessly furnished, that can be abandoned without regret and replaced, almost exactly, a thousand miles away in the time it takes to drive there. Replaced with new friends, clubs, schools, and amenities all complete, all interchangeable and unrecognizable one from the other. But in this great social advance a few things have been lost. The things a man would die for. His roof tree, his hearthstone. It is hard to imagine a man defending a mobile home or a shell-pink prefabricated ranch-type house. But we don't need men who would defend their homes. The minuteman is obsolete. Now we do it with rockets and mirrors.

Handwork, even chopping people up with axes or shooting them down with guns, is obsolete and for peasants. Now death must be mass produced and the dead anonymous, even their bones atomized, gone forever.

Mr. Chao said that the geisha houses are disappearing from Japan. The girls are now hostesses and taxi dancers. This is considered more moral, just as the call girl is more moral than the streetwalker. Not that geishas were prostitutes in the usual sense, though they might have favorite customers. But how many virgin stenographers are there in New York City? One reason for abolishing the geisha houses appears to have been that the expense for parties at them was deductible and immense costs were chalked up and kicked back.

JANUARY 6

It is still cold and there are quite big rollers. We pass a Japanese trawler, drifting with her nets, riding up on one wave and disappearing into the trough behind it. She may come from either Hawaii or Japan, the captain says. There are many good fishing banks here.

A typhoon is what we call a hurricane in the West, though it sounds worse somehow. Talking of lifeboats, our Captain Bergan said he did not like those with engines. They can run for only forty-eight hours and the gas and water take up a lot of room. During the war he took out the engines of his lifeboats and relied on oars and sails. I have heard other sailors say the same. All say they would never get into a lifeboat with a motor if they could help it. I personally hope never to get into a lifeboat. Sails are not compulsory now, which seems a pity. Not only can a great distance be covered by a small boat sailing before the wind, but the sail itself makes the boat much more visible and likely to be sighted by a passing ship.

None of the officers seem to like the Filipinos very much. They say they are liars and thieves, though of course the only people they see are the customs officers and stevedores. Apparently the Japanese are the most honest people of the Orient. For two reasons: the law is very hard on thieves, and they lose face by stealing.

We were told that the most notable feature of the Philippines is the houses of prostitution, which are the best in the world after those of Tokyo. The whole question of red-light districts is interesting, and it may be better to have this profession localized than spread all over a city. Better for keeping order and for the protection of the public. This was brought up in a discussion I had with a parson from a seamen's mission in Port of Spain, Trinidad. He put it this way: The man who wants a woman is going to get one, and the man who does not want to have anything to do with one only has to keep away from the red-light district to be safe. If, however, there is no red-light district and the women are scattered, he will inevitably be accosted and may succumb to this very natural temptation. These evil inclinations of mankind cannot be eradicated and the government might just as well control them. All gambling, lotteries, casinos, and horse racing should be government run. As it is, in spite of all the nonsense talked and written about it, the government is in the liquor business in a bigger way than the manufacturers through the taxes it collects on the sale of liquor and on the profits of the makers, the wholesalers, and retailers who handle it.

The passengers on this ship are all self-sufficient, each with his own habits and way of life. The honeymoon couple we see at meals. Mrs. Finlay comes to meals. She reads a great deal, writes a great number of letters, studies French, and walks up and down the deck one hundred twenty times a day. Miss Johnstone, the missionary, does not come to lunch and we see her only at dinner. We do not go to breakfast. We get up late and spend the morning writing and reading on deck. After lunch we paint, read, write, and sleep. When dinner, which is at 5:30 P.M., is over we go to our cabin after having been on deck to look at the stars and the sea. By ten o'clock we are asleep.

The adult gooneys, if they are gooneys, have left us. But we have eight others, or the same eight, flying, soaring, and swinging in loops about the ship. Their wings often tremble as they adjust to an air current, like the extended arms of a man on a tightrope. Their feet stick out behind the fan of their tails when seen close up.

When I was a boy I would have wanted to shoot one. Though not at sea where I could not have picked it up. The idea now horrifies me. Though I would still go out and shoot a few flighting ducks, or partridges over a good gun dog if I had the opportunity. Man is not a logical or rational animal. I hate the idea of animals' being butchered, yet I have bred a lot of slaughter stock when I was ranching in Africa, and I like good meat. We live by tastes, prejudices, and habits, some innate, most the result of education and environment, but nonetheless real. To an Italian garlic is a lovely smell. To Frenchmen snails are a delectable dish. In one nation women hide their faces and expose their breasts. In another they never show their feet.

Tonight we took an empty whiskey bottle in to dinner with a piece of paper on which we had written our names and addresses. After dinner we forgot it and went back to the saloon to find the steward and stewardesses had fished out the paper and were adding their names to the list. We had written no real message, just given the name of the ship, the date, and our position as being near Midway.

We screwed the top on tightly and went up on deck, where I threw the bottle into the sea. Tiny could not bring herself to do it. It was so irrevocable, she said. Some gooneys dived down to see what it was, and rose again in disappointment.

Everyone seemed to think this message in a bottle was a fine idea. All had said they had thought it would be fun to do it, but none of them ever had done it. It was Tiny's idea and made a pleasant little ceremony. I do not think the bottle would last long, as the metal cap would rust, particularly as it floated on its side. A wine bottle with a wax-sealed cork and weighted a little at the bottom so that it would float vertically should last for years at sea, unless it hit a rock.

The only bottle with a message I ever heard of being found was discovered by a friend of ours in Africa who was not sufficiently curious even to open it and just threw it back into the sea. I suppose every child has heard of messages in bottles, so ever since I was old enough to walk along a beach I have picked up every bottle I found, looking for one. Perhaps some child may find our message and be stirred by something out of the ordinary occurring. Anyway, that is our hope when we throw bottles overboard, and we have thrown a dozen or more in one way and another, dreaming like children ourselves of their adventures in the seas they will travel and the beach upon which they may land or the rocks that will founder them.

Tonight is the sixth, Friday. Tomorrow will be Sunday, the eighth. This was the notice on the board:

Advance watches 30 minutes. We will pass the date line during the next day so tomorrow will be Sunday, 1/8.

The half hours we have been advancing our watches have now caught up with us and are consolidated in the loss of a day. The date line is curious, running straight down the map except where it makes a dog-leg bend by the Aleutians in the north and another around Fiji in the south.

SUNDAY

We are beyond Midway now and bearing toward the Marianas, Guam, and Manila. An army plane flying below the clouds has just passed over us and turned back, satisfied we were not going too close to the base. These are strategic waters that still echo the sound of battle.

Some of the gooney birds have left us. We have only four now. Midway is a gooney breeding ground and at one time the Navy thought they would have to destroy the whole colony, as they caused too many near air crashes. They were saved by a naturalist who persuaded the authorities to level all the dunes that were near the runways. It was the air currents rising from the dunes that attracted the birds. Collisions were immediately reduced by sixty-five per cent.

The sea today is a magnificent rolling country of hills and valleys decorated with the white shrubs of the breaking waves. A flight of small flying fish, the first since the Gulf of Mexico, breaks out of the ocean like a scattering of silver coins. The sea is deep blue, marbled with white veins. The whitecaps whipped into manes by the wind, caught by the hand of the sun, become prismatic, transparent rainbows. The sky overhead is a cerulean blue with white clouds that look like shredded wool. The horizon astern is dark with squalls.

We have had some more interesting conversations with Mr. Chao. He said the Chinese do not like and apparently cannot digest dairy products such as butter and dried milk. The banquets in Japan are cooked in the Chinese style, just as ours are French. Many Norwegians take back firecrackers from China, as they are illegal in Norway. This was the first use made of gunpowder by the Chinese, who discovered it. They used firecrackers to scare devils rather than kill men—a much better idea.

Mr. Chao told us that they no longer have fighting crickets in Hong Kong. It has been stopped—theoretically because it was considered cruel, but actually too much money was lost betting on the outcome of the battles. The Chinese are great gamblers. The crickets came from the mainland or Japan and winning insects exchanged hands at high prices. Every day they were fed a grain or two of cooked rice and given water to drink. At one time there was a shop in Hong Kong that sold nothing else, importing them by the thousand. He also said that many retired men take their caged birds out for walks in the morning and evening, and sit at tables in eating houses and feed them tidbits. This would be nice to see. Old men and their birds in the East. Young men and their transistors in the West. *Plus ça change . . .*

STILL THE PACIFIC

Eight

Today the sea is rougher, the rollers attack like lines of cavalry across the plains of the sea. We have only two birds with us now. A rough sea is uncomfortable even if one is not sick. It is hard to read, write, or move about. Every act must be calculated, from eating soup to shaving.

After twenty-four hours the sky cleared and the sea lost much of its turbulence. The waves now are bigger but much farther apart, with wide green valleys between them and no whitecaps. If this were land it would be described as rolling country, almost flat in appearance, till one got into it, and then it is filled with dips, hollows, valleys, and dead ground.

To look at, from the deck, it is rather like the pampas must have been in Hudson's time, and that is not so long ago, almost within the memory of living men—with the killing grounds on the outskirts of Buenos Aires and the gardens enclosed with walls of cattle skulls.

A hundred years ago is not far away in time. There are men alive today who were babies then, two hundred or more centenarians in the United States alone. One, a member of the National Arts Club, is a friend of ours. Ten such lives overlapping one another by even a day would take us back to the Battle of Hastings. Five to the discovery of America.

As we have just left California it is interesting to trace the evolution of the Western saddle and horse gear back to Spain, where it was brought by the Moors from North Africa, right down as far south as the Sudan and Nigeria. The wide trousers worn by the gauchos still can be found for sale in the stalls of the old market in Kano, Nigeria. Even the blood of some of the Western painted horses is North African, rather than Arab. They are Barbs and resemble such breeds as the Bar el Gazal and the horses of Chad, Maiduguri, and Sokoto—blotched and spotted horses with blue eyes and pink noses. The wild horses of America now being hunted for dog meat are of this famous stock.

The ship's work is proceeding faster, the bad weather having slowed it up. A ship is like a woman, never satisfied with her appearance. Like a woman who, when she has made up her face, finds she has to do her hair again.

Some of the ship's noises are like those of a dentist's surgery, multiplied a thousand times. Electric drills whine. Winches sound like drills. There are hammering and mixing sounds, as if great cavities were being filled, and the decks are being scraped clear of their rusty tartar.

At twelve noon, so that there shall be no mistake, all hell breaks loose. A loud hoot at six minutes to twelve, at twelve another hoot, two whistles, and then the dinner gong.

The sea is seldom beautiful. This is an illusion, one of the clichés that deceive us. The associations of the sea are beautiful, the wide horizons, the skies, the clean fresh air, the gulls, the mystery of this vast emptiness. The real fascination of the sea is the changing expression on its face, the way, flecked with white dimples, it smiles in Mediterranean blue, or turns dark gray with rage, spitting gobs of yellow spume as the great white-maned stallions of the deep roar in combat with the wind.

Another day there is a hypocritical bottle green—a "butter would not melt in my mouth" kind of calm—as smooth as a satin dress stretched over a woman's thigh. I have seen this off Cape Verde, West Africa, a favorite place for suicide and famous for its sharks.

The sea can be a sheet of beaten pewter or a coat of mail worn by a man, rippling with the swell of his muscles. Sometimes small white waves appear like lovely butterflies on the blue crests; the sun is reflected by a thousand winking triangular mirrors, each bursting like an exploding star. And always one is in the center of it, in the very bull's-eye of the sea, like a crumb in the middle of a blue plate edged by the horizons.

Only at sea is a man in the center of his world. No matter where he goes the horizons move with him, frustrating him, leaving him equidistant from 12 and 6; 9 and 3 in the very middle of this great clock, alone with the ship's company in an empty world.

Ashore the horizons are much closer. Hills, houses, trees close us in—a man-made womb of security. Our fellows, instead of being the ship's complement of passengers and crew—all strangers—are our friends and relatives, a closed corporation of interest and blood. But only at sea does all this become apparent; only here do we realize our own insignificance and the fact that each of us is always, wherever we are, the center of his own private world, the axle around which, as far as he is concerned, all public affairs and private emotions must revolve to be relevant.

The sea is very calm except for the great rollers. The ship going through them makes the water sound, as it breaks away from her sides, like the little waves that uncurl themselves, soft as lace, on a sandy beach. The horizon is not flat but broken by distant rollers; some, seen sideways, look like little valleys, others like low hills stretched out to infinity. Its edge is like the skin of a dog, flat but edged with the undulations of its hair.

We are about level with Wake Island now, possibly five hundred miles to the north of it. The island is only three spits of coral a dozen feet above the level of the sea, and a thousand Japanese soldiers starved here when our submarines blockaded it in World War II. There are wrecks and guns rusting, half buried in the sand, old hangars and defense pits built by the Japanese and Marines, and a guided-missile checking installation at one end of the island is part of the Western world's defense warning system. Wake is a fuel stop for Pan Am, Japan Air Lines, and British Overseas Airways, being equidistant from Japan and Hawaii. It has a 9500-foot runway that is now being extended another 1500 feet. One thousand people live here—service people and air lines personnel. The skin diving and spear fishing around the wrecked Japanese submarines and the hulk of a torpedo supply ship that were sunk here less than twenty years ago is said to be the best in the world. Proud ships, full of men eager for the kill, are now a playground for fishermen and a refuge for fish.

Several of our crew are Chinese: the second carpenter, second cook, two deck hands, and a laundryman. There is something very homey-looking in seeing the sailors' pants whipping in the breeze as they hang on lines strung over the hold. Sometimes we have ladies' undies, too, but they are segregated and flap seductively on a line of their own on the boat deck.

The carpenter was working on deck today, finishing off a plywood filing cabinet. He was varnishing it with a pad of rags wrapped around a stone, instead of a brush. A much better idea. He was a small man exactly resembling the ancient Chinese drawings and carvings I have seen. A type that has probably been fixed for a thousand years. The calf development of his leg was tremendous. He carried no fat and worked with unbelievable speed and concentration, never looking up even when spoken to.

Chinese carpenters, Mr. Chao told me later, are apprenticed to a master craftsman for as much as seven years, and when they leave they know as much as he, for he has taught

them all his secrets and the bonds developed between the
master and his apprentice are very close, resembling those of
father and son.

All the birds have gone now. We are beyond their beat.
Perhaps we may pick up some new ones as we approach
other islands. A few flying fish today, rather large ones, solitary, and appearing to be thicker set than those of the Caribbean. We have always noticed that the bigger the school the
smaller the fish. These big ones that swim and fly alone may
be the sole survivors of quite big schools. Their flight out of
the water is probably a desperate effort to escape some
enemy—in this case the ship.

The sea changes like a landscape from hour to hour, its
color and texture depending on the wind, the color of the
sky, the currents, and the topography of the bottom. These
factors, continually rearranging themselves, produce the variety of the marine landscape. The ship's charts show ocean
depths that are contoured like those of a physical map on the
surface, and, in principle, it is no more than that, since much
of it is the surface of the earth that has been submerged,
though it is hard to visualize it and think of it that way until
we remember the raised beaches we have seen, the sea shells
found inland, and places where the sea is losing ground to
the land, as on the coast of South-West Africa. There is a
kind of endless war between the water and the earth. An
endless tearing down and building up. An endless erosion
of the earth and wearing down of rocks. A pulverization of
stones into sand, of rain washing soil into the sea; water being sucked up into fog and clouds that fall again—all in a
never-ending cycle, like the wheel of life itself, only revolving
much more slowly. In geological aeons instead of biological
moments. We, too, and all living things are eroded by age
and accident, die, and change our form, but are not destroyed. Like the rain that was once the sea and the sea that
was once rain, our souls are like the rainbow that is only a
shower, caught in the hand of the sun.

Our American fly has gone from the saloon. I expect it has been killed. In the ten days since we left San Pedro we had become quite attached to it and looked for it every day. It is curious the way we feel about anything alive, perhaps because so little is left alive now. I remember back when there were thousands of flies, when ceilings were black with them. Today they are rare insects. You have to hunt for one if you want it. So rare that in Trinidad a lady tourist at the Queens Park Hotel became quite hysterical when a fly landed on her lips.

"Imagine it on my lips," she cried.

I nearly said, "Lady, I have been where flies were so thick on a bit of bread and jam that we often ate some."

While she was doing this the gentleman with her was complaining about a pen. It was a regular pen with a pen point that had to be dipped in a bottle of ink. I thought of my father teaching me how to sharpen and split a goose quill to write with. He used a small, sharp pocketknife—a penknife in fact.

Everything is a question of numbers. One fly or one mouse is a pet. More are a nuisance or a curse. There is no man in the world who does not want a beautiful girl around. But twenty beautiful girls, twenty Bardots, Marilyns, Lollobrigidas, would send him mad.

The sea is much calmer here and without rollers. It must now be broken up by the hundreds or even thousands of islands and atolls that separate us from the antarctic. In this it resembles the Caribbean calm behind the barrier of the West Indies.

It is blue again, dark ultramarine, and much darker than the sky that is a pale washed-out cerulean, paling still further into an almost light ocher on the light horizon. The little whitecaps are more than white. They are almost incandescent because there is no glitter on the sea to steal their glory.

JANUARY 12

This morning we passed Marcus Island, a white spot dropped like a handkerchief on the horizon to the north. This is an important radio station with a tremendous mast. Who lives there? What do they do? Or think about? How strange to be so alone and yet in touch night and day with the whole world.

At sea we do not fly our flag, the Royal Mail flag of Norway, red with a white cross on it and a blue cross on the white, and, in the middle of it, because we are entitled to carry mail, there is a crown. The edge of the flag is serrated —a swallowtail. Some captains fly their flags on the ocean, but most do not as the wind whips them to tatters.

But in harbor and near land it is fascinating to recognize the different national flags and think of their meaning, which must be different for every one. The American flag with its stars and stripes is the most beautiful flag in the world—Old Glory—though less beautiful now with its fifty stars, since the proportion of star-spattered blue to the striped red and white has been changed. The American flag means home, though it means less America than New York to me, the place I have lived the longest and in which I have been most happy and unhappy. It is the strength of any emotion, not necessarily its pleasantness, that makes a place important. The British flag, the Union Jack, the red ensign of the merchant service, and the white of the Navy give me a feeling of security, of roast beef and bitter beer. I was born English, was at school in England, and was a soldier in the Coldstream Guards in the First World War, so the flag means a lot to me. The Union Jack and the Royal Standard over the palace ring silver bells in my heart.

The tricolor of France, where I lived as a child, touches me too. I think of the parks in Paris where I played, of lovers entwined under the trees, of good wine and food—mostly wine and food and the language that I love. As I grow older

I pine for France, particularly for the food. I have a theory that old men tend to go home to die, not for some reason of sentimental nostalgia but for gastronomic reasons. They want to taste again, before it is too late, the food they were weaned on, the first solid food they ever ate.

When I see a Belgian ship I think of the Congo. That is the last place I saw the striped red and yellow and black flag on a black and white striped flagstaff over the office of a *chef de poste*. I think of the work that has gone to waste there and the men who died for nothing, for a dream, for a great tropical civilization that they hoped to build in the basin of the river. I think of my friends there, of their homes, their possessions, heirlooms, of the women raped. Did I know any of them? Of Kivu, the beautiful lake where there is fighting now. I think of Leopold and the horrors of his Free State that the Belgians seemed to have forgotten when they thought the Africans loved them. Six years ago when we were there I saw no smiles, no love. That was the time of the Mau Mau emergency in Kenya. It is difficult to explain to anyone who does not know Africa that an African is not a black European. It is three thousand years of time rather than the color of our skins that separates us.

The red sun on the white ground of Japan excites us. We want to go to Japan. There is something very special there, some sense of values that we do not have, in their idea of miniature gardens, of dwarfing trees, of breeding goldfish with popeyes and tails like clusters of chiffon scarves. We want to see a people who will work for generations to produce such things. Things that are of no practical value.

The Russian ships look sinister. They lie by the dock with no sign of life on board. The portholes are frosted glass. The red flag with the yellow hammer and sickle seems menacing. Is this due to conditioning, to propaganda? Are we too brainwashed in some subtle democratic fashion into believing everything in Russia to be evil? There seems to be no valid public information about Russia. One article by an expert says they are ahead of us in everything. Another says we are ahead of them. Probably neither is true. All the Russians can no more be bad than all of us can be good. In world affairs they are getting the best of us because it is easier to make trouble than to cure it. In a world of powder barrels it is no great problem to create explosions if you have a box of matches. Our difficulty is that we have no creed, no slogan, no positive attitude other than to be against communism. A hundred negatives do not equal a single positive. I personally do not fear Russia as much as China.

I am still allergic to the German flag. I have fought the Germans. I have been shot by the Germans. They killed my favorite brother. With their concentration camp atrocities they destroyed my faith in civilization, culture, and religion. Without doubt they are a master race. To recover from two wars, to achieve what they have done, makes them what they claim. But there is madness in the German soul, some tribal or racial memory of their ancient gods.

Italian ships make us want to go back to Italy—to Venice most of all. If one could only see one city in Europe this is the city to go to. It is unique and in a sense the most westerly city of the Orient. Byzantine. Venice was the center of all trade with the East for centuries, queen of the seas for years.

The Argentine blue and white stripes make us think of the River Platte and Buenos Aires. The green flag of Brazil with its blue globe takes us back to the wonders of Rio, the great harbor that the Portuguese thought was the estuary of a river and named it for the month it was discovered.

Greek ships, ships flying the Liberian flag. Danish ships, Swedish ships. Ships of all nations, all kinds, all colors, all shapes, carrying every kind of cargo, each with a flag and home port. Each manned by men whose hearts are miles away. To them the flag at the stern is more than a declaration of nationality. It is a symbol of their homeland, a testament of their eventual return.

Our fly is still alive. It looks fatter. Perhaps it is a girl.

MANILA

Nine

To an air-minded person there are no boundaries. To a
sailor the world consists of ports joined to each other by
the sea. The sea is no barrier to him. Quite the contrary.
To our ancestors a wide river was as much a separation
from the land on the other side as an ocean. If they could
not see the opposite bank they had no means of knowing
that the world did not end on their own riverbank.

A man on foot can cover ten to thirty miles in a day, a
mounted man thirty to seventy miles, a modern ship three
hundred to five hundred miles, a plane several thousand
miles. It is inevitable that these thoughts should be in one's
mind as one travels, or that one should forget for an instant
that the early voyages of discovery were made by canoes and
sailing ships, and the first explorations of the land were made
by men on foot—the despised pedestrians of today.

SATURDAY, JANUARY 14

Last night was unbelievably beautiful—great stars blazed
like headlights out of the dark blue velvet sky; some were
bright enough to rule a line of light across the sea. The stars

seem bigger in the Pacific, brighter, nearer even than in the high veld of South Africa. Everyone knows that the starlight we see set off on its journey through space hundreds or thousands of years ago. We know it but cannot realize it—at least I cannot. I have no wish to travel in space, little curiosity about the firmament. It is enough for me to stare at it and to wonder. Next time I looked out of the window the moon was up. Almost red. A half-moon on her back bright enough to put out the stars, to dim them the way candles in a dining room are dimmed when the electric light is turned on. The wake of the ship was snowy with feathers of white water. The sky was much paler now with a few dark clouds, their edges illuminated with silver.

So, till I slept, I lay on my back and looked out at the sky and the pale stars, swinging and softly swaying overhead. Always, as I watched them, it was the stars that moved, rolling through the sky, coming into view and going out of it again. The ship seemed to be stationary.

It would be wonderful to be able to walk on the bottom of the sea, to climb over wrecked ships, go through seaweed forests, to see the monsters of the deep in their lairs and watch them hunting. To be among thousands of small fish in shallower waters bright as butterflies. We had a taste of it on the reefs at Tobago. Skin diving is a fascinating sport and I can imagine its taking a man over. The exploration of a new dimension, of a mystic and silent world.

This morning the deck was very gay, strung with flags—twenty-six of them, all the letters of the alphabet. These are the signal flags. They are all colors, shapes, designs, and sizes, checkerboards, stripes, sideways, and longways. One was twelve feet long. Their great diversity in size is due to the country in which they were bought and the ship chandler who made the replacement of the worn-out flag. They had been brought out to check, to give them an airing. But it has begun to rain and now they are limp and bedraggled.

SUNDAY, JANUARY 15

More rain, more gray rollers, gray skies, and empty, lonely seas.

MONDAY, JANUARY 16

Still gray skies and gray rolling seas that slip under the ship, flatten into a vast saucer of melting blue and white ice cream, and then rise into sharp dunes crested with spray. Between the blue marbled water beside the ship and the white horses there are patterns and streaks of translucent aquamarine. How aptly the stone is named.

We are used to the noises of the ship now and all we hear through the open port is the tearing-silk sound of the sea as we knife through it. Sometimes it sounds like great sheets of tissue paper being crumpled into wads.

We are heading for the San Bernardino Lighthouse. According to the officers, it sometimes has a light and sometimes it doesn't, and again we were told that the Filipinos were difficult to deal with—that they would remove anything movable from the ship if they were not watched. There is apparently corruption everywhere in public life and there are still communist-led Hukbalahap guerrillas in the mountains. There is great poverty and misery among the nineteen million barrio residents, and United States aid, we were told, is being improperly distributed. Of course stevedores are not as a rule the pick of the population and all people tend to steal when hungry. But hungry people are sitting ducks for communist propagandists.

We shall be in Manila before long and able to see for ourselves something of what is going on.

There must have been a big storm somewhere to stir up the seas we are getting. Tiny, after three days of it, says, "It always rains in the Marianas. Didn't you know?" Certainly we have been misinformed about the South Pacific. The books and films don't mention this kind of thing. I thought the battles were all fought in sky-blue Technicolor lagoons amid palm-fringed islands, all rather like the Bahamas and the Caribbean in general.

This part of the run, between Midway and San Bernardino, is usually calm and was for the first day or so. The bad part is supposed to be between California and Midway. There, we were lucky because the sea was very quiet, but it can, when ill-tempered, be mountainous.

When a wave rises, the angle of incidence is dependent on its base, which is itself related to the width of the trough. When the wave can reach no higher, it curves over and falls, blue and transparent, against the light for an instant, then snow white with foam as it slides back into the ocean. There is no end to these patterns of the sea.

TUESDAY, JANUARY 17

The sun came out long enough to get a sight about 9 A.M. We are seventy-five miles off course to the north, with a typhoon building up behind us and racing seas that lift the stern as they pass under us. Some rain and the skies still gray.

We see a few flying fish, but the seas are too high for any spectacular skips. The captain has been on the bridge for three days and nights, being worried about our position. In all that time we have not seen the sun by day or a star by night.

After lunch, at about 1 P.M. we pass San Bernardino on our left and approach Luzon. It lies to our right and twists and turns like a serpent. There is an active volcano of five thousand feet half hidden in the clouds, with a fishing village on the shore at its foot. This is rolling, tortured country with green hills sculptured by wind and storm, deep valleys, and what appear to be lines of palms. Columns of smoke are going up in several places where the bush is being burned.

Beyond San Bernardino, looking as if it is attached to it, is a great jagged black cliff that continues as a reef out into the sea and is probably the cause of the lighthouse's being built. The seas, as we came near, were beating against it, sending up great splashes of white water.

Soon we were surrounded by Japanese-looking islands that rise like the furry humps of animals out of the sea and seem to go on in depth for miles, one behind the other. The scenery is like a Japanese print in monotone, the nearest to us almost black, the farthest pearl gray. There are no gulls. Are they afraid of the storm that is following us?

This is the East—the Orient—all right. Like nothing we have seen before geographically. The colors are different, the quality of the light and the water, the shape of the hilly islands—hunchbacks, crocodiles, hippos—half submerged— all a blackish blue-green or gray, rising out of a dull sea, sharp against a pale sky, the highest tone the breaking waves, like white plumes thrown at the islands' flanks.

JANUARY 18

A pale blue sky and bottle-green sea, ruffled, but without whitecaps. We come to a large mountainous island on our left that has been planted with trees—conifers of some kind.

There is some cultivation on the flats. A fat woolly cloud, white, tinged with the rose of dawn, lies like a ball of eider down along the crest of the hills. Between us and the big island are some smaller, alligator-like islands. There are more mountains in the distance, and we now pass what looks like an oil refinery with large tanks and smoking chimneys.

From early dawn we are among islands that were burning bush or cane. "Sparks," who acted as the captain's secretary, gave us a circular about currency regulations in the Philippines from which I made some extracts.

During the past, there have been so many persons, visiting, returning or entering the Philippines who have encountered insurmountable difficulties, inconveniences and several have been prosecuted and convicted and are now serving prison terms at the New Bilibid Prisons of the Philippines having violated Central Bank rules and regulations. These transactions in U.S. dollars and Philippine currency are most oftentimes done without willful violation on the part of the persons affected due to their ignorance of Philippine laws concerned.
(Nevertheless)
Any violation . . . is punishable by ₱20,000.00 fine and five (5) years imprisonment.

WHAT YOU CAN DO:

(1) You can bring with you any amount of U.S. dollars in any form and you must declare the same upon arrival in the Philippines at any point of entry with the Central Bank representative who shall exchange into Philippine currency any amount you want.
(2) You can only bring into the Philippines ₱20.00 every time you enter the Philippines.

WHAT YOU CANNOT DO:

You cannot exchange U.S. dollars with Philippine currency in foreign countries and bring the said Philippine currency into the Philippines if it is more than ₱20.00.

This was all quite serious and it could not be very pleasant to be incarcerated, even in the new Bilibid Prison, so we declared our money and had no trouble of any kind when we went ashore.

Manila can at last be seen, a dark streak against the gray smoke of the hills. Some tall buildings and spires are distinguishable.

Suddenly the anchor goes down with a roar and a cloud of rust dust from the unwinding chain. The black ball that shows we are at anchor goes up. We have been flying the Filipino flag since morning. It is a white V against the staff with a round golden device that looks like something between a water lily and a Rotarian wheel, and three golden stars. The rest of the flag is dark blue above red. A few moments later the ship is alive with officials, small brown men with semimilitary caps and brief cases, and we go through the usual formalities of health certificates and passports in the saloon.

The deck is a litter and a maze of lines, ropes, and hawsers, strung from the booms that stick out from the masts like gargantuan toothpicks at a giant's cocktail party. People begin to assemble on the dock. People with services to sell, like the barber with a pair of clippers in his hand, and the small boy with newspapers—the Manila *Times* and *Evening News*. Idle people. Some dock workers. In appearance they seemed small, thin, and wiry when young, thickset later if prosperous. Their complexions varied from dark African brown to a golden Chinese yellow; the features were Mongol with a touch of Negrito. Many showed white and Japanese blood. These islands have been occupied for hundreds of years by Spaniards, Americans, and Japanese. Each race has left traces on the population. The illegitimate children left by invading and occupation forces may be a kind of dividend that to some extent offsets the ravages of war. These are men in their prime, the pick of their respective nations. It is an interesting idea anyway, and one does not need to be an anthropologist to pick out the various strains.

We saw our first man in a barong, a kind of short embroidered nightdress worn outside the pants with one button open at the neck, and long sleeves fastened with links. This is the national full-dress costume and must be very cool and comfortable. The toenails of everyone who was barefooted, and many people were, looked as white as if they had been enameled. Something we had never seen before.

Our Chinese friends, the Chaos, were happy to be back in the Orient. This was home to them, to him at any rate, for though a Chinese his wife had never been to the East. Born in Trinidad, she had only been to England, where she was trained as a nurse before meeting her husband. But the psychological effect of race is very interesting. Here everyone looked more or less like them, as people look like us in Europe, or as Africans look in Africa to a Negro, though to some extent this does not really apply to Americans, white or black, because they have moved so far away from the countries of their origin and are separated from them by a culture that is so entirely their own. The American Chinese are probably an exception to this, living as many of them do in their Chinatowns.

We attributed the lack of gulls to the oil slick of this almost landlocked harbor of Manila Bay. The only birds we saw were two swallows.

We went ashore carrying two small bags which the customs officer insisted on going through most meticulously on the open dock, much to Tiny's horror. He was a man entirely without charm. The officials here are liable to search people's persons and in no gentle manner, I was told, unless they receive some tangible reward such as a carton of cigarettes. It was either here or in South America, where conditions are very similar, that the customs men who each had been given a carton of cigarettes came back with the guard from the gate, who would not let anyone through until he had one too. The taxi was stopped at still another control area, and then drove us to the Everett Travel Agency, where we made some inquiries about our visa to Vietnam and got them to book us a room at the Manila Hotel. Here we were "had" with the taxi fare. We paid three pesos (one dollar) instead of about fifty cents, which was the correct fare. But this is tourism. The first time anywhere you are taken.

Our room was very large and paneled with very wide two-foot boards of mahogany. It had a radio by the bed and an air-conditioner in the window, and looked out over the park and the bay.

We had a glass of beer in the Jungle Bar, which was decorated with large artificial jungle trees, lianas, and a real waterfall. The walls painted with jungle scenes made it all most realistic. The beer, San Miguel, is excellent and is made here. We then had a Filipino lunch in the Bamboo Room. It was full and we were the only white people in it. Most of the men wore barongs. Some were very fancy, cream with white embroidery, others white with black needlework. A number of materials are used. Some are made of abacá, a kind of banana fiber. The same plant is used for making Manila rope, which I had no idea came from a tree that I could not distinguish from a regular edible banana. Others are made from a fiber that comes from the pineapple, others are cotton or cotton and silk. The lunch was excellent. The best thing was a fish soup made with the front half of the fish and decorated with vegetables. There was some unrecognizable meat mixed up in a dish of steamed rice, a pudding, and coffee.

At two o'clock our car came. Our driver, Johnny Agsalud, told us that the population of Manila was 2,000,000 and the total population in the republic 27,000,000. The first thing we noticed was the number of jeeps, brightly painted, that had been converted into miniature busses. There are ten thousand of them—army surplus that was sold cheap at the end of the war—and they are still running well. Twenty-seven different dialects are spoken in the islands. The official languages appear to be English and Tagalog, a Malayan language with Spanish additions. It is interesting that English should be official here and used in the schools, whereas in Puerto Rico, with closer ties to the United States, very little English is used.

The town is divided in two by the river, which was once filled with the lilies that gave Manila its name. Until recently this was the main thoroughfare and Manila a kind of oriental Venice. Even now there are a lot of barges and other craft tied up or plying up and down.

Our first stop was the Intramuros, the old town, which was almost demolished by the war and which has not yet, after all this time, been rebuilt. Thick walls of colonial Spain still stand, pock-marked by explosives, the empty sockets of their windows staring like dead eyes into this desolation.

Against these ruins are some of the worst, most ramshackle and extraordinary slum dwellings, shanty towns, Hoovervilles and Bidonvilles that I have ever seen. Sordid as they are, they have an extraordinary artistic fascination. Tottering—two and even three stories high—they are built like card houses of sheet iron, mats lashed to bamboo uprights, with part iron, part flattened kerosene can, part thatch roofs that have a Chinese pitch; roofs that are worn like rakish hats; roofs that seem to hang by only a thread. Yet almost every house has a plant or two. A palm or flower in a pot—an effort toward some beauty, for some symbol of life. They must see something grow. Gray washing, washed without soap, hangs wherever a place can be found to hang it. People swarm, people who are unbelievably poor, with naked children and starving dogs; people who, as has happened everywhere, have come in from the country, attracted to the bright lights of the city. This is the world problem that makes slum clearance a near impossibility.

We saw the church of San Augustín, where the Japanese imprisoned all the padres and then killed them by throwing hand grenades through the windows. We saw the ruined fortress of St. Iago, where first the Spanish imprisoned their recalcitrant subjects, and where later the Japanese secret police imprisoned and tortured the Filipino patriots and where, at the end of the war, the Japanese made their last stand in the dungeon and were blasted to death by American bazookas. The Japanese had their prisoners confined so closely in this low, domed vault that they could never lie down to sleep. In the walls there were the slots that had once held the ring bolts to which the Spaniards used to fasten their captives' arms above their heads. The water for the prisoners of the Japanese came from the river alongside, which often contained the rotted bodies of the dead. A curious thing about this place, with its memories of horror spread over the centuries, was that we had no feeling of it. Something had canceled them out. Time, victory perhaps, or the physical destruction of most of it—as if it was the very stones themselves that had held the memory.

At the entrance gate there was a heroic Spanish man of arms carved in bas-relief with his lower part blown off by modern gunfire.

The fort in general, what was left of it, resembled the one we saw in San Juan, with exactly the same-shaped stone sentry boxes. I do not think either the Spanish or the Portuguese are given the credit they deserve for the amazing feats of courage, endurance, and initiative that they performed in colonizing these distant parts of the world. Mexico and Brazil were bad enough. But to go around the Horn every time they came here, or around the Cape and through the Indian Ocean and China Sea strikes me as fantastic.

We passed the shrine to the Unknown Soldier with a burning flame. The last one we saw was at Rosario in Argentina on the River Platte. Is there a country in the world without one now? But in the history of the world, how many lost and unknown dead have there been? It certainly has taken us a long time to commemorate them.

Our next stop was the market. It is in the markets that one sees a cross-section of the people and examples of the food they grow and eat. In the place where we parked there were not only cars but a lot of small, very gaily painted

carriages with high wheels and covered tops that held up to
seven people. They were drawn by very tiny horses that
looked quite different from any I have ever seen except on
the Jos Plateau in Nigeria. These were Mongolian-type
horses, related to the wild horse of Mongolia and the Norwegian horse. They were of all colors, including one piebald.
Duns, creams, mouse grays predominated, though I did not
see any buckskins. They were almost all stallions with very
short, thick necks. All had bearing reins that were much too
tight but presumably necessary to control them in heavy
traffic and stop their fighting. The horse I was looking at
suddenly reared and chopped at another that was passing
him, all in the twinkling of an eye. There was one quite
ordinary-looking horse that Johnny said was an American
horse. It towered over all the ponies. What they call an
American horse is a descendant of some American cavalry
horses that escaped or were abandoned by the U.S. cavalry
after the First World War. Any Filipino who can capture

one of these animals is allowed to keep it. The harness is complex, heavily ornamented with brasswork, again derivative of Spain, just like that in South America, and stemming from North Africa. For that is how all this type of horse furniture, bridles, saddlery, and so on, reached the Iberian Peninsula. The Moors brought it with their other arts and it can still be seen in its original form all over North Africa and the Sudan.

The first stall we went to sold plants. Orchids by the dozen hung from the ceiling: there were asparagus ferns in half coconuts, Christmas-tree-like araucarias in pots, palms of various kinds, and lovely artificial flowers. Inside the building there was every kind of food, household utensil and material. There must have been ten stalls that sold nothing but different kinds of rice. There was a big fish section, empty, as it was afternoon, except for the smell. It would have been interesting to see the varieties of fish caught in these waters. There were stalls of meat, also mostly sold out. But there were some sides of horse meat easily recognized from the dark, almost brown flesh and cadmium-yellow fat. There were dried pig's bowels for making sausage. I had not seen these since I was a child in France. We used to use them at home to make our sausages, fitting them onto the end of a machine. The meat was stuffed through a nozzle and I was sometimes allowed to tie the joints.

We saw most of the ordinary vegetables that we are accustomed to, but some nice exotic stuff, too—white radishes a foot long, long beans, little red scallions, breadfruit, banana flowers—a kind of not quite round purple-colored ball which is eaten as a salad (I had no idea one could eat them); big beans, turmeric, coconuts, and greens of various kinds.

Many of the stall keepers were asleep, sitting among the goods with their heads on their arms. It was siesta time, the hottest part of the day during which only tourists, mad dogs, and Englishmen wander about.

We next went to the zoo, as we always do everywhere. In Rome we went six times, and most people do not even seem to know that there is a zoo in Rome. In Manila it is combined with a kind of amusement park with loud-speakers endlessly blaring popular songs. The most interesting feature was probably the animals' spoors, deer, lion, and so on in the smooth cement of the pavement at the entrance, reminiscent of Grauman's Chinese Theatre in Hollywood, and a small enclosure at the gate marked "Lost Children" in large letters.

The bears were in poor condition and seemed short of water. There was a young lion with rickets that would not last long, and a small wild pig with a bad case of mange. On the other hand, I have never seen a finer pair of cheetahs. All the deer and buck looked well. There was a particularly fine eland cow. There was a big aviary with eagles and vultures, and a nice little sun bear called a Vietnam bear who was very much at home here. There were also some nice jungle fowl, including one variety in which the hens had no tails and looked like quail, that we found most appealing; some lovely Burmese peacocks, bronze and green instead of blue, slightly bigger than the Indian variety, with faces covered with bare skin that was half blue and half white; a pair of silkies described as Chinese fowl. No animal or bird had the country of origin given. It had the name of the donor instead. There were four or five very fine pythons that I imagined to be local. This should be a very good place for them climatically, well wooded and watered with plenty of small game. Our driver said there were nine universities in Manila, but I am inclined to think he included high schools and technical schools. On trips like this one has to accept information as it comes and then check it if possible later.

We dined in the Bamboo Room again and after dinner went to a couple of night clubs. We went first to D'Wave on Dewey Boulevard, which at one end consists of embassy after embassy, and at the other of clubs of all kinds—taking "kind" in its widest sense. D'Wave was a sort of taxi-dance hall *cum* club.

The girls here were among the most beautiful I have ever

seen, with long, slim figures. They wear their clothes so tight that they look like mermaid tails and the zippers go down the back almost to their thighs. One girl in white satin had to go up the low steps at the entrance sideways, and the steps were not more than four inches high.

In the club they go into a kind of enclosure from which the men in search of partners pick them and pay thirty pesos, or ten dollars, per hour for their company. I do not know if this was only for dancing or included other activities. American dancing would have been impossible with such tight skirts. The couples danced separately, the girls coming forward, stepping back, and twirling about in a most provocative manner. At times they would take the man's hand and he would turn them around. It was beautiful to watch, a teasing, courting dance from which it seemed to us that our jitterbugging might have been derived. The orchestra was superb. We drank only beer. The lighting was low. The comfort rooms were labeled "Kings" and "Queens."

There was an interesting notice at the decorative, flower-embowered entrance to the club.

Fire arms and other deadly weapons must be presented at counter for safe keeping.

As we left, more beautiful girls were arriving in taxis.

At ten o'clock we went to the Safari Club. It adjoins the zoo, and has a floor show. There was a dance team, and three sisters who sang that were like all other singing sisters and dance teams. But the contortionist was one of the best I have ever seen. She worked with three lighted candles in tumblers and turned herself inside out in every direction, holding one candle in each hand with the third balanced on her forehead. Among other things she picked this one up between her knees when lying on her back, and in the end replaced it with them.

There were some very pretty girls in family parties. One,

quite lovely, with a wonderful neck and back, had a head of hair like a Chinese Bardot.

In general, the prettiest girls were rather Merle Oberonish with Bardot touches. Their waists are high, their legs long and beautiful, with slim, rounded hips and thighs. Their breasts are small and delicate. Their carriage is superb—they stand as straight as wands.

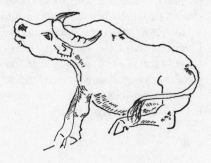

THE BAMBOO ORGAN

Ten

Orange juice for breakfast was three pesos, that is to say, a dollar. So we had pineapple. It was as good as any I have ever had. It then occurred to me that these were probably our own California Sunkist oranges. We had brought a cargo of them on the *Pleasantville*. I do not know how many cases.

The car picked us up at the Manila Hotel at 9 A.M. Our first stop was to be the Bamboo Organ at Las Piñas Church. The drive was fascinating. Once we were out of Manila into the suburbs the atmosphere changed completely. There were more gardens, more trees—big trees: mangoes, breadfruit, some that I did not recognize, and one group of very old frangipani of all colors—white, pink, dark red, and canary yellow. They were planted a few yards apart and made a kind of little forest that was quite fascinating.

Near the sea we saw some catamarans, boats with three bent poles running across them at right angles and socketed into large bamboos that prevented them from turning turtle

under sail. Crossing a river, we saw bamboo rafts each with
three or four tall masts lashed together at the top and curving outward, on which lanterns are hung for night fishing
with nets in the shallow waters where the rafts must be poled
along.

The houses became more and more oriental in appearance
—more mat walls and windows with small panes only four
inches or so square glazed with clamshells that had been
ground down until they were transparent and set in lead
frames. Every house had plants, in pots, in tins, and window
boxes. From the main road short feeder roads ran off into
really sordid rural slums. The windows of some houses were
movable sliding screens, and a lot of the architectural and
decorating ideas that appear in our slick magazines, such as
these screens or use of decorative bird cages containing
plants, are not at all original but came straight from the
Orient. We passed large paddies of water hyacinth, which
I was told they have found a use for and can make into
paper, and there was one beautiful white water lily standing
up out of the water on a six-inch lotuslike stem. The petals
were turned back from its center like the skirt of a ballet
dancer. We passed a man carrying a gamecock in his arms
as tenderly as a baby. We saw other cocks tethered by the
leg along the road, and small, neat game hens walking about.
Cockfighting is a national sport in the Philippines.

Bicycle taxis now became numerous. There is a kind of
economic or status taxi-and-jeep scale. Regular taxis for the
rich, the horse cabs, called *calesas,* for the middle classes,
and in the country bicycle taxis for those who can afford
them.

We passed a nursery area, at least a mile of plants of all
kinds—shrubs, creepers, and small trees in pots and tins. This
love of potted plants may be a holdover from the Spanish
colonialism, as it is so characteristic of Spain.

We came upon the church at Las Piñas suddenly. We

were driving along a village street, saw a crowd of school children playing in a yard, and there we were. The church is a part of the mission school.

This is an old church with four-foot walls, the roof held up by great arches with columns four feet square. Built in 1762, this church is now in a glorious state of disrepair. The blue sky is visible through the wide whitewashed window-less windows, through which the chirping sparrows fly. From outside comes the noise of children playing.

We went up into the organ loft and saw this wonder of the world, the only bamboo organ. Its construction was begun by Father Diego Cera, an Augustinian Recollet friar, in 1818. The nine hundred fifty bamboos he needed were selected and buried for six months in salty sand to preserve them from the ravages of bamboo bugs. The organ was finished in 1822. In 1862 it was damaged by an earthquake. In 1882 it was damaged again by rain when the church's

roof was blown off in a storm. In 1917 it was repaired by a Belgian missionary. In 1932 an electric blower was installed, replacing the hand bellows. It was repaired again in 1943.

This is the story of the organ according to the leaflet that is given to visitors. But there is no explanation of how Father Diego Cera came to think of building an organ of bamboo, or of his tools or his skills. Had he seen these big bamboos growing and thought they looked like organ pipes, and decided to try to build one?

A sister played "Ave Maria" for us. The tone was beautiful and the sparrows, excited by the music, fluttered and chattered a loud accompaniment which somehow seemed utterly in keeping with the solemnity of the occasion. Paradox has its own importance, the chattering birds punctuating in some way the grandeur of the music, as if their little voices, their fluttering in and out of the glassless windows, brought God closer.

Below us two black-clad women prayed and some children sat on the pews with folded arms. In the belfry a big bat flew around us a couple of times on silent leather wings, and disappeared, while a sparrow sat sideways clinging to the bell rope. The sparrows here seem to be a subvariety of the European, rather smaller, neater, with whiter cheeks.

The church needs restoration. It is only to be hoped that it is not overrestored. What it needs is a new roof and some new floors and stairs. If windows are put in and it is replastered and whitewashed it will lose a great deal of its charm. This is, as it were, a working church, and one of the few that were spared war damage. Restoration of anything old is always dangerous. The qualities that give it importance are so ephemeral. Square up the walls, paint them, scrape off the moss, repair the doors, replace the steps that have been worn down by a hundred thousand feet, and nothing is left but a building. Its spirit . . . its soul—the very things that caused the restoration to be begun—has vanished.

We now set off for the American cemetery, which is on a slight rise overlooking Laguna de Bay. Before reaching it

we passed through what I called the Filipino Beverly Hills
—an area inhabited by millionaires. Hollywoodlike mansion
was followed by still more Hollywoodlike mansions, each one
more ornate, its garden more tailored and neater than the
last. Some walls had borders of dwarf poinsettias no higher
than geraniums. They flowered on stems thinner than a pencil and appeared to be a semi-creeper.

The entrance to the cemetery is hedged by mixed bougainvillaea, all unpruned, sending up long shoots of color that
burned like flames in the sunshine.

The cemetery itself is one of the most impressive sights I
have ever seen. A miniature forest of marble crosses set in
battalions along the contours of the grassy slope. Seventy
thousand young men lie dead here, their bones collected
from every island battlefield. Some are Jews. Driving slowly
past, we saw several surmounted by the Jewish six-pointed
star.

At the top of the hill (it is really little more than a big
mound rising out of the flats) is a great circle of enormous
marble slabs all open to the air. This is the Book of the Dead
and the Missing. Inscribed alphabetically on the left are the
names of the missing, the dead, their units and their states.
The marble pages that support the roof are twenty feet high.
They are separated from each other by carpets of black stone
cobbles.

First came the land-war maps in colored terrazzo, great
plaques made by Italian craftsmen. Then the names.

To the right are first the maps of the naval engagements
with names of the places that we have passed near and that
had never had much reality for us before. Then came the
marble pages of the naval missing, the men who were killed
in action or went down in a scum of burning oil. The horror
of death in a battle at sea has always seemed greater to me
than being killed in action on land. Perhaps this is the normal
reaction of a soldier.

We walked over lawns of velvet green and looked out into the blue distance that not so long ago had been a battle-field.

There were some big flat-topped trees nearby that re-minded me of Africa. A group of Filipino gardeners in wide Chinese hats squatted among the crotons they were weeding and paused to look up at us. I wonder what they made of us? What their memories of the war were? If they related the American dead to their own experiences? We saw no birds, but heard one that made a sound like a gong at in-tervals.

Between the two wings of the great stone hedgelike circle was a tiny chapel that pointed its square finger to the sky. It was tall and narrow, no wider than the altar it contained. Above the altar was a tall Virgin Mother in mosaic on a pale blue mosaic background. Outside, the chapel had a tall nude male figure holding a sword, with his foot on a Japanese crocodile-faced dragon. Behind him, all in bas-relief, were the figures of peace and plenty.

The whole concept is wonderful, a combination of the classical neo-Greek and the modern up-and-down monolith —a place where the dead can lie peacefully in the honor that is their due.

The arrangement of the pages or slabs is such that there is a central passage between them as if a book had been torn apart at the spine and the pages set apart. The armorial bearings of every state are set in the marble floors.

We drove back in silence, for this had been a moving experience. First the Bamboo Organ and then this. I listed some of the trees we saw in my mind: bougainvillaea—purple, cherry red, cyclamen pink, mauve, purple, yellow, brick red, and white. The yellow I had never seen before, though some in Port of Spain came near to it. Few hibiscuses were out. There were double and single poinsettias everywhere, a lot of papaya and frangipani, and the masses of mango trees, coconut palms, and breadfruit a heavy backdrop against the sky.

Our next visit was to the official residence of the President, the Malacanang Palace, built in the later stage of Spanish colonialism, a bad period, lacking in charm or even dignity. We were shown the immense reception rooms. The best things in them were the Spanish carpets, a gift of Spain, reminding us of those we had seen in the Palace Hotel in Madrid. There were some mediocre portraits of former presidents, one of them wearing a barong. The dining room was enormous, with a very fine long table made of two different-colored native woods. The chandeliers were modern Czechoslovakian, of a Victorian design. The palace gave onto the river and was surrounded by a wide veranda. The whole place was simply one for official entertainment and had rather the atmosphere of a big, old-fashioned hotel. The double doors of the entrance were made of stained glass and portrayed two old-time Filipino warriors in their ancient costume.

The teahouse, which the President often uses, was built largely of bamboo and had great charm. It was altogether more personal and had some very good water-color portraits of native types and costumes. In the garden I found a new kind of white poinsettia with small leaves. It was very floriferous and covered with thicker, smaller flowers than the red variety. In the grounds there was a small, sad zoo that included a dog that had been born with only two hind legs. None of the animals, chiefly birds and deer, looked happy, comfortable, or seemed well cared for.

Our final adventure was to visit a pet shop in Chinatown. This was, though we did not know it at the time, a preview of Hong Kong. Dirty, overcrowded, a mixture of slum dwellings and small shops, overrun with people of all ages and all sexes. There were so many and they were so varied in appearance and dress that it was hard to believe that they were all either male or female.

The pet shop was tiny, crowded with animals, and dirty. The most interesting thing they had was a tank full of bright electric-blue tropical fish, fish as blue and as bright as the morpho butterflies, whose wings are used for jewelry. There were some very large Japanese pigeons, and some very small short-legged Japanese bantams. One cock—he was white with dark hackles—had a long black tail that hung down like a bunch of ribbons. There were some other, small buff-colored hens with no tails, and a very attractive baby Australian sulphur-crested cockatoo. He was all complete but only about eleven inches high. Both cockatoos and macaws must go on growing for several years, thus differing from most birds, which attain their full size the first year.

We left the shop depressed, and as usual wishing we could have bought everything they had, particularly the cocky. I have a great weakness for all parrots and cockatoos.

We sailed after lunch on Friday, the twentieth, passing close to Corregidor. What a terrible island to take, with as far as one could see only one small landing beach set in a neck commanded by two heavily wooded hills. There seemed to be some ruined buildings at the top of them.

The alligator-shaped island that guards the Bataan Peninsula was very clear today as we came upon it from behind.

There being no gulls is a noticeable feature of these waters. We saw no insects and few birds other than sparrows around Manila, but of course we did not have time to get into the bush or visit any of the other islands that are quite wild and unspoiled. Nor did we see any agriculture, sugar and rice, which are produced in quantity, or even any working carabaos—the water buffalo that is the draft animal of the Far East.

We now had time to read all the books, magazines, and newspapers we had bought.

First the history of the Philippines and some facts about them. They are an archipelago of 7107 islands with a population of 24,000,000 people speaking 87 different dialects, whose national average income is 200 pesos per annum. That is to say, less than 100 U.S. dollars. The total area of the islands, more than 114,000 square miles, is a little greater than Great Britain and Ireland. It is the only Christian country in the Orient.

Until Spain colonized the islands in the sixteenth century they had been subjected to four great influences—Malayan, Indonesian, Chinese, and Indian.

It was Ferdinand Magellan who first sighted eastern Samar on March 16, 1521. He later lost his life here fighting the Filipinos in the name of Christianity and the Spanish Crown.

There were continual troubles and revolts that burned up and died down, culminating in a three-sided war among the Filipinos, Spaniards, and Americans in 1898. The Americans acquired the Philippines and all armed resistance to them collapsed in 1901, with the capture of President Aguinaldo in Palanan. American teachers followed the soldiers and businessmen followed the teachers. But even though civil American governors followed the military the Filipinos never ceased their struggle for freedom and finally achieved it with the establishment of the Commonwealth of the Philippines in 1935.

Their freedom did not last long. In January 1942 the Japanese captured Manila and it remained in their possession till liberated by the American forces in February 1945.

It was only now, after crossing the Pacific and seeing the devastation of Manila, and the great cemetery where so many young Americans lay dead, that we began to appreciate the war that had been waged here.

There was, I think, a kind of regional attitude to the war in America. Those who lived on the East Coast were more concerned with England, France, Germany, and Russia—the European Theater in fact. The term "theater" is more than apt applied to such great dramas. On the West Coast they were much more vitally concerned with Japan and the operation in the Orient. We each stood, as it were, on our own shores looking out to sea, and ignored to a great extent what went on behind us.

And this was only the beginning as far as we were concerned—the beginning of the area occupied by the Japanese and the beginning of the Orient, though actually so Westernized and Christianized that it was not really a preparation for what was to follow. All it did was give us a taste of it, a whiff of the oriental incense which once smelled is never forgotten. This was the first of the lands of the lotus for us. The threshold of a new and beautiful world.

We had bought dozens of papers and magazines—copies of the Manila *Times*, the *Philippines Free Press*, and other publications. I now set about clipping the most interesting items, that is to say, those which in a kind of haphazard manner gave some insight into the lives and problems of the people.

From the papers it would appear that the charges of corruption are valid. Funds vanish, salaries are not paid, and U.S. aid does not reach the people.

The final clipping is about the weather—the bitter cold snap of sixty-two degrees which we have been going through.

Manila Enjoys Cold Spell

Chilled noses ducked even deeper into warm blankets yesterday morning as the weather bureau announced that the thermometer at 6:40 A.M. yesterday slid down to 62 degrees Fahrenheit, the lowest in many months.

The weather has been exceedingly pleasant for the last few days: chilly in the early morning, snappy and brilliant when the sun comes up and chilly again at night. Baguio weather, they say.

Curiously enough, the cold seems to make the air sparkle, and Manila's buildings have a special jewel-like quality that they acquire only at this time of year.

So enjoy it while it lasts, folks. We won't have this again till next year.

In general the picture is one of corruption and bad organization leading to lack of employment and malnutrition. There seems to be a general lack of confidence. Someone has said that only a thin line separates order from chaos in the rural Philippines. In the hands of a demagogue they would be lost.

It is difficult to understand why the old city has not been rebuilt and why so much of Dewey Avenue is still in ruins.

The Filipinos are a free, charming and proud people. The trouble is that you cannot eat freedom, pride and charm. And without integrity in the legislature, without a stable civil service, there can be no stability.

SAMPANS AND JUNKS

Eleven

JANUARY 22

We approached Hong Kong early in the morning and saw the mountain clothed in mist. The city at its foot was climbing up the slopes. A slow entrance by sea into a fairyland, a vast, organized confusion of vessels anchored and moving. Big junks with nautilus-shaped sails, sampans, great liners, tramps, motor launches, rowboats propelled by a single oar in the stern. We were flying the red ensign of the British Merchant Marine. Again about us were the ships of every nation. We saw no gulls, but a number of kites were sailing over the bay, some very high, some low near the water.

It is impossible to overestimate the charm and variety of this harbor. Rio is the most impressive harbor we have ever seen—its shape, the Sugar Loaf and the immense Christ on the mountain they call the Hunchback. But this—this was out

of this world. Literally. For we were really out of our world
and into something new.

But to remind us, and something always did, of the near-
ness of war, was a magnificent American aircraft carrier. It
looked as if it was a mile long. On the flight deck there were
a group of brilliant red planes ready to take off.

Her side was open—a kind of great panel—and we could
see into her—a great womb filled with red planes. There she
lay like an enormous queen ant, her belly full of death and
destruction. This was the last word, except for the hydrogen
bomb, in man's ingenuity. And about her were the circling
sampans, unchanged in a thousand years.

This strong contrast hit us hard and was to go on hitting
us. The so-called primitive still worked. It had lasted, stood
the test of centuries.

The passport and health authorities who had come on
board took only a few minutes to clear us.

The sun struck the tall monolithic buildings. A ferryboat
passed us. Our tug took hold and nosed us into the dock.
We saw Mrs. Finlay's daughter and Mr. Chao's parents.
His mother is a most beautiful woman.

We were hardly out of our cabin with our luggage before a fat, Buddha-like, and benign Chinese, Mr. Johnny Chik of the Dragon Company, had seized it out of our hands and was leading us to his tailor shop.

"You stay hotel?"

"Yes, the Peninsula."

"You booked there?"

"No."

"There no room. Booked to November. I fix it up." And he did, in his office—for the Esther Hotel. This turned out to be the Astor.

We reached his shop by ten, by ten-thirty we had been measured, I for an Indian raw-silk sports coat and Tiny for a two-piece suit and a dress, also of Indian silk. Then we bought two silk dressing gowns, one cashmere sweater, and one red *cheong sam.* Things move fast in Hong Kong. By eleven-thirty we had booked into our room, parked our luggage, and were off on a tour of Kowloon—also arranged by our new friend, Mr. Johnny.

This was the Orient, its festering pearl. Only now did we begin to understand what was meant by "teeming people." They swarmed, all moving fast, in all directions. We saw lines of red rickshaws in ranks like taxis, cars of all kinds. No horses anywhere. Just people. Shops of all sorts, open-fronted, selling every kind of thing. Many of the women in trousers. Men carrying enormous loads balanced on shoulder poles that bent like bows beneath their weight.

Our first stop was in the resettlement area, great blocks of low-rent flats that seemed to drip with people as if the buildings were receptacles, vessels that leaked humanity at every pore and seam. They overflowed. Each window had poles stuck out into and over the street with laundry threaded through them, hanging in flapping flags. These apartments, built by the government, house more than a quarter of a million refugees from Red China. A family that may number a dozen people inhabits each room. The blocks are marked by letters and have balconies running around three sides of the U overlooking a courtyard. They have five stories. Each floor has one water faucet and one kitchen. Each block is an anthill where overcrowding is the price the inhabitants pay for freedom. But they seemed happy and cheerful. They smiled and laughed—no children cried. They know what they have escaped.

The noise was a subdued roar of thousands of voices with the dull, muted throb of thousands of wooden-soled slippers on the pavement. There were children everywhere; running children, children sitting in the street, children crawling, women with children on their backs, tied on with cloths that had wide tapes, like the four legs of the animal cradle-skins of the Africans, that went around their waists and over their shoulders. Some carried bigger children piggyback. These are the last refugees. No more are allowed in now, so they are the lucky ones. The impression was one of noise, color, and ordered confusion. The prevailing color was red. Many of the streets were arcades with round pillars. The pillars were painted with Chinese letters in red on a white ground or white on red. Everyone seemed good-tempered.

There were big London two-decker busses in the streets (so this is where they went), more cars, more rickshaws, more men carrying buckets and packages on poles. Pawnshops and teahouses, shops full of dried fish hanging on strings, Chinese sausages in strings, dry ducks pressed flat and split down the back, their orange feet a decoration against their sides.

We stopped at Sandy Field station to see the view. We passed Taipo market and went on up to Wan Fu Shan—Yearning for Husband Hill—to a hotel with a view of a valley and the railroad that led like a silver snake into Red China. This was a farming area. The ground below us was a pattern of different greens, all vegetables, with patches of orange that turned out to be little kumquat trees loaded with fruit. Then on up to a point, Lokmaachow, where we actually saw the Chinese border over the flats. It was divided from us by a river. It was extraordinary to see this other world, to see white houses there surrounded by trees. They looked like any other houses. The trees looked like other trees. But we were looking through an invisible Bamboo Curtain at the phenomenon of our time. This new sociopolitical religion whose aim is our destruction. There are police posts on both sides of the border and it is constantly watched. Both sides have machine-gun posts. Refugees, Chinese wetbacks, are sent back if spotted. If caught they are then tortured by the communists as an example. The Hong Kong police send them back at night so that they have a good chance of evading detection. Some do succeed in running the double gantlet and reach their friends in the city. One of the tragic features here is the china vases—the big funeral urns of the richer refugees who have died in freedom and have had their bones placed looking toward the land of their birth. The bodies of the poor are cremated and buried at sea.

We had lunch at the Dragon Inn. It was full of people, all Chinese, and very gay. We had fish soup that was most excellent, and noodles. Some of the more exotic things on the menu were bird's-nest soup with quail eggs, mushroom and bamboo shoots and greens, kale and oyster soup, quail eggs Lo Hon, chicken and duck feet with greens, dried cuttlefish and kale, preserved eggs, beef and cashews, chicken-blood soup, stewed abalone, minced quail with lettuce, frog cutlets and shark-fin soup with crab. I should like to have tried them all. There was a tame chained monkey here in a house on a pole, a very flat-faced Chinese-looking monkey with sad eyes.

On the way back we passed some old brick fields full of water where they were breeding goldfish; other abandoned brick fields, which were used for breeding edible fish, were alive with ducklings, a symbiotic association profitable to the ducks, the fish, and the owners. We saw hundreds of ducklings about two months old. A number of cottages had pigeons in wire enclosures. There were big black pigs and water buffalo, some of which had calves (this is probably the only young animal that is really ugly), and local cattle that were dark brown and semihumped. In all we saw only about a half-dozen dogs, all chows (the edible dog of China, hence the term chow, no doubt!), except for two black-and-white large spitz-like dogs and one that was woolly, and looked like a Thibetan terrier.

We now saw an old fort some distance off the road and went with some difficulty over the cultivated ground to see it. This is the miniature walled city of Kam Tin—Fertile Field—built centuries ago by the Teng family. These tiny fields, fifty yards square, were all irrigable and were crossed by the narrow eighteen-inch dikes of hard yellow clay. In one patch that was underwater children were grubbing for the corms of a plant that had leaves like an arum lily, which they call mushrooms. The inside of the fort was a maze of little dwellings that ran off the narrow alleys. We saw a number of chickens, two tortoise-shell cats, and a tethered heifer outside the walls. The fort was of brick and was several hundred years old, built as a defense against the pirates who at that time lived on the island of Hong Kong.

Many of the vegetables were new to me and I have never seen such cultivation. Every cabbage, every lettuce, was as well tended as a bedded-out geranium. The soil, a sticky clay, was dug with a heavy hoe and dried into big clods. I saw one portable irrigation trough that worked with a handle and scooped the water out of a furrow in cups that rotated as the handle was turned. Another method of irrigation was by splashing the water up with a scoop on a long handle. But most of it was done by little watering cans, the water carried in four-gallon kerosene tins slung on either end of a pole. The carriers, many of them women, moved at a slow trot. All workers wore big straw hats. Those of the women had a four-inch border of black cotton that hung down from the brim. Some red-flowered peaches were beginning to bloom. They were small trees and all had their branches tied together so that they looked like brooms upended in the soil.

Green peas were in flower and there were pole beans growing on crossed sticks as we do it at home. We saw bananas,
papayas, and what looked like mango trees and groves of
guavas. The smell of the night soil, which was not as bad as
I thought it would be, explained the beautiful green of the
vegetables. In each garden there is a concrete pit where it
is mixed with water to weaken it before it is used. This is
what accounts for the fertility of this soil that has been used
for hundreds of years without any deterioration. Until comparatively recent times the size of even European cities was
based on the distance night soil could be carried from its
center during the hours of darkness. Near all the paddies
there were stacks of unthreshed rice. The cattle and buffaloes
grazing in the stubble were all in high condition.

We now came to the industrial district of Tsun Wan,
which was alive with working girls, walking fast, laughing
and chattering like magpies. Without exception they were
dressed in fitted pajama suits of cotton in all colors. The tops
fastened on the side with zippers from armpit to hip. The
trousers clung to their slim figures. The wages are low, only
one to two dollars U.S. per day, for a ten-hour day and a
seven-day week.

We got back to the Astor in time for tea and a bath. At
seven-thirty we set off again on a night tour that was to last
until midnight.

We dined at the Far East restaurant. We were the only
Europeans and had real Chinese food. Two famous Chinese
picture stars were there. The woman was most beautiful.
She was not mobbed as she would have been at home.
She was not even stared at. Tommy, our guide, a friend of
Johnny's, gave us a lesson in chopstick eating. It is rather
like golf. You have to concentrate, not press, and keep your
eye on the ball, that is to say, the bit of food you are trying
to pick up. The important part is to keep the sticks level at
the bottom, the food end, and prevent them from crossing
at the top. Our dinner consisted of peanuts marinated in
some sauce, a tasty salad of white cabbage cut into thin

strips, steamed fish with a green vegetable and one that
looked like a black lady's-slipper, fried prawns, fried chicken,
chicken with noodles (noodles and their European offspring
macaroni originated in China and the method of manufac-
ture was brought back to Italy by Marco Polo). We had fried
rice with green peas, and hard-boiled eggs, and ended with
soup. The Chinese eat their soup at the end of a meal, a very
good idea, as it then flows into the gaps instead of filling up
the stomach. We drank perfumed tea all through the meal.
When we had done they brought warm wet towels to wipe
our faces.

This food and the lunch made me change my mind about
Chinese cooking, which I had never cared for in America.
In the East it was wonderful. Rice is eaten with chopsticks
by the shoveling method, the bowl held near the mouth and
the rice pushed in with both sticks held close together.

Our next stop was the Cantonese Opera. To get there we
drove down Nathan Road, another of the world's famous
thoroughfares. There is one in every big city. Nathan Road
is a sister street to Piccadilly in London, the Avenue de
l'Opéra in Paris, Fifth Avenue in New York, Canal Street in
New Orleans, and Adderly Street in Cape Town. This was
brighter than Broadway and more beautiful, with lights of
all colors, red again predominating, and the names of stores
in Chinese characters made lovely designs against the blue-
black sky. I have no doubt that even "Coca-Cola" in Chinese
would look beautiful.

We climbed out of the city proper, the view becoming
more spectacular every moment, till we reached the terrace
of the Carlton Hotel, where we had coffee.

Of all the night-lighted cities we have ever seen this was
the best because of the variety in the color of the lights.
They were white, yellow, reddish, orange, greenish, spotted
here and there with the scarlet and bright green of distant

neon lights. It was quite cold now and we were glad we had coats.

The Cantonese Opera was held in an amusement park, a sort of Disneyland, with ferris wheels and merry-go-rounds where blue Chinese horses went round and round and up and down, racing Chinese tigers and giraffes. Children were driving miniature motorcars. People were playing a kind of bowls. Others were roller-skating. Going past all this, we entered the auditorium where the opera was taking place. These operas last several days, going on for four or five hours each day—one act a day. That is to say, with four or five intervals twenty hours long. The Chinese is so classical that many Chinese do not understand it. There were quite a lot of small children in the audience with their parents, all beautifully behaved.

The scene was a trial. A judge, a girl, a hero with a sword, and a lawyer were the main characters. There were also soldiers with swords and the judge's attendants, a small girl, and other extras. The costumes were magnificent, shining with sequins. The heroine had hair that hung to her thighs. The hero wore two five-foot-long argus pheasant tail feathers, like horns, in his helmet. He expressed rage by bending them down on either side with his hands. Every time he moved they waved. The make-up was curious. The face, except for the forehead and nose bridge, which were white, was heavily rouged. The singing was high and nasal and the music bore no relation to anything Western. It came nearer to that of North Africa and the Near East. The whole effect was fascinating and we could have watched it for longer than we did.

The Chinese grand opera is an art that consists of dancing, acting, singing, acrobatic display, all fitted into a classical tradition of folk tales, legends, and stories that go back to a dynasty of the seventh century. It was perfected in the fifteenth century and has remained more or less unchanged since then. A great deal of the performance is symbolic. The characters are recognized by their dress and make-up. A red face indicates courage, a black means cruelty, and so on. An emperor wears a hat of pearls, a warrior pheasant feathers or foxtails. An actor holding a tasseled whip that represents a horse mounts and dismounts from it. Invisible windows and doors are opened and closed, non-existent stairs are climbed. The music is made by wooden clappers, hard leather drums, by gongs and cymbals. To the Western ears the singing sounds rather like the caterwauling of highly talented cats—tomcats and lady cats—but it has a charm of its own. We had no difficulty in following the plot. There were the usual archetypes. The brave soldier, the wise judge, the wicked lawyer, and virtuous maiden.

At ten o'clock, when we left, children were still playing in the amusement park and the streets seemed thicker with people than ever. Women with small children on their backs now had them wrapped in quilted coats with little hoods over their heads and they all seemed to be sleeping happily. In Hong Kong the oldest boy baby often wears a hat with little ears. This is so that the devil will not realize his importance and will pass him over, thinking he is a mouse or a rabbit. We often see such hats on children at home. Their mothers just think they look cute and have no idea they are fooling the evil spirits that must be just as common in Central Park as on Nathan Road in Hong Kong. There are parallels in Africa, where some tribes do not use real names or use such a name as "cesspit" for a favorite child, so that the gods will not bother to destroy such an inferior creature.

The night club we went to was the High Ball. We saw two floor shows. In the first, two strong European girls did balancing acts, and then one of them, a big blonde, did a scarf dance. In the second a big West Indian Negro sang with a guitar and did some limbo dancing, and his partner, a beautiful part-white, part-Chinese, and part-Negro girl, danced first alone and then with him. The people at the club were mostly Chinese so the floor show to them was exotic in the extreme. The best place to see a Chinese floor show would probably be in Paris, Berlin, or London.

The women were beautiful. Their cheong sams split up to their mid-thighs, showing their pale golden flesh, were unbelievably seductive. This, with the dignity of their carriage and behavior, was paradoxical and only added to the attraction. Slim as wands, straight as arrows, these long-legged girls had a quality of femininity peculiarly their own. As opposed to the Filipinas, with their split skirts they could take a long stride in dancing. We did not think they were as beautiful as the Filipinas, for among them with more mixed blood there was greater variety. But both had the charm of slimness and carriage, both carried their heads high on long, slim, swanlike necks. Of course the stiff three-inch collars of their dresses helped to keep their chins up.

We got back to the hotel at midnight and left a call for

seven. The telephone was blue plastic, very light in weight, and shaped like a microphone, a pattern I have never seen before.

At 8:30 A.M. the car picked us up and we crossed to Hong Kong Island by ferry. We went up Victoria Peak, where we had a magnificent view of the harbor, the big ships, the flattop, the liners, the small boats all leaving a wake that was like a spoor in the water. On the ferry, as we went over, a Chinese gentleman with a little mirror in one hand and tweezers in the other was removing the odd hairs of his beard from his face. The Chinese have very few hairs and do not have to shave.

We next went to the Tiger Balm Garden. This is a remarkable construction, carved out of a stone hill, all in virgin rock. An example of Chinese rococo in the worst possible and most imaginative taste. It took years to build and hundreds of men must have worked on it. First the mountain, for that is what it is, a small mountain, was cleared of earth. Then the exposed rock was carved into whatever it suggested —dragons, rhinos, bears. One ridge is carved into waves in which fifty or so seals, each of which has a different expression, are disporting themselves. The interior of the hill is honeycombed with passages, steps, and small rooms with seats and tables, all cut out of the rock and all leading up to the white six-story pagoda that crowns the top. Everywhere where there is space for them are allegorical figures in concrete, all painted in full color. There is a war of white rats against brown, complete with Red Cross stretcher-bearers, a monkey hill, a collection of nude, long-legged, small-breasted Chinese goddesses. There are Buddhas, mermaids, gods, skeletons, illustrating Chinese folk tales, myths, and Buddhist stories, all with a moral exhorting people to do good and commit no crimes.

The garden was founded by the Chinese millionaire philanthropist Aw Boon Haw, who died in 1954. He made his money with a patent medicine, Tiger Balm, after which the garden is named and which he dedicated to the public for their pleasure. In his lifetime he is said to have given twenty million dollars to charity.

The nude lady was young Kwai Fi, who was fond of bathing, possibly, the guidebook says, to show her charms and please the king. Anyway she came to a bad end. Her lover was beheaded and she was allowed to kill herself.

There is a series of paintings representing the ten courts of hell with the horrible tortures of the suffering of the wicked fully illustrated in Technicolor brightness. People are being sawed in two, having their eyes gouged out, tongues cut off, being fried in a boiler, and run over by a truck. There was, I was told, at one time some erotic statuary that the authorities had removed. But I have no idea if this is true or just a nice story for the tourists.

The most prominent feature of the garden other than the pagoda that crowns it is a stone waterfall. The rushing stone water that pours down the hill is whitewashed and ornamented with streaks of Ricketts blueing in varying shades.

Painted concrete tigers, the Tiger Balm trademark, are prominent and prowl over the rocks in several places. There is also a smallish statue of Mr. Aw Boon Haw, who built the garden, looking out at the view—the garden and the home he built for himself. In the garden of his home there are some old trees in china pots—dwarfed and tortured into curious shapes, dahlias, and the variety of poinsettia that flowers on low stems that we saw in Manila.

As a contrast to this rich man's home, the opposite hill, not three hundred yards away, is terraced in little strips of garden as wide as a bedside mat. Up they go, step after step, strip after strip, for five hundred feet, till they look no wider than bright green threads drawn through the tapestry of the hillside. All are watered by hand, every drop carried in four-gallon petrol tins from below. Each can full of water weighs forty pounds—ten pounds to the gallon—so at each trip they carry eighty pounds of water up the mountainside. We watched them climbing the little paths that feed the strips of garden—women, bent beneath the carrying poles, shuffling along at a trot.

None of these farms or gardens belong to the peasants who work them, and work they do, like slaves, with a hundred ready and willing to take their place if they are fired.

The rich here are very rich and getting richer. The poor, who number millions, can get no poorer. Nothing cannot be subtracted from nothing.

The only flowers out now were chrysanthemums, which originate here—China, Korea, and Japan—and some dahlias. There were also some golden shower, a bignonia that is common in Africa but comes from the East, and a tall yellow Indian marigold that smelled like honey. Some dark purple bohinia trees were in blossom. They seem to be indigenous and grow in profusion in the bush, which is almost jungle on the steep sides of Victoria Peak.

The flower gardens in which the Chinese take such pride I thought lamentable. Formal and without charm, everything growing in china pots, they did not compare in beauty with the truck gardens of the farmers that were like green garlands spread over the hills.

As to the villas and apartment houses on Victoria Peak, they had nothing to recommend them but the view, which was magnificent, overlooking the sea, which was an interesting dirty turquoise blue dotted with cones of islands that were a gray olive-green, some almost obliterated by the mist which sprang up as we watched, so that they looked like the Japanese woodcuts we had so often admired. In the distance was the typhoon shelter in which the sampan dwellers seek refuge when there is a storm warning. But in spite of this protected enclosure many lives are lost each year. On this drive we stopped for gas at a roadside garage and saw a very pretty Chinese teen-ager playing with her dog—a woolly Lhasa-type terrier. We were struck with her natural charm and vivacity. Europeans never seem to associate this quality with the Chinese, but as time went on we found it an outstanding characteristic.

Repulse Bay Beach, the best in the Orient, came next on the itinerary. This is a good beach surmounted by a castle built by a Chinese millionaire. Conspicuous spending seems to be common here. Houses, feasts, and the possession of beautiful concubines are the most popular expressions of Chinese status.

The fishing village of Aberdeen was one of the most sordid and remarkable sights I have ever seen. Here there are several thousand sampans side by side in black, muddy ooze. Many of them are rotting and incapable of floating. They are about twenty feet long with a covered portion that is curved like the top of a covered wagon about eight feet long. They are covered with canvas, straw mats, and a kind of sky-blue linoleum. Whole families live in each and have lived like this for generations. This sampan village probably looked like this one hundred, five hundred, or even a thousand years ago.

It would be interesting to get a psychologist's opinion of the effect of this on the children who must of necessity witness every primal act, from birth to death, apparently without ill effects. For, despite cold and poverty, the people seemed remarkably well and not unhappy. Perhaps the more we have the more we want. These people looked well and tough. They were the survivors—the sickly died as children. All our previous ideas of poverty and squalor were now invalidated. The only worse places we have seen were in Lagos. But there was a big difference. These people were workers, which the Africans are not. It occurred to me that in Africa the women work, in the West the men work, and in China everybody works.

Farther down the waterfront the situation improved. Here the sampans could float and did. They were of a better quality. The blue linoleum that covered the living quarters predominated. There were fewer mats and less canvas. We were out of the slums and in a floating suburbia. Quite unconcerned about anything going on around them, the women on board kept house—cooking food, making lace, sewing, and cleaning. They all swim well. Even children of three can swim. Again these must be survivors, those that didn't fall overboard when they were a year or two old.

Big junks were moving in the open water with whole families working them, the women side by side with the men. They were fishing junks going out to sea. One passed us with the number 2108 on her bow. They are licensed like taxis. Some were "Red Junks" flying the red flag and had come in from Communist China. This is an interesting feature of Hong Kong. The way communist ships come into the harbor with impunity, whereas if a Hong Kong fishing vessel gets blown by a storm into communist waters it is seized.

Reaching a relatively open space where the sampans were not actually touching each other, we got into one and sat in rattan chairs in the stern. The people in the sampans about us did not look up. Tourists were no novelty to them, as irrelevant in their lives as people from another planet. A young woman with a baby strapped to her back was preparing some lovely flaky rice in a conical rice pot. An older woman sat sewing beside her.

Our sampan was worked by two nice-looking pajama-clad girls in their twenties. One worked a single long heavy oar made of two spliced pieces of timber in the stern. The other fended off the boats around us and, as soon as we were in open water, picked up a little round stool with four-inch legs, sat on it and began to row, pulling on another long oar with all her strength. All the sampan oars are fastened with a loose cord to the boats so that they cannot be lost overboard. We were on our way to the Tai Pak, one of the gaily painted floating sea-food restaurants for which Aberdeen is famous. The young ladies who taxied us over were employed by the Tai Pak. Each restaurant—there were three of them—had its own sampans and its own girls. Each of them tried to inveigle customers into their craft.

On board we were shown the live fish in big baskets that hung over the side—a small shark that had the bulldog face and whiskers of a catfish, immense prawns, big crabs, a parrot fish with a beak, its gray body ornamented with bright blue and yellow markings, a big pink grouper, large lobsters that snapped their tails against their bellies. They were brilliantly colored with red, blue, and yellow markings and had enormous feelers that stuck out from their heads like antennae. They made me think of the feathers worn by the hero in the opera and the decorative clothes and armor of the ancient Chinese warriors.

The lunch was good but not as good as I had hoped. The soup of crab meat and sweet corn was excellent and could be made at home by adding a can of crab meat to a can of sweet corn. This was followed by fried prawns—too dry. Next came a crab-meat omelette—very good. Then a fried cutlet of grouper—too dry. This was followed by sweet-and-sour pork—too rich. Then we had fried rice and, last, oranges cut into sections.

On the side I had an extra—shark soup with crab meat—one of the best soups I have ever had. Much better and richer than turtle. By this time I was eating pretty well with chopsticks and they gave us each a pair as souvenirs. We also bought two plates for one Hong Kong dollar each.

A large group of Australians now came in to lunch, all of them, both men and women, six feet or more tall. This is a tourist restaurant, and the food, like the Chinese food in New York, was overcooked and fried in batter to suit Western tastes. In this way they avoided people's asking what this was and that was. Some people would not like to see strange black discs floating in a fish stew or to have the fish's head staring up at them with blind eyes from the bottom of a bowl. I think few Chinese go to these floating restaurants unless they are entertaining occidental people.

Most Americans and tourists in general will not eat local food, however good it is—even in Paris. And this is one reason they get ill. By insisting on European-type food they get it, but it is seldom fresh, most of it being imported and so expensive that anything not used is popped back into the refrigerator to await another sucker.

Local food is always fresh, since it is eaten at once, and,

except for raw green vegetables and some fruits, much safer.
A fish is, after all, a fish. You can see it, smell it. But who
knows what's in an oriental hamburger—a dog that was run
over last week, maybe? We drank big glasses of another kind
of scented tea, some hot, dark brown rice wine in small ones,
and went back with our pretty rowers to the shore.

All through lunch the restaurant swayed at anchor. It was
two decks high and from where we sat we watched the junks
draped with nets set out for the open sea to fish. Two small
girls, singing as loud as they could, passed by standing up
and rowing, each with an oar twice her own length. The
little one was so full of life she danced a little jig in time to
the tune she sang.

As we went down the grand staircase to the boat deck our
guide proudly pointed out photos of American film stars
Elizabeth Taylor and Mike Todd, Errol Flynn, and other
celebrities from overseas—all of whom were apparently devoted to the cuisine of Tai Pak and had signed their auto-
graphs with a bold flourish.

Ashore we wandered around looking at the shops, and
Tiny bought some coat hangers for her new clothes in a small
store filled with oddments of all kinds, including wooden
back scratchers. I examined a Chinese feather duster. I had
seen them in other shops but had not picked one up before.
They are sticks about two feet long on which the skins from
cocks' necks are threaded so that the hackles look like plumes.
Feather dusters are fascinating. In Africa they are made from
hen ostriches, in America from turkey tails, in the Argentine
from rhea feathers.

We now drove back to the Dragon Company on Ashley
Road, to try on our clothes. They were perfect. We paid our
bill and left, utterly exhausted, in a welter of handshakes and
good wishes.

The company car took us to the dock entrance and we
went on board. It was 4:00 p.m. At six we sailed.

The other passengers who had sailed with us from the
States had left the ship and been replaced by three middle-

aged American couples who, like all passengers when first one sees them, looked frightful, but as usual turned out to be quite nice, well traveled, and well informed. I have no doubt they thought the same of us. All passengers think all other passengers terrible when they first see them. This seems to be a normal reflex.

How can the lot of all these Eastern people be improved? What help can be given and by whom? And how much of the help that is given really reaches the needy?

One is overwhelmed by a kind of hopeless sadness and again I wondered at the sympathy given to the Africans who live in greater comfort than the Chinese and have, in all the millennia of their existence, done so little to help themselves. It is interesting to compare the Congo, where chaos continues to increase, and Hong Kong and the Philippines, where hard-working people are starving for lack of opportunity to exercise their skills.

Our guide in Hong Kong was Mr. Tommy Teng, a young man of eighteen who was studying to be an engineer and acted as a guide to improve his English—a most poised and sophisticated young man of immense charm. He liked rock-and-roll, and we arranged with him to send us some modern Chinese records. They have their own rock-and-roll singers. We had heard some and liked them. They sounded wonderful coming over the water as we were rowed over to lunch at Aberdeen. Not being very musical and loving cats, we may be intrigued by the catlike quality of the singing.

Tommy was a most interesting character, a very modern Chinese and amusing in his contempt for the very rich, their houses and concubines, who were a great worry and expense to them but a status necessity. Tommy's father was dead and he was running the family business—a small shoe factory—as well as studying at the university. He was full of gossip, news, and ideas about everything. Among other things he told us about the secret dog-eating that now goes on. It is against the law to kill and eat dogs but many Chinese are very fond of them. So a party goes on a picnic into the country with a dog and when they come back they have no dog. This kind of party is called a dog picnic. He told us about imperial feasts that take two months to prepare and three days to eat. The guests sleep between courses and get up and gorge some more. A great delicacy is raw fresh monkey brain. The monkeys are killed *in situ*. Here we get into homeopathic gastronomy, things that are eaten to produce certain effects—qualities such as courage, intelligence, potency, and so on. They are related to ritual cannibalism, where a man eats parts of his enemy to acquire some of his virtues.

Back on shipboard we now had time to think about our experiences ashore in Hong Kong. The general impression was one of an almost hopeless fecundity, of an ordered chaos possible only because the Chinese are a hard-working, law-abiding people, of the immense wealth and conspicuous spending of the few and the almost unbelievable poverty of the masses.

We were profoundly affected by what we had seen, felt, and not felt. The population explosion which hitherto had been a phrase, an idea which I knew to be correct, now became a shocking reality. We found that the emotion of pity is expendable. That one only has so much pity. That when misery is so great and poverty so appalling, the mind, acting self-protectively, refuses to accept it. We can be sorry for one man, share with him, and both live. We can help ten people, but when it is a hundred, a thousand, a hundred thousand it ceases to be a personal problem. We give up. This is a matter for the government or God. We wash our hands of it.

Give a penny to a child and the child is crushed in the rush for more. Pat a dog and you have to stone it to make it leave you. These are ethical and spiritual dilemmas that leave you shaken. The will to live, the will to work, the feeling that prompts a slum dweller to tend a flower in a pot or hang a caged bird in the window are all things to be considered and to try to understand.

We had learned a lesson, but what it is exactly we do not know—even yet. But we were left with a picture, a composite, three-dimensional picture of sights, sounds, and smells, almost all of them new and bearing little relation to those of Europe or America. Elements in each were the same, but their resemblance was that of distant cousins, not of brothers. The skyscrapers were like those of New York but much smaller. Only the scaffolding was different. Instead of tubular steel they used bamboo. The idea of tubular steel may have come from some smart guy seeing these vegetable tubes and duplicating them in metal. Bamboo is the only beautiful scaffolding I have ever seen. It decorates the buildings like lace. The music, and there is plenty of it, is atonal. It is music and it is not music, not till Elvis Presley's voice bursts out of a dive from a juke box going full blast. Men in skirts, some men. Women in trousers, some women. Babies and children everywhere, picture pretty, with eyes like black plums. The architecture is not functional, not straight up and down, vertical and horizontal. It curves, bends, twists, spirals. The roofs all seem to have backs that are about to break. The gables are voluptuous.

People and ever more people. This is more than a crowd. Bamboo shoulder poles, rickshaws, taxis, cars. The explosion of firecrackers. The sound of hammering, of pneumatic drills, brass bands. Old women in coolie dress. Young women in cheong sams and pajamas, in European dress. Men in all kinds of clothes from new business suits to rags.

This is the city of Hong Kong and Kowloon. Then there are the new territories on the Chinese mainland altogether some 398 square miles on which three million people manage somehow to live. There are twenty thousand junks and sampans in these waters, and nothing is ever still.

Our last impression was the same as our first—the great harbor alive with traffic, the bare, bleak, barren hills, the towering peak with its villas and the shanty towns of the poor clinging like limpets to the rocks.

But now we know more. We have had a glimpse into this anomaly. This tiny, flourishing Western enclave set like a window in this new great wall of modern China. China could take Hong Kong tomorrow. But it won't. Hong Kong is useful to both China and the West. China sells goods here and uses the city as a base for intelligence and financial operations. Red China has a seventeen-story bank in Hong Kong and operates a tourist agency. On our side we have a close view of China, an easy means of getting agents into and out of the country, and above all as far as England is concerned the greatest international department store in the world.

GIRLS LIKE ANGELS

Twelve

NEXT DAY, JANUARY 25

The sea is very calm and very blue. Not a bird in sight and no flying fish. I have reached the conclusion that one does not see flying fish even if they are there in calm water. They swim near the surface and fly only when they come out of a wave. They fly to escape danger, a very effective mechanism, I should imagine, and most of them that do get caught must be captured in smooth water.

Certainly we had never seen so many as we saw in the China Sea, which was roughish the day before we reached Hong Kong. There were thousands, with hundreds of little ones in the air at one time.

About four o'clock we saw great numbers of gulls fishing. There are banks here but no fishing junks. We were off Red China now and the fishermen of Hong Kong are afraid of this coast and steer clear of it. At 6:00 P.M. we sighted the mountains of communist North Vietnam about twenty-five miles away.

Looking at a copy of the *South China Morning Post* we bought on board, we saw that the cashier of a restaurant in Shatin had been found with kitchen utensils, three baskets of dog fur, and a bloodstained jute sack. He admitted he had killed the dog. We wondered if Tommy Teng had seen the item. We wondered who had eaten the dog. Not tourists! The Chinese would not waste a nice dog on tourists.

SAIGON, THURSDAY, JANUARY 26

We woke early and found ourselves anchored near some dark hills, black against the blue, in a still, star-speckled night. Slowly the sky paled and the stars went out. There were a few lights from a village on the shore. Then the dawn came up out of a golden glow behind the blackness of the mountain silhouetting the bush that crowned it, a filigree of black against the yellow sky, and the sun itself, a great yellow ball, appeared swiftly as if thrown into the air. Two white gulls materialized out of the golden glow, dived at some fish, and flew on. They had had their breakfast. There was a strong wind and it was cold on deck. Our pilot must have come on board, for we began to move.

For four hours we wound our way up the river that ran curving and twisting like a snake through the vast alluvial delta of mixed black soil and gray clay that was covered with low bush. We passed fish traps marked by poles in the water, small junks with triangular, ribless sails whose booms were set high over the deck, sampans that seemed heavier and clumsier than those of China and were rowed by two men— one in the bow and one in the stern. The long oars were fastened to posts set in the boat and were tipped with small crossbars like spade handles. Some were fishing boats, others carried timber and bricks.

We passed huts roofed and walled with reed mats in lands cleared by woodcutters, and a brick field. I have the impres-

sion that this scrub has been cut over many times for a thousand years perhaps. Some of the sampans had sharks' faces
painted on the bows in red, white, and black with frightful
staring eyes.

There were more clearings as we got upriver. Rice paddies
where people were harvesting the crop with sickles and
threshing it by beating it into a kind of high wickerwork
barrel with one part cut away. The unharvested rice looked
almost like wheat except that it grew in tussocks. The villages
were sepia-colored and all but invisible among the plumes
of the nipah palms that surrounded them. These palms
fringed the fields and canals and were evidently cultivated
as a crop. Conditions here must be ideal for mosquitoes and
snakes.

Water buffalo were grazing in the stubble. We saw a flock
of white egrets, some kites, one heron, two crows, and one
big white-bellied hawk. The fields, divided by straight canals,
were spanned by graceful oriental bridges. We passed several big tributary rivers and a number of slow streams that
ran out of dark tunnels through the bush.

Far ahead we saw low white buildings rising out of the
water. The effect was Venetian and beautiful. Saigon. But it
was not Saigon when we got up to them. They dissolved into
a Caltex oil depot. So even oil tanks can be beautiful in the
right setting and far enough away.

Some sampans now drifted near the ship, coming downstream and manned by two men, one with an oar and one
crouching in the bow with a long, twenty-foot boat hook.
Coming close to the ship, the man with the hook clipped it
onto the lower deck and swarmed up it with a plastic bag in
his mouth. As soon as he was on deck he cast off the hook. It
drifted away downstream behind us till it was picked up by
the man who had brought him. Three men came on board
this way. They were money-changers who offered eighty piasters to the dollar and had several hundred dollars' worth
of change in their plastic bags. They had time to do very
little business before they were ordered off the ship and

jumped overboard into the river, where they were picked up
by other sampans, like the pickup men in rodeo bronc-riding
competitions, that had drifted down to meet them.

At last we saw Saigon, a tall, white, sunlit city rising out
of a gray mist of smog. We passed a wrecked ship, one of
those bombed by the Japanese. Mud and earth had piled up
against it, forming a small grass-covered island out of which
the steel masts projected at an angle of forty-five degrees, as
if they were trees struck down by some bygone typhoon.
Farther on we passed another ship sunk more deeply in the
water, and some derelict and rusty tramps. More tramps,
very small ones, had been pulled up onto the bank and were
being used as dwellings. There were more and better native
huts here. Two small gray warships, gunboats, passed us flying the South Vietnam yellow flag with three red bars.

The city was close now and we anchored to wait for the
immigration and health authorities. We handed over our
passports and were given receipts for them. There must have
been ten officials on board, all checking typed lists and each
filled to the point of bursting with authority.

At lunch the agent warned us not to go out of the city after
dark, as there were communist gangs within twenty miles of
us. At one o'clock we went ashore and took a taxi to the
Caravelle Hotel, where we got a room. On the dock I noticed
and picked up a long bamboo ladder. It had bamboo spokes
fitted into holes drilled into the uprights and was lighter than
one I once had that was made of aluminum. Bamboo is certainly a wonderful material.

Having parked our gear in a beautiful air-conditioned
room, we went out for a stroll. The town was dead. This was
the siesta hour, from twelve to three, and all the shops were
shuttered. We bought tickets for a tour from a very pretty
Vietnamese girl, six hundred piasters for the two of us, and
at two-thirty set off for the country in a small bus with three
other Americans.

I was very happy to be in a French-speaking city, this
being in a way my native tongue. The city is beautiful, with

wide streets lined with high trees. I have never seen such high trees in any town. They went up thirty to forty feet before they branched. The things that struck us were the number of bicycles and Vespas—one million, we were told—for two million inhabitants. The pedicabs are not sidecars like those in Hong Kong, but are propelled from behind so that the passenger, or victim, is thrust defenseless at the oncoming traffic. The street stalls sell everything from flowers (real and artificial) to fountain pens. The girls—tall, slim, with hair down to their thighs, and small, high breasts—were beautiful. They moved like angels floating on silken wings. Many were dressed in pure white.

The national costume consists of a tight blouse reaching to the hips, and wide satin or silk trousers. Over this is worn a long silk garment, tight to the waist and then split all the way up on both sides, which blows back in the wind and gives an effect of wings. I can imagine no garment less suitable for cycling, but they all wear them, either holding them in their hands on the handle bars or floating out behind them. The wide trousers worn without clips looked dangerous too, though all bicycles had chain guards. The costume of these young ladies was completed by a Chinese hat that was like a large, closely woven basin of straw, with a pointed bottom. The bottom of course was worn upwards. They were covered with cellophane and held on by a wide ribbon worn under the chin.

The dogs were ordinary, most of them what Tiny calls "pure mongrels." Others were recognizable crossbreeds—relics of the colonial period. But I did see one extraordinary animal, quite large, with prick ears, yellow in color and spotted like a leopard with circular black marks. The pure mongrels are types that can be found everywhere in any country, that show no trace of any breed, but fall into a half-dozen categories and probably resemble the original ancestors of the dogs of today.

Our old friend, the European sparrow, chirped everywhere, all cocks, since the hens were busy nesting.

Another thing that struck us was the number of butter-flies in the streets, none strikingly beautiful but butterflies nonetheless.

We crossed several wooden bridges guarded by soldiers with fixed bayonets and Tommy guns. In spite of the activities in the village markets and the people working in their gardens one did not feel that the country was at peace. As in the time of the French war, here—in Indo-China—the peasant of the daytime could become a bandit in the night.

We passed a number of small, two-wheeled, horse-drawn carts. The horses were Mongolian in character but were not stallions and had not the quality of those we saw in the Philippines. Many of them had plumed ornaments on their heads.

The water buffalo were the fattest and best-looking we have seen, their legs so short that the calves suckled their dams from between their hind legs. So fat and so wide that in one field we saw a quite big boy as comfortably asleep on the back of one as he would have been on a sofa.

This is the most fertile and most highly cultivated country I have ever seen. It is either divided into small, mud-walled rice paddies which can be flooded, or into strips of black alluvial soil twenty feet wide separated by ditches full of water. Here the irrigation is by the scoop-and-splash method, being spread by a kind of big spoon on the end of a long stick. In other places the water comes from wells. A bucket is fastened by a rope to a long beam mounted on a pole that acts as a counterbalance. It is forced down into the water and the counterbalance pulls up the loaded bucket. We saw no big bamboos growing and the shoulder sticks on which they carry their baskets and four-gallon cans are the ribs of palm notched at either end.

We saw big patches of sugar cane, rice paddies, and some mango plantations, but most of the cultivated strips were a mixture of everything, all planted in neat lines. Lines of papaya interplanted with pineapples, koko yams, lettuces, and strange greens, and a plot of what looked like white convolvulus. All were neat, weedless, and orderly. Palms everywhere. Bananas, mangoes. Hedges of yellow allamanda, of white gardenia, of hibiscus. Poinsettias blazed in the sunshine. There were great patches of cannas—red, pink, and yellow. There were the small wild red cannas such as I have seen all over West and Central Africa. I have an idea that these cannas and their round seeds, sometimes called Indian shot, had some juju significance there. Africans do not plant flowers for decoration alone. As we drove by a rubber plantation, slouch-hatted soldiers, armed to the teeth, passed us, hooting wildly and paying no attention to anyone.

There were numbers of neat little houses standing back from the road behind vegetable gardens, all with flowering trees, plants, and shrubs in pots. Bougainvillaea, frangipani, yellow and red coxcombs, crotons, and fine, feathery bamboos. We saw some pink lotus in flower and a lot of water hyacinth. This is as ubiquitous as the common sparrow.

The digging was done with hoes shaped like the ace of spades on long handles. The world could be divided into the races that dig by pulling the ground toward them as they do here and in Africa, and those that turn it with spades and throw it forward as in the West.

We passed a number of bullock carts drawn by beautiful

zebu humped cattle. Some were a golden yellow, others gray white. All were fat. We saw two small herds of goats, a number of ducks, and several white Chinese-type knob-nosed geese. The commonest vegetable was the cassava, or manioc. This, with rice, must be the staple food, the basis of the peasants' diet. There were also plenty of coconut palms. We saw one magnificent traveler's palm and one patch of corn, one kapok tree heavy with green pods. In several places we saw short, fat, black and white pigs. No children were carried in slings or piggyback as in Hong Kong, but there were small children walking about everywhere with the greatest confidence. Older children were plastering the irrigation ditches with mud which must harden before the rains begin in six weeks' time. The roads, according to American standards, were narrow and badly surfaced.

Our first stop was a shoe (clog) factory, a series of open sheds and cottages, obviously a family or clan industry of immense charm. Women, half-naked children, dogs, and chickens wandered about as the men, stripped to the waist, worked sitting on the ground. First the thick planks from which the shoes were to be made were sawed into chunks. Then, on a kind of assembly-line principle, they were passed to the rough shaper, who trimmed them down. Next they went to the finishers, who, working by eye, with spokeshaves, produced the finished article in all sizes, from infant to adult, including a fashionable high-heeled model. Finally they were painted with a kind of plastic lacquer. The shavings were fragrant. No one paid any attention to us or stopped work to stare. On the other hand, there was no feverish activity. It is possible that, provided a living is made, these people are happier than our factory workers at home. It may be better, psychologically speaking, to work ten hours a day in the open air with your family about you, see your work completed, and market it yourself, rather than work eight hours at a routine job on an assembly line at a forced pace, alone among strangers, miles from home.

All the poultry we saw here and in the Philippines or in

Hong Kong, other than game fowl, was pale yellow in color. I saw no black or white fowl except for the bantam cock in the pet shop in Manila.

We saw numbers of big brown Ali Baba pots with heavy lids that would hold at least ten gallons and were presumably used for storing grain. The pots with flowers and shrubs growing in them were all ornamental, varicolored, and of many shapes. There was a general feeling that beauty and utility should be combined and that beauty had a certain utilitarian value through the pleasure it gave the eye and the sense of touch, with which we certainly agreed. This is something we have lost and it was even further impressed on me at the next stop, the lacquer factory at the village of Thudaumont. My previous impression of lacquer was that it was merely wood covered with several layers of paint, each of which was rubbed down before the next was applied. This was a gross oversimplification.

First the lacquer. It is the product of a shrub, *Rhus vernicifera*, and had been used by the Vietnamese only to varnish their boats and as an export to China, until in 1443 a craftsman was sent to China to learn the art of using this raw material on furniture and the method of obtaining the characteristic gloss.

The wood to be used is first coated with a mixture of kaolin and gum, which prevents the lacquer from being absorbed. The lacquer, a creamy liquid "the color of a cockroach wing," is mixed with iron oxide and colophony and stirred for forty hours before it can be used. The article to be lacquered is now coated with raw lacquer; next a piece of thin calico is stuck on to it with a mixture of glue, *blanc de Meudon*, and crushed slate. This is allowed to dry for a week and then coat after coat (up to ten) of lacquer is applied, each being pounced, that is to say, rubbed down with a mixture of pumice and crushed cuttlebone. After each operation it is allowed to dry. The final polishing is done with coal dust. The actual superfinished gloss is produced by rubbing with the heel of the hand, topped off by a coating of car polish.

Decorations of gold and mother-of-pearl are put on before the other work is begun and are actually lacquered in. We saw mother-of-pearl shells being trimmed down by hand and then cut into intricate designs with a hack saw. We watched a cherry blossom branch being made, all cut by eye. The pieces are then fitted into a drawing on tracing paper that is laid out on a tray. When completed it is carried to the master craftsman who will glue it onto whatever he is making, and lacquer it on, adding gold leaf where it is required.

A quite young man was making an eggshell lacquer dish. He was fitting crushed duck eggshells into the lacquer, producing a cloisonné effect. Outside on the lawn onto which the rooms of the factory faced there were more duck eggshells drying in the sun among the flowers.

In another part of the factory china was being made. Intricate human figures—horses, horsemen—and vases were cast and finished by hand from pencil drawings. Pots were being thrown on potters' wheels turned by small boys who gave the wheel a twist like a roulette wheel with their feet while they molded clay with their hands. Other men were painting china, getting it ready for the kiln.

In the carpentry shop they were making and carving furniture. The carving was done with small chisels that they struck with a short piece of heavy wood, using it as a mallet. Two hundred hands are employed here, spending weeks making things that could be made in hours by machines. But they make things that will last for centuries, things that will acquire a patina with age and never become so shabby that they have to be thrown away as junk. They were also working in a traditional way, with pride in their own craftsmanship under ideal conditions, a modern factory open on one side to a garden that blazed with flowers.

We bought a little tray and two chopstick holders, little souvenirs that would bring the place back to us when we handled them. But there were beautiful pieces—large pictures in gold and red and black of tigers and fish and fighting cocks—wonderful work and cheap, too, for anyone who was rich.

We passed a number of Buddhist shrines, small temples, and cemeteries that were overgrown with weeds. We saw children flying kites—another Chinese invention—and ended up at a small local sugar refinery. This was really primitive. The most modern thing about it was the Victorian steam engine that turned the little crushing mill. Standing in an open shed was a two-wheeled cart with homemade tires; they were made of little lumps of rubber pressed against each other. The cane, which is very thick (as thick as a woman's wrist), was brought in in small bundles a foot in diameter on hods that consisted of two Y-shaped tree forks fastened together in the middle to form a yoke.

The cane was fed, some dozen sticks at a time, into the crusher. The juice then ran into the caldron—a big flat iron saucer, divided into three sections. The fuel was the bougasse, the residue of the crushed cane. As the cane juice

boiled, some powder, I don't know what, was thrown into it.
Then as it thickened the syrup was bailed by hand from
Number One section into Number Two, and from Number
Two to Number Three. From here, where it was very thick
indeed, it was poured onto a straw mat on a table where it
coagulated at once. The mat had horizontal divisions, and
when the man who was in charge of the operation pulled it
toward him whole long ribbons of sugar fell off and were
broken into pieces—small rectangles marked by the woven
straw—and packed into baskets. We were given some. It was
still so hot we could hardly hold it, but it was not sticky,
and quite delicious. As nice as any candy I have ever eaten.
It would certainly sell anywhere.

By five we were back at the hotel, having woven our way
through, it seemed to us, all the bicycles of Saigon.

We had tea on a terrace on the ninth floor, overlooking
the city. Many of the buildings had penthouses and roof
gardens with trees and shrubs growing in pots. One was almost a miniature jungle of palms and bougainvillaea. Till I
came to the East I had no idea of how much could be done
with potted trees. The entrance to the hotel is flanked by two
gnarled bushes eight feet high, trimmed into tiers like little
tables. The art of topiary must have originated in the Orient.
We had seen peacocks and even deer complete with antlers
growing in some of the gardens we passed.

After tea I had my hair cut, one of the best haircuts I
have ever had, for only sixty piasters. The barber was an
artist with the most gentle touch. Like everyone here he
worked with utmost concentration. When he had done he
gave me a friction rub with eau de cologne. It was only then
that I realized the strength of those fine-boned fingers. He
ended it with a massage of the head, neck, and shoulders
that left me completely refreshed. This over, we went back to
the hotel. We bathed, rested, and went out for a drink, a
Dubonnet, which we had sitting at a table in the street, and
watched the world go by.

At nine we dined. A European-style dinner geared to the

American taste. The menu was in English and the burgundy had been iced. The orchestra was good, the service excellent, and the meal neither bad enough to complain about nor good enough to remember. The best thing we had was the vegetables, grown, no doubt, with night-soil fertilizer. The baked tomatoes with garlic were wonderful and so was the spinach.

They use the term "boy" here, not "*garçon*." We had, for instance, *deux boys* in charge of the room, which was a beautiful big room with Parisian draperies—a French material patterned in big roses on a black ground that let a little light through them. The sheets were blue linen with drawn threadwork at the top. The counterpane was pink. The bathroom was superb, complete with a bidet. The beds were most comfortable with foam-rubber mattresses over wooden slats and a kind of low, triangular-shaped bolster under the mattress that raised the head about six inches and sloped away to nothing. The air-conditioning was if anything too good.

In the room I found a brochure and discovered that Vietnam is one of the best big-game-hunting areas left in the world, with five varieties of buffalo (gaur, Asiatic water buffalo, banteng, Kupray, and Mithan). There are tigers, panthers, wild pigs, bears, elephants, and seven kinds of deer. But what with the difficulties of language in the bush, climate, bandits, and transport, I felt the brochure to be overoptimistic.

The dawn had been remarkable. When we woke the city below us was wrapped in soft white mist, out of which a white sun rose like a luminous tennis ball. Breakfast was the usual French one of coffee and *croissants*. After breakfast and doing our packing we went shopping. Tiny wanted a local blouse. We inquired at the American Express, which is combined with the Pan Am office, and the girls there all offered to introduce us to their tailors and said such things could not be bought ready-made, nor would they fit a European woman. They smoothed their slim shapes and looked coy. These girls are beautiful, but they do not seem to mature as well as the Chinese. Their faces are fatter and become jowly. They do not have the same good bones.

Ten minutes later we had bought two outfits and had to wait while they were taken in. This pleased Tiny, who had said that these oriental girls made her feel crude and gross. We sat at a café in the street and drank coffee and were soon surrounded by hawkers. We bought four shell necklaces, but had trouble getting rid of the men who had pictures to sell. We had bought six good ones on silk at the hotel and kept saying we had some. Finally, as a last effort, one of the men whispered in my ear, "You want dirty pictures?" and Tiny, who had not heard what he said, said, "No, we have plenty." She was annoyed when I laughed.

Then we heard chickens and found a man selling little clay and rubber toys that made chicken noises: hens if you squeezed them and cocks if you blew in them. We bought two, went to collect our clothes, and back to the hotel for our luggage.

The taxi went too far and had to come back through slums that I have never seen equaled elsewhere. On one side of us were open-fronted shops, on the other a kind of endless mixture of market and dwelling. The dwellings went out over the water where they stood on stilts above the river. Between the two was a solid mass of seething people. We drove through smells, odors, and stenches of unbelievable variety —burning fat, rotting fruit, fish, perfume, urine, excrement, sweat—all so strong that they were almost visible.

This is a powder barrel. There have already been explosions here. In October, Vietminh guerrillas engaged the army in an action that lasted a week. In November an American police adviser was shot down in broad daylight near the seaside resort of Cap Saint Jacques. Two hundred civilians, mayors of small towns, village headmen, and others known to be anti-communist are murdered every month. We in our short drive into the country were shown a bridge that had been blown up only a week before.

It is difficult to see how these small new countries came into existence or how their planners ever expected them to survive. Vietnam, a long thin strip divided into a communist north and a theoretically Western south. Laos a landlocked fairyland. Cambodia helpless. Thailand alone seems to be strong, spiritually at least. Burma is another strip. Malaya a peninsula. These are all miniature countries with coast lines and frontiers hundreds or even thousands of miles long. All are overpopulated; the cities swarming with people who have come in from the country in the hope of something: something new, something better; following the rumor of rich pickings in the towns that has seeped into the mud of the rice paddies and black shadows of the rubber plantations.

There is no answer to this teeming fecundity. A million dollars would keep a million families for one day. Contraception, even if it were practicable, would not be accepted by races who regard children, sons particularly, as necessary to their salvation after death and as an insurance against penury in old age.

The ship tied up next to ours was a Chinese communist freighter. We were again struck by the magnificent physiques and rippling muscles of the stevedores working stripped to the waist. On the other side of the river a tangle of reed huts straggled out over the water on wooden legs. Below them snow-white ducks paddled in the muddy garbage. In a boat a few yards from the shore a woman was washing a small boy of three or four, and ended the proceeding by dipping him overboard as she held him by the arms.

And this was the last we saw of Saigon, a golden brown woman dipping a naked golden boy into the silver river.

SILK AND WHITE ELEPHANTS

Thirteen

SATURDAY

We are now in the Gulf of Siam. The sea is smooth, with small whitecaps, a beautiful dull green, opaque like poor quality jade. The clouds are the usual long thin clouds of the Orient, like squashed cigars, so different from the voluptuous snow-white forests that one sees in the Caribbean. Every sea seems to have a quality of its own—its own water, its own clouds, its own sunrises and sunsets, its own stars. We have now left what was once French Indo-China and is now North Vietnam, South Vietnam, Laos, and Cambodia. A lot of Frenchmen lie dead there. Whole classes from St. Cyr were killed almost as soon as they graduated. But they left behind a language, a modern alphabet and a Western culture that has been grafted onto this ancient oriental scion. There were not many settlers here. It was not like Algeria, where, as has been said, the settler's choice is a coffin or a suitcase. After Hong Kong, one of the noisiest cities in the world, Saigon was very quiet with relatively few cars. The hundreds of cyclists ring no bells. The people talk softly and even the clatter of their wooden shoes seemed muted. Nevertheless, one's impression is not of peace or progress, rather of stagnation and a slow running down of the machine. No building is going on, and away from the city itself there is neither peace nor security, with a troubled Laos on the west and a communist Vietnam to the north. One wonders what the future will hold for this little Paris of the Orient with its tall trees and white buildings, with its girls that are like golden angels winged with silk; its butterflies, and the sparrows in the streets.

All my life I have wanted to go to Indo-China. Now I have been and the hope has turned into a memory that time will dim. Again we are glad we did not come by air. There must be time between one place and another. The mind and heart must digest too if there is to be no confusion.

SUNDAY

The moonlit sea was oily, glass smooth. The dawn beautiful and the sea as it grew light a pale, unruffled turquoise with a paler sky—a faint blue tinged with pink that turned to gray on the horizon. At breakfast a lady passenger complained about there being chickens on board. That was us with our chicken toys. I made a noise like a hen laying an egg and Tiny blew in hers and did a most realistic cock crow. We said we had heard chickens too.

The sea has now turned green. We have passed two large, semicircular fish traps that have hats on them and are moving up a channel marked by buoys topped with small black flags on bamboo poles. The captain was very careful to give the traps a wide berth, for if damaged the owners make enormous claims, which is not surprising as they are very expensive to build. I found that they are called *kelongs* and that the nipong palm, from which the traps are made, is imported from Indonesia. A nipong pole eight fathoms long costs twelve dollars Malay and since a *kelong* in three fathoms of water requires about seven hundred poles the capital outlay is very large and, with the net, may cost forty thousand dollars.

A flock of gulls, rather like herring gulls, have appeared. There are nine ships nearby. A small gunboat, some fishing junks. A beautiful turquoise-blue freighter with a red waterline, the *Estelle Maersk*, came past us. All the Maersk Line ships are this color. We were to see plenty of them before we got home. The first one we had seen was in Lake Gatun in Panama. The sea changes color again; it becomes tinged with the yellow mud that gives it a golden glow. The visibility is low as we go into a light fog of heat in which the horizon is lost.

We docked and while waiting for the immigration and customs had lunch. Then we took a car to the Hotel Rama, four or five miles away. We passed some installations, ramshackle houses, swamps, cultivated ground where a herd of buffalo were grazing, and finally booked into the hotel. It is brand new and beautiful, air-conditioned, and decorated in a restrained oriental manner. Having left our gear in our room, we went out to look at the city. After Saigon, Bangkok seemed sordid, grubby, treeless, but very active. Building was going on everywhere. Most of the shops had their names written in both Thai and English. Thai script looks like a mixture of Chinese and Arabic. Almost everyone spoke some English and all were most charming, helpful, and polite, but there were no beautiful costumes or people. The peasants are a strong, thickset race, the women tending to have bowlegs and to walk with bent knees. Some wore European clothes, some oriental wide trousers and some sarongs. We looked at jewelry, Thai silver, rather dark in color, that looked a bit like stainless steel, star sapphires, some a dull blue and not the best I have seen, others black, which I had never seen before. Among other things offered for sale were wood carv-

ings and bronzes of Buddhas and dancers, tiger and leopard
skins backed with silk and not well tanned, and ties made of
hooded-cobra skins.

The art of weaving Thai silk, a cottage industry, had almost been lost until revived by an American, Mr. Jimmy
Thompson, who has built it up into a great business of world
importance. This would seem to be the ideal way of helping
people—helping them to help themselves, building up their
pride, and filling their pocketbooks at the same time. Thai
silk is fine, thin, much of it in checkerboard designs of all
colors. I bought one shirt for two hundred ticals, or ten dollars U.S. The only other thing I saw that I should have liked
was a tiger skull beautifully mounted and embellished with
silver.

It was hot, though not too oppressive, just sweating hot,
and after a bath and a drink we dined. A set dinner and one
of the best I have ever had anywhere. *Consommé au
nageoires de requin* (shark fin), *loup de mer poché,* a fine
fish resembling turbot, with a *sauce hollandaise,* which was
followed by roast beef, potatoes and spinach, a pineapple
dessert and coffee. We drank a half bottle of Rhine wine.
And so to bed in preparation for an early start to see the
floating vegetable market.

We were called at six and had breakfast in our room—
coffee and a rather dry red-fleshed papaya with a hard green
melon-like skin, eaten as we watched the sun come up like a
red ball out of the South China Sea, and went down to the
lobby to wait for the car. It came at seven and took us to
the dock by the Oriental Hotel, where we got into a launch
and went up the Chao Phraya River, the Grand Canal of
Bangkok. It is lined with houses and temples; alive with craft
of every kind, from Thai warships with the biggest flags I
have ever seen to tiny one-man sampans no bigger than a
canoe and paddled like one. There were children by the
dozen in boat-busses that were taking them to school. All
were laughing and wore navy-and-white uniforms. Launches,
big lighters roofed with flattened-out corrugated iron bent

over like the canvas tops of Western wagons, and junks of all
sizes moved like great insects over the water. We passed
temples and warehouses, and then as the river narrowed
came to the real Bangkok of the past. Here all the houses
stood mounted on stilts with steps leading down into the
water. Beside almost every one were canoes and rowboats,
tethered between two thin bamboos, plunging like horses in
their stalls as the wake of every passing vessel struck them.
Many houses had landing stages made of bundles of floating
bamboo poles that were lashed together and looked like logs.
Similar bundles were used to retain floating gardens of a
vegetable that looked like a giant water hyacinth. Every
house had flowers in pots on its veranda or at the windows.
Roses, poinsettias, red ones and the white double poinsettia
we had seen in the gardens of the President in Manila, bougainvillaea, some of which were colors we had never seen
before. Bright scarlet and rose pink were mixed with purple,
magenta, cyclamen pink, brick red, and yellow. Cannas six
feet high were growing almost in the water. So were many
trees. Some had their roots submerged, others grew on
patches of land less than a foot above it. Coconut palms,
bananas, kapoks, mangoes, and breadfruit seemed to thrive
in this black waterlogged soil. Some of the old houses leaned
at every angle. New, almost ranch-type, wooden houses were
being built. The roof was always put on first. Many of the
houses were ornamented with fretwork and looked rather
like Swiss chalets. There were shops, open-fronted to the
river, selling groceries, others selling vegetables and tinware,
and everywhere life was going on. Home life merged into
river life. Girls were cleaning their teeth, children urinating,
clothes and dishes being washed, and people stood waist
deep soaping themselves, all in the same water. These are a
very clean people in an unhygienic way. Floating in the
river was vegetation of all kinds, escapees from the water
gardens: palm ribs, coconut shells, banana leaves, a dead
dog, and a dead cat.

Many of the houses had orchids growing under slatted

shades. Some of them were long-stemmed purple blooms growing in the open like regular flowers. We had seen similar ones in Saigon and Puerto Rico. I saw several pigeon lofts, quite a few ducks swimming beneath their owners' houses, one wicker bird cage, and a gibbon disporting itself upside down on a private landing stage. There were any number of dogs of the classic mongrel type, very like the native dogs of Africa, mostly yellow with prick ears. Some had curly, almost corkscrew tails that went both ways—that is to say some curved to the right and some to the left. Several, though smooth-haired, had the wide faces and wrinkled foreheads that showed an infusion of chow blood. We saw one short-legged, woolly Thibetan-type terrier and saw a fair number of cats, most of them orange. There were no wild birds except for the kites. We saw several dogs in boats and wondered if any of these animals ever got ashore except on their own front stoep.

Everywhere there was activity, a proliferation of life amid the unbelievably fecund vegetation between the houses on the riverbanks. Women cooking, sewing, washing babies in the river, washing clothes, dipping up water in buckets to water their potted plants or wash their floors. Old white-haired women that from a distance looked like blondes watched the river traffic. Naked children, like pretty little golden statuettes, stood beside them, watching too, as once the elders had stood beside their own grandparents watching the same unchanging scene. Everywhere subsidiary canals, *klongs,* as they are called, watery side streets, led off the main artery. This is a water city and these are water people. The first road, called the New Road, was built in 1869. It was formerly an elephant track and was built at the request of the foreign community who used it for walking exercise, to the great amusement of the Siamese.

Launches loaded with beautifully packed green vegetables passed us and we finally reached the floating market—a flotilla of sampans loaded with yellow papayas, green vege-tables, pink tomatoes, and white roots that looked like giant

radishes or turnips. Among the vegetable boats were vendors
of tinware and one floating butcher with a big straw hat
cutting up revolting-looking bits of meat and weighing them
out on a brass scale in the bow of his sampan. A florist with
a boatful of potted plants and cut flowers plied his trade. The
plants were mostly roses, for which Bangkok is famous. I have
an idea that the polyantha roses, among others, came from
the Far East. Many of the ones we saw were small-flowered
and very floriferous.

Having seen the market, a ride upstream that had taken
almost two hours, we turned around and headed back, stopping to look at the royal barges, which had been pulled out of
the water and rested in their shed. These superb boats, giant
canoes, are a hundred fifty feet long and are entirely covered
with gold leaf. Each is sculptured into scales or feathers with
great figures at the bow. One is a swan, another a kind of
many-headed snake. The others are human figures with
painted hats and rather indecently spread legs. When used
at festivals they require sixty oarsmen who are all dressed in
scarlet and use golden paddles. Thick ropes of flowering
jasmine trail in the water from the bow to stern. The open
sheds were dark, but the carved prows were bright with
reflected light.

The straw hats worn here are wide-brimmed, flat-topped,
and appear to have a liner that fits close to the head, resembling the Fulani hats of Nigeria and the Sudan.

The food in the local eating houses was not attractive. In many of them there were chickens hanging from hooks by their beaks, plucked and shiny from scalding.

The first temple we went to was on the river, its entrance guarded by two granite crocodiles whose noses had been daubed with red paint. On the dry grass between the river and the temple were stalls where plastic crocodiles, slides, postcards, articulated cobras, drawings on rice paper, and rubbings of Buddha in gold on black cotton were being sold. We bought two rice-paper pictures for a dollar each and went in. In this temple we did not have to take off our shoes. It and the surrounding buildings were an amazing sight. Great stone statues of gods, heroes, and animals that had been brought from China as ballast in the trading junks stood at the foot of every building. The buildings themselves were ornamented with fragments of china in a most brilliant baroque and rococo manner. Whole plates, and plates smashed into segments, were used to make flowers. Flowers made of big cowrie shells went from the ground level to the pinnacle of some towers. Ancient tortured trees in china pots stood alone and in groups. There were big shade trees with seats below them. It was like nothing we had ever seen before. The nearest thing was the Byzantine mosaics of St. Mark's in Venice. In fact the whole of the older part of this city with its canals and houses overlooking the water made us think of Venice, a tumble-down, rickety, wooden Venice, rich with temples, trees, and flowers. The two cultures might be related, too, since Ayudhya, the ancient capital of Siam, or Thailand, was a great trading center in the fourteenth century, doing business with China and Japan in the East, and England, France, and Italy in the West. The Western trading center at that time was Venice and the Arabs were the link between the two.

Some confusion still exists in my mind about the names of the various parts of the temple, but it would appear that the term *wat* applies to the whole enclosure. The *bot* is the most important though not necessarily the largest building. It is marked by eight boundary stones, called *bai sema*, that surround it. The *vihan* is the hall in the temple area where meetings are held. There may be several *vihans*. The *phra chedi*, or *chedi*, is a circular monument with a sharply tapering spire. This is also known as a *stupa*, or *pagoda*, and usually contains some sacred objects in a vault at its base.

The *prang* is a Cambodian development of Hindu architecture and was often used to contain the wealth of gold and jewels that belonged to the temple.

Except for the *chedis*, the *phras*, and the temple itself, the other parts remain unclear to me, such is the grandiose confusion of this architecture. The tiled roofs are sway-backed and each ends with an upward curl like a horn that at first seems meaningless but later, on closer inspection, turns out to be a stylized peacock's head, the long part of the horn being a vastly exaggerated crest. From the eaves small brass wind bells with heart-shaped clappers modeled on the leaf of the sacred *boh* tree dangle and ring with every breeze. Pigeons coo. The pigeons too are reminiscent of St. Mark's. Birds sing in the trees and monks with shaven heads and bright orange robes move sedately about their affairs. This is a fairyland world utterly removed from the present, a world of Madama Butterfly, of Gilbert and Sullivan, and *Chu-Chin-Chow*. Old, spiritually, beyond a Western concept, and yet historically new. No temple is more than a hundred seventy years old and the newest, I believe, was completed only sixty years ago.

By now, only a few hours after visiting so many, these temples are somewhat blurred. In some we had to take our shoes off, in others we did not. They all had magnificent teak doors, some painted with pictures in gold leaf, others with an intricate and tiny design of mother-of-pearl inlay running from the ground level to twenty feet above our heads. The doors were six inches thick. There were big tiles painted with flowers, bas-reliefs and intaglios, china and glass mosaic

in every color. In none of them, vast as they were, could a
silver dollar be placed without its touching some decoration.
Some temples were in wonderful repair, in others bits of
colored china had fallen off and lay scattered like autumn
leaves on the ground.

Two temples we shall never forget were those of the
Reclining Buddha and the Emerald Buddha. The Reclining Buddha is a hundred sixty feet long and thirty-nine feet
high. It is made of cement-covered brick and plastered with
gold leaf. No joints are visible. This immense gold figure lies
full length on a platform, resting its head upon its hand with
the elbow bent. As we looked at it, children were playing
outside and the sound of their laughter rang through the
walls.

The Buddha's hair was curly, each whorl in the shape of a
snail. The ten toes of the enormous feet are all the same size
The soles are covered with a hundred eight figures in mother-
of-pearl inlay contained in squares surrounding the Wheel
of the Law.

The temple of the Emerald Buddha is one of the most magnificent. This Buddha, cut from a single piece of green jasper, is twenty-three inches high and is set above a series of life-sized golden statues holding umbrellas. It has three changes of jewel-studded garments that are worn, respectively, in the rainy, cool, and hot seasons.

The story of this Buddha is that it was made by the gods for a Naga king in Ceylon, and after being captured by various people in a number of wars finally ended in the hands of King Rama I and was brought to Bangkok in 1785. The ceilings and beams of this temple, like those of all the others, are highly decorated with gold on a red and black ground. And the walls, for their whole height of forty or so feet, are painted with scenes of Buddha's five hundred fifty previous recorded existences.

None of these Buddhas resemble our Western concept of the fat, smiling figure sitting in the lotus position. They all wear tall conical hats and none are fat.

Outside, in the wat, there is a great courtyard surrounded by a cloister in which dozens of statues of Buddhas are lined up against the wall, which made us think of the clay figures in some of the courtyards of the juju houses of West Africa.

I have always had the conviction that we know very little of the early movements of man, and think that the Chinese penetrated deeply into the African Continent in search of tin and ivory. They mined tin at Rooiberg in the Transvaal and may even have reached the Jos Plateau with their ponies and there taught the natives to mine and make tin straws— raw tin which was smelted and flattened into sheets and rolled. There are pottery fragments that appear to be Chinese in origin. In the museum there is one piece that is known as the Pagoda Fragment. There are places with Chinese names in Ghana and Nigeria, Jos among them, umbrellas, hats, and dogs, all of which appear to be oriental, as is the practice of dog eating. So far no anthropologist has gone into the matter, but stranger things have happened. It is even possible, too, that the Romans reached down along the West Coast bringing their architecture, the atrium, and the toga, the Gold Coast national costume, along with them. It is these speculations that make travel so interesting.

In the wat here, on one of the balconies, are several magnificent gilt figures, half man and half bird, called Kinnari and Kannara, that are said to live in a wonderful forest in the Himalayas. There are also statues of elephants captured in wars during the reigns of Rama II, IV, and V. The Thai history, like that of most nations, is one of war after war, in their case chiefly with the Burmese and Cambodians.

The Thai were pushed out of China about A.D. 500 and overran the Cambodian and Mons people, with whom they soon amalgamated. By 1250 they were strong enough to form a kingdom of their own, and in 1350 established their capital at Ayudhya, forty-odd miles from Bangkok. This town was sacked by the Burmese in 1767. In the sixteenth century it was probably larger and cleaner than the London of Elizabeth I, and had a higher and more sophisticated culture than any town in Europe.

Bangkok replaced Ayudhya as the capital and is therefore, as cities go, relatively young. Thailand has the highest living standard of any country in Southeast Asia and is even able to export food—rice. Its other exports are rubber, teak, and tin. Of secondary importance are wolfram, soya beans, tapioca flour (cassava), stick-lac, and oil seeds.

For the tourist the most interesting buys are Thai silk, silver, some precious stones, wood carvings and goldwork, and Buddhist temple rubbings.

Perhaps the most outstanding impression of our temple visits occurred when some small girls, eight or nine years old, dressed in navy-blue skirts and white jumpers, carrying schoolbooks, passed the gates of one of them. Most turned toward the temple and with their hands folded in front of them bowed slightly. But one put down her schoolbag and knelt on the pavement in the conventional attitude of prayer. There was something unbelievably touching in this act of faith. What did the future hold for her? She had no more past than a flower. For an instant unknown to her, her path had crossed ours, mystically touching some chord in the depths of my personality by an act of beauty, of purity. It was like seeing a butterfly poised on a rose, as ephemeral, as beautiful, another comma in the long book of life, another of those moments of beauty that are always sought for and so seldom found.

At the last temple we stopped for refreshment. They had orange bottled drinks, Coca-Cola, and ice-cold coconuts. We each had a coconut. They were full of delicious milk, a pint at least, and had a soft pulp that tasted like delicately flavored, creamy toothpaste.

We next visited the snake park—a couple of walled snake pits filled with cobras that lived in small round concrete houses that looked like big pudding basins. Each had two small holes for the snakes to enter and four iron handles so that they could be turned over when the snakes were required for milking to make serum. There were several moving about on the grass and two swimming. One most obligingly half reared and put up its hood. It was 1:30 P.M. They were going to be fed at 2:00 P.M. But I had no great desire to see them eat. They knew the day and time, because before we left more came out of their houses. We saw one frog and one white mouse, the smartest of those that had been given them a week ago (they are fed every Monday), a doomed survivor running helplessly from one snake house to another. In one way I was curious to see the exact method by which a snake caught and killed and swallowed a mouse. In another I did not want to see it, and I knew it would upset Tiny, so we left.

Our general impression of Thailand was that the people were most charming and polite, bowing deeply at every request, but in no way obsequious to anyone.

The things we should like to have done and seen were:

Thai boxing, which is very formal but where all means of attack except the teeth are used. I should like to have seen the Golden Buddha, that weighs five tons and until recently was believed to be of no great value, having been plastered over with stucco. The gold was discovered only when it was moved. We should like to have gone up country to see the elephants working in the teak forests, to have flown up to the Angkor Wat, and to have gone to the zoo to see the king's white elephant.

This elephant, when young, roamed about at liberty with his keeper. He was playful, the guidebook said, liked children, and was a bit of a show-off. Then on the tenth of November 1959, he was raised to the peerage, given the name and rank of Phra Savet Phumiphol Pahana, and now stands hobbled and tethered in his pavilion to receive the worship of the people. There is a moral here. Perhaps even among elephants it is better to be happy than important.

We should also like to have seen some Thai dancing. There are four styles. In one of them elongated false fingernails are used. We should also like to have seen a game of Ta-Kraw played with a rattan ball, and the theater in which jointed figures, cut from leather, are manipulated between white sheets lit from behind.

Here are some extracts from the guidebook:
"Toilet facilities outside of Bangkok are very primitive.
Drink only selected bottled drinks. Use a straw and no ice.
Do not eat any fruit that does not have to be peeled and
see that the skin is not broken. There is no city sewage disposal system, each house providing or not providing a septic
tank at will—the people living on the river have no problem."

The Thai are very fond of children and value girls as much
as boys. In a jeweler's shop we went into the owner was
playing with his six-month-old son, who was lying naked,
head down, in his lap. This is perhaps why the children are
so fearless and friendly.

Thai gardens do not compare with those of Vietnam,
though we did not go into the country to see any real agriculture. But the gardens around the houses were poorly kept,
and overgrown with weeds. They seem to specialize in pot
plants, flowers, creepers, and small trees cut into designs.
Some of the street trees were bohinias, their heads trimmed
into big balls.

We saw people on two separate occasions collecting algae
from ponds with muslin nets. Is this edible? Or do they use
it to feed fish?

The cars drive on the left as they do in England. Many
of the taxis are tiny open vehicles that will hold only two
people.

We saw no wheelbarrows. Sand and gravel were brought
to the working point by truck and then carried in baskets
slung on poles.

There are several ways of visiting foreign countries. There
is ours, the quick superficial view, where impressions are
received with tremendous and exhausting impact, and a
longer visit, where more is seen but the impressions are often
dulled and the knowledge gained is not necessarily accurate,
and often prejudiced; and finally, by living and working in a
place, which may mean living in a small white enclave. The

ideal would be a swift look and then a return later for a longer stay. There is always the danger of trying to see and do too much. The human mind's ability to absorb impressions is rather like a cup: when it is full, it is full. And ours after twenty-four hours are full to overflowing. They will hold no more.

With no previous knowledge of the Orient we shall, after nearly six months at sea, return enriched by this experience, far more able to understand and appreciate everything we read about the Far East—its arts, crafts, its peoples, and way of life, which, provided they can obtain enough to eat, may well be fuller and happier than our own. In general they seem to work well together and are often surrounded by their families. Their wives bring them their food at work as their children play at their feet. This is not a sentimental point of view. It is in accordance with the nature of man and was followed in Europe till the industrial revolution destroyed the cottage industries and craft guilds of our ancestors, and left us, today, with a surplus of material possessions that are no more than toys, and fail to fill the spiritual vacuum of our shattered homes. We have lost our belief in the possibility of happiness. To talk of it is corny. Love is only sex, sex is only glands. Children, the product of sexual union, are democratically regarded as entities long before they are capable of rational thought, a woman and man instead of co-operating compete with each other for the worldly success that is our substitute for happiness and content. These are the new ideals that we are giving to the undeveloped nations in the name of progress and freedom and democracy.

We have finished loading—tapioca flour (cassava), thousands of duck eggs as deck cargo, and great baskets of small white onions. The immigration people have come on board for a final check of passports. One of them, having lunched with us, burps happily and unapologetically. To burp is polite in the East. There is a great bunch of brilliant flowers in a vase in the saloon. Red and orange roses, tall fragrant tuberoses, orchids, goldenrod, yellow chrysanthemums, and a lot of what look like big double Barberton daisies—red, mauve, pink, and orange in color. Nothing goes with anything. The colors all clash and burn like fire on the table. There is no Constance Spry nonsense here.

The tug pulls us around and we set off down the river past the gray naval ships all flying the royal standard, the red, white, and blue stripes of Siam with a white elephant on a red ground in the center. Past other freighters loading and unloading cargo onto the dock and lighters. Past all the small craft—sampans, canoes, and launches—almost all of them with flags. Everything here has a flag, including the taxis.

Down the river, past little villages half hidden in the jungle, each with its temple and pagoda. Past fish traps and nets hanging out to dry on tall bamboo poles.

Night fell and a big pink full moon came up in a rosy sky. Then the sky and the moon turned to gold, casting a golden track over the sea, the Gulf of Siam, as we went down the channel, marked by buoys flashing intermittent red lights that shone like single ruby eyes. Outside the channel we saw the dark shadow of a two-masted fishing junk. It carried no lights. It was just a little darker than the sea and we waited, leaning on the rail, to see it caught on the bright moon track, silhouetted for one instant—black on silver—and then disappearing into the night as we steamed on.

Below in our cabin our temple wind bell, which we had hung on a curtain, chimed softly, the air was perfumed with the scent of the tuberoses the girls had put in a vase on our table. Later I was awakened by the sting of the mosquitoes that had come in with the flowers. The sting was almost as sharp as a tsetse fly bite.

We have now left the Gulf of Siam and are back in the South China Sea. Tonight we shall be in Singapore. We mark our progress on a big map of the world we bought in New York for a dollar. It is extraordinary to remember that this is a better map than any used by the mariners of the sixteenth century. Each captain, each trading company, guarded their knowledge. Every trade route, the name of every king or chief with whom they did business were a "top secret" on which the success of their enterprises depended.

All but two of the other passengers are sick with dysentery, other stomach trouble, and headaches, due to being out in the sun without hats, drinking too much, mixing highballs, Coca-Cola, John Collinses, coconut juice, tea, coffee, and beer, eating ice cream, putting ice in their drinks, and buying hamburgers of doubtful origin. They said how good the vegetables were (and they are) but seemed shocked and surprised to find they were fertilized with human excreta. We were blamed for everything because we had persuaded them to drink coconut milk. Persuaded? Not at all. We drank it because we always do. We like it. And they followed suit.

A CONCRETE BUDDHA

We lie in the Roads outside Singapore all night. From the cabin we can see lights and low hills. In the morning we steam into a narrow channel past numbers of beautiful islands, many of them studded with Victorian country houses and gardens. We passed the watchtowers and radio station and the hidden batteries that should have made Singapore invincible, and would have, if the Japanese had only attacked it from the right place. A water boat passed us. Evidently there is no water on some of these islands.

We come in through a mass of shipping, British, German, Dutch, and Japanese, and after twisting around this way and that docked against the quay. Immigration is no problem. Everyone is charming, the dock police the best turned out we have seen so far, really smart spit-and-polish boys. A mark of any highly disciplined body of men. At Gate No. 5 we picked up a taxi and drove to Raffles Hotel. This is another dream achieved. How many men in their lives have this good fortune? The hotel is big, old, and rambling. The gardens have white frangipani and rows of immense, fanlike traveler's palms.

A gin sling is the first thing, the traditional drink—gin,

cherry brandy, lime, and a touch of Angostura bitters with soda water and ice. We take it in the big open lounge. The bar, once said to be the longest in the world, has gone. The longest now must be at the Rand Club in Johannesburg. We looked at the shops in the arcade and arranged for a taxi in the afternoon. The lunch was mediocre and moderate in price. The two generally go together. But the pineapple was excellent, outstanding, sweet as honey.

The town, after the others we have seen, seemed dull, and the residential areas very residential. Big oldish white houses, with red roofs set in big well-kept gardens.

We saw a so-called death house. A kind of flophouse where the very poor sleep in tiers and someone dies each night. The Thieves' Market—there seems to be one in every city. Here things can be bought cheap. Shoes by the hundred are stolen by children from the mosques and temples where people have to take them off to go in, silver cups, flatware, luggage, china, clothing, and so on. If something is stolen it can often be found here, exposed for sale a few hours later.

We saw one mynah bird hopping about the docks, a young one, very bold and tame, one dove, and a few swallows. No gulls again. We visited a pet shop and saw only white Java sparrows and doves. There were whole blocks where nothing but rattan furniture and baskets was sold. Another, a short one, that had all kinds of noodles exposed for sale. There were shops and barrows full of fruit—bananas, durians, jack fruit, and a red fruit that they call hairy fruit and that looked like a cross between a gigantic strawberry and a spider. It had long black spines sticking out all over it. I saw several very fine long-legged gamecocks, black, flecked with white, but the driver said they no longer fight cocks here, which I do not believe. He said they did fight fish which they import from Siam.

We were both much struck by the big street trees in the older parts of the town, all of which were covered with orchids. High up we saw some in bloom. The cannas were magnificent. We saw bohinias, bougainvillaea, poinsettias—

the small white ones and big red kind that were almost trees —crotons, masses of Hawaiian creeper, mauve convolvulus, coxcomb, both yellow and red, in pots, and in the botanical garden a pond full of pink lotus. It is easy to understand why this flower is thought so much of in the East. The delicate pink water-lily-like flowers stand up on long stems out of the water. Their leaves, also like water-lily pads, have long stems too. The dining room at the Raffles Hotel had a big mural of lotus flowers in a tropical lake that was most attractive. Crotons, spider lilies, and big zinnias were also grown in china pots. There were palms of many kinds, Eastern almond trees, and big rounded and flat-topped trees that we did not know.

We passed a doctor's shingle in the street which said, "Specialist—eyes, piles, and weakness," and I wondered at the common denominator. There are whole areas where Indians live, but the majority of the population is Chinese, with some 10 per cent Malay. The total population of Singapore is a million and a half. In 1959 some 37,545 ships, totaling sixteen million tons, were handled here—the second largest tonnage in the shipping world. The exports are mainly rubber, tin, palm oil, copra, pineapple, timber such as mahogany, and rattan furniture.

We visited the Gaya Buddhist Temple, where there is a Buddha fifty feet high made of three hundred tons of concrete. It is guarded by two very large yellow tigers with white whiskers, white feet, and white private parts. The Buddha is hollow and contains a second reclining Buddha in his inside that is approached from the back. There is also one of Buddha's footprints in ebony decorated with mother-of-pearl.

There are a lot of very nice gray monkeys in the botanical garden that take peanuts from your hand, and among the flowers we saw the biggest butterfly we have ever seen, black with white wing tips, that was as big as a bird. Perhaps the most interesting thing about this garden is that it was here that the rubber industry of the Orient was born. The first rubber sapling was brought here from Kew Gardens, having reached England from Brazil.

The variety of insects of all kinds in the museum makes one realize that this is another entomologist's paradise, like the Congo; the thought of it filled Tiny with horror, but she could not resist torturing herself by lifting cover after cover on the showcases and finding bigger and bigger beetles, tarantulas, and centipedes in every one.

We visited a lot of shops and bought some batik shirts and dress lengths fom Java. These have to be smuggled out, as their export is forbidden. The work involved is tremendous, a form of etching with wax, and the prices—ten dollars for a shirt and seven dollars for a piece of material, enough for a dress—seemed remarkably low. We priced some jewelry and it was dear. Large, very poor color Burmese ruby rings are two thousand dollars U.S.

Singapore struck us as a comfortable Victorian colonial city, with its slums very neatly hidden away. The Raffles Hotel epitomized it. Our bedroom was immense. There was also a big dressing room with a basin in it, and a large bathroom. Both had the walls covered waist high with white mosaic. Above, it was soundproofed, for bathroom singers no doubt. This suite was air-conditioned and almost cold. Between it and the open cloistered corridor was a sitting room furnished with rattan furniture: table, sofa, chairs, and a writing table on which there was note paper with our own name printed on it—a highly personalized service that we have never had before. The open cloister outside was supported by whitewashed columns and looked down on the garden that was illuminated at night with small individual floodlights. The flowers of the big white frangipani were level with the balustrade. The black painted floors were covered with coconut matting and each room (ours was No. 41) had a little metal lantern at the door.

But we were conscious that we had missed something here. We were not here long enough to get the flavor of the city, or the flavor was not strong enough for us to appreciate it. It seemed too colonial and Victorian after Hong Kong, Saigon, and Bangkok. We had mislaid the key that would open this lock. But we were coming back. That was what we said—"We shall be back," as we paid our bill, got a taxi, and drove to the docks.

At 11 A.M. we sail for Jakarta—it used to be called Batavia—past Sumatra to the west and Borneo to the east, into the Java Sea, and the republic of Indonesia. We came out of Singapore by a different route through an archipelago of tiny, palm-fringed islands, each more like something out of a fairy tale than the last. They rise like furry animals out of an olive sea, striped with the pale, almost *eau-de-Nil* green patches of what must be shallow water.

The islands seem endless, rising in solitary heads or distant ranges out of the water that is millpond calm but ruffled with tiny, lacelike whitecaps that are scattered like feathers.

Indonesia is one of the world's greatest archipelagos, with over three thousand charted islands.

We now had time to look at some of the local statistics and history in the guidebook.

Singapore Island lies at the bottom of the Malayan Peninsula, to which it is joined by a causeway. It is an oval-shaped island, twenty-six miles long and fourteen miles wide. The colony administers the Cocos Islands and Christmas Island. It lies eighty miles north of the equator, has a uniform hot, high, though not unbearable temperature, averaging eighty-seven degrees, with a high humidity and a rainfall of seventy inches. This is the cool time—October to February. December is the wettest month. The population is 77 per cent Chinese, 12 per cent Malay, 8 per cent Indian, and 3 per cent European and Eurasian and others such as Arabs and Parsees. There are forty-odd outer islands, and the whole area is rich in natural indigenous fruits, both wild and cultivated.

Its history, as far as the West is concerned, is young. In 1819 Thomas Stamford Raffles obtained an agreement from the Sultan of Johore to build a factory on the island of Singhapura. The ancient City of the Lion that had been destroyed by the Javanese in 1377 was then reborn. Its population at the time of the concession was only a hundred fifty souls. By 1824 it had risen to ten thousand. Until 1856 it was ruled by the East India Company. After the Indian Mutiny it was taken over by the India office and later by the Colonial office that ran it till it was overrun by the Japanese in February of 1942.

We begin to sort out our impressions, and they are no more than that. The Chinese seem to have a great sense of humor and no chip on their shoulders. The Indians are serious. The Filipinos are touchy and color conscious. The most beautiful young women we had seen were Filipinas and Vietnamese, the costumes and the long hair of the latter being a great help. The most sophisticated and beautiful women were the Chinese, who retained their looks long after they had ceased to be young girls.

SUNDAY, FEBRUARY 5

During the night we crossed the equator (for me the eighteenth time).

We pass more islands, infinitely mysterious and fairylike, rising out of a jade-colored sea marked with almost purple patches of plankton. Our new passenger, Mrs. Hester Henderson, the wife of the Acting Ambassador to Indonesia, gave us a lot of information about the Far East. She has been here thirteen years. She told us that the boh tree is a wild fig sacred to Buddha because it sprang up to protect him from the sun when meditating. The snails which cover his head in some instances crawled out of the sea to protect him from the sun on another occasion. It is nice to think that the snails were so worried about Buddha's getting sunstroke that they came up out of the water to protect him with a sort of hat or skullcap. In Thailand, Siamese cats are, or were, temple and palace guards, trained to make a noise if strangers appeared and attack them. We once had a Siamese cat that went for any new servant we had until properly introduced. But we saw no cats in any temple here.

Mrs. Henderson told us that in South China the tin mines are worked by children of seven. Few live to ten. These mines were once owned by British and other Western nations and managed by white men. It is hard to imagine the mentality of the engineers who drew a good salary for such a job. Were they married? Did they have children of their own?

Bangkok is apparently full of snakes. Cobras are sometimes seen in the main street. The Thai, being Buddhist, will not kill them, but call upon the Chinese to do so. Residents are told on arrival where to go if bitten by a snake or mad dog. (Except for those in the snake park we saw no reptiles of any kind.) There is a great deal of rabies in Thailand and the poor-conditioned mangy dogs we saw were probably suffering from venereal disease. Crocodiles are a menace in Indo-China, and in Saigon they have monthly hunts to kill them. Some come to within two miles from the city. In Indonesia most of the game, which includes tigers, is to be found in Sumatra. Much of Borneo is marshland. None of this area appears to be fully explored and there must be many species of small mammals and insects still to be discovered.

Mrs. Henderson naturally knew Sukarno and said he was a man of great charm and very popular. She had driven all over Java and Bali and thought things were much better than in the Dutch colonial period. The Dutch were hard and inconsiderate taskmasters.

When we returned to Jakarta—the ship was going on to other parts and then coming back—we were to come and spend a couple of days with her and she would show us around. This sounded wonderful.

In the Raffles Museum in Singapore most of the labels on animals were unspecific: ". . . believed to be common in . . ." ". . . said to have been killed at . . ." Attached to the case containing a very nice small tiger was a notice saying that its stomach "contained nothing but frogs."

There was a stuffed crocodile fifteen feet long and the skull of one that had been thirty-three feet long. This must be about a world record and bigger than the biggest killed in Africa. . . . The hornbill exhibit was fascinating. These big birds resemble the South American toucan except that their beaks have a second story like a big nose. . . . There were also some stuffed peacocks, which clarified still further our concept of the peacock ends of the temple gables. This peacock has a longer and more solid crest. The Indian peacock's crest consisted of several thin feathers, each tipped with a little blob.

It is much hotter here and there is some question about whether we shall be able to get off the ship, as we have no visa for Indonesia. In New York we did not think we were coming here and in Manila the Everett Agency said we would not need one. But the Indonesians, though charming, appear difficult at times. If we can't get off we shall simply stay aboard. So there is no real problem.

Several of the Chinese we have met seem, in a guarded way, to be pro Red China and impressed by its achievements under communism. To hope for a breach between Red China and Russia seems to be wishful thinking, and to feel optimistic because of the present famine in China both inhuman and absurd. We should really wish our enemies well because if people are full fed and prosperous it is much harder to lead them into war than if they are desperate with hunger.

BASKETS OF PIGS

Fifteen

We anchor in the roads outside Tandjongpriok—the harbor for Jakarta—at dusk and see the lights come out on the
shore. At 3 A.M. we come into the harbor, at 4 A.M. we are
alongside.

The harbor is a good one, a row of rectangular basins protected by a big breakwater. If there were no clouds we should
see mountains. All we can see are mountains of coal dust,
shabby shacks, and godowns, as the warehouses in the East
are called.

A twelve-foot shark came to the side of the ship to inspect
the garbage we had thrown out. The orange peels he left
alone, but a floating can he nosed right out of the water,
and for a while appeared interested in a bottle of ketchup.
We have seen other sharks in African waters and in the Caribbean, but none swam in the conventional storybook way
with a triangular fin out of water.

The sea about us was spotted with tiny fishing craft with
square sails. One passed near us later, a very beautiful craft

—a proa with a big flat decoration shaped like the ace of hearts on the bow, and a large oblong sail hanging obliquely from the mast. The sail was bronze and patched with white, black, and red. These ships look like big canoes, but they must have a keel or centerboard.

A chestnut kite with a white head and breast came down quite low over the water.

The immigration people came on board at about lunch time. There was no trouble about our lack of visas. It cost us twenty Singapore dollars to get them and everyone was smiling and happy. They all spoke good English. But I heard several Dutch words used such as *"pas op," "Hoff kantoor,"* and *"emigrasie."* The general opinion seems to be that the Dutch exploited Indonesia and did not prepare the country for freedom. The result is that the standard of efficiency is low and the machinery in general of the country is slowing up.

More red kites now appeared, at least a dozen of them, looking like a smaller and cheaper version of the American bald eagle—the emblem of the U.S.A.—that appears to be in some danger of becoming extinct.

Meanwhile, Mrs. Henderson was waiting on the ship, and her husband, the Acting Ambassador, was waiting on shore. She finally disembarked at 4:30 P.M.

At 8 P.M. we went ashore with the captain. Carbon black for the Goodyear Company that manufactures car and bicycle tires here was still being unloaded. This is about the dirtiest cargo we have seen, a black powder as fine as face powder, in heavy paper bags that still manage to break. We were unable to leave the harbor area, as we had some money with us. The customs officers stopped us at the gate and our choice was to leave the money with them in return for a receipt, which I had little confidence in, or go back to the ship. No one can take money ashore. It was no use trying to smuggle it, for after we passed the harbor guards at the gate there was still a second check by soldiers who were liable to search you very roughly and lock you up if you had broken the law. I can imagine nothing worse than being a white man in jail here.

This money business is very curious. Most people want your money. I did not know how we were going to pay for a taxi to see Jakarta, but this was arranged in some way by the captain. The company paid the taxi through the agent, and we paid the captain.

The port is unattractive, dirty, and unkempt. There is grass growing where there should be no grass, barbed wire where there should be no wire. The station, a fine building built by the Dutch a hundred years ago, is now half occupied by troops as a barracks. This country is not at war. The revolution is said to be over, but one has a war feeling here, a feeling of "What's the good?", of lethargy, and a feeling of "Let's get to hell out of it if we can."

The road to Jakarta is straight, narrow, and poor. It is edged by trees, some of them flamboyants which, when they are out, must be beautiful, which were reflected in the canal that runs parallel to the road.

We passed some good truck gardens, ribbons of vegetables sewn together with silver stitches of water. We passed quite big ships, fifty feet or more, being built on land under roofs beside the canal. We passed several hundred acres of fish farms; cottages, red-tiled and no bigger than bathing cabins. Little houses beautifully constructed of reeds, bamboo, and rattan, thatched with palm fronds. Banana trees were reflected in the water. A small herd of buffalo heifers ran by, pursued by two dogs, the only dogs we saw all day. We saw one heron standing in a fishpond, but no other birds.

Jakarta, once Batavia, the pride of the Dutch, famous for the cleanliness of its streets, the whiteness of its houses, and the excellence of its *richstoffel*, has degenerated into an immense slum, if a slum is defined by an unpainted, dirty, and deteriorating built-up area.

The White House, pillared neo-Greek and strongly

guarded, was about the only place we saw, other than the museum, that was not coming apart at the seams. Of course it was raining and rain does nothing to improve the look of any place. Still, dividing our impression by two—cutting it in half—it still stood. There is one new big hotel that is always so full that three or four people, irrespective of sex or relationship, are put into one room. Another, fourteen-story hotel is being built with Japanese capital for the Asian games that will take place here in 1962, and for the tourists of the future. All the Dutch business and private houses have been taken over, largely by the government. There is a great deal of hatred for the Dutch. Much of it may be justified, but the Indonesians, like most other freed colonial people, are confronted with the problems of freedom. Freedom is not a solution. It is a difficulty, rather resembling a divorce. Something no one will ever find out, of course, is how much the peasant masses anywhere in Asia and Africa really enjoy their freedom, or even if some of them know they have it. The passion for education that is sweeping the undeveloped countries is often less a longing for learning than a preparation for a jump onto the government band wagon. The day of colonialism is over. The marriage of a rich metropolitan country to a poor dark-skinned virgin has ended. She will no longer be either exploited or protected. The British, French, Dutch, and Belgian husbands have been pushed out of the bed. But the lady is still nubile and the bed warm and inviting.

Of course all nations should be free. But this upsurge of freedom has been so rapid that few nations are prepared for it, or able, like so many divorced wives, to make a living, and must therefore subsist on the international alimony of the UN, which really means the U.S.A.

More and more do I question the value of foreign missions. Why don't they preach the word of God in our own slums? Why do so many of them pose as heroes when they live in unbelievable comfort in air-conditioned houses with fine gardens and plenty of servants? How many missionaries could earn a living at home? And finally, except for the

medical missionaries, their work probably does more harm
than good, by destroying the fear of devils, which controls
most native morality, and failing to instill the love of God
that might replace it.

The museum at Jakarta, a Dutch legacy, must be one of
the finest in the East, containing sculptures, and ceramics
from all over the Orient. Vases and dishes of all kinds; costumes, artifacts, models of houses and canoes; coins and
temple gongs. The archaeological finds all are wonderfully
arranged. Days could be spent here. There were a number of
Indian (Hindu, I think) gods with elephants' heads, all holding the tips of their trunks with their left hands. But of them
all one stood out, no bigger than the others, just more endearing. Later, in Bangkok, we mentioned it to our guide,
who delighted us with this legend:

Once upon a time a maharajah, half god and half man,
was madly in love with his human wife. One night, having
imbibed rather heavily, he made his way to his wife's apartment with amorous intentions, only to be stopped by the
guard outside her door—a greedy fellow, slow-witted, but
loyal to his mistress, who fed him well. The husband, in fury
at not having been recognized, drew his sword and slew him.
He proceeded to his wife's apartments and she was horrified
when she heard his story, and swore she would never sleep
with her husband again until the guard had his head replaced. The husband, realizing the enormity of his mistake,
sent men to the four points of the compass with orders to
bring back the first head they could find. The men from the
north arrived first, bearing an elephant's head. The husband,
half god, half man, placed it on the deceased guard's shoulders—and entered his wife's apartment for her forgiveness.
That is why to this day the god-made, elephant-headed
man is still sacred and worshiped as a potbellied, greedy,
elephant-headed minor god, and why, throughout the East,
it is considered bad luck to sleep with one's head to the
north.

One room in the museum was entered through a revolving cage guarded by an armed attendant. It contained jeweled weapons—scimitars and krises with golden hilts and sheaths embossed with rubies, sapphires, and diamonds (or zircons), all beautifully kept. Here too were examples of gold plating rather like that of the Gold Coast in West Africa and found in the ruins of Zimbabwe in Rhodesia. Some of the bronze heads reminded me of those in Ife, Nigeria, which always seemed much more Eastern than Greek (as some people believed) in spirit.

It rained softly almost all day. Indeed it could hardly be called rain. It was more of a light, soft, warm vapor, a sort of steam to which few people paid much attention. Some had Chinese umbrellas of bamboo slats; others had very large hats made of bamboo that were wider than their shoulders and really amounted to umbrellas. Many of the men, particularly the longshoremen, wore more or less ordinary panama-shaped hats, brightly painted with red, blue, and orange. Some women wore no hats and carried no umbrellas. We saw a few wearing batik sarongs. The pattern had run in none of them, but of course none of these people do their laundry in hot or even clean water, nor do they use detergents. All along the canals we saw girls washing clothes. There were a lot of pedicabs. They are called rickshaws here and belong to Chinese entrepreneurs who hire them out. The drivers, who work in six-hour shifts, are said to die before they are thirty. There must be a great deal of TB here, and a lot of the people have no way of drying their clothes when they get wet. The carts have very short shafts that do not reach to the horse's shoulder. They are generally loaded too far back so that the weight is on the horse's girth, under his belly, and he runs like a dancer, almost on his toes. The ponies are the usual type, geldings, driven without a bearing rein, and not as good in quality as those of Manila, where almost all of them were fat. It is curious that a stallion seems to hold his condition better than a mare or gelding.

In the museum some of the horses' bits and headstalls were tiny and would hardly have fitted a Shetland. One had a broken snaffle bit, so that invention, like so many others, was not an invention at all, merely an adaptation of an oriental idea.

One thing that interested us very much was the furniture made here for the early Dutch East India Company merchants. This resembles almost exactly that of the Cape. This is natural enough, since Cape Town was established by the company as a halfway house to India and the first technicians in South Africa were slaves imported from Batavia.

Near the abattoir we saw numbers of zebu skins neatly threaded onto wooden frames. We also passed three two-wheeled horse carts loaded with pigs, packed individually into long, pig-shaped openwork baskets. They must have been dropped in head first and then stacked like cordwood. They made me think of the baskets in which the druids used to burn their victims. In spite of having been a rancher for years and sold hundreds of cattle I still hate to see animals going to slaughter. This is no doubt a sentimental approach, but there may be a time for sentiment, even a reason for it, if we are to remain fully human.

We saw no wheelbarrows, but a number of very crude, heavy, small two-wheeled carts pulled by harnessed men and pushed by others. Somehow all this seemed worse than in Hong Kong. There, however bad things were, the people seemed happy and laughed. There were plenty of laughing children. They knew they were free. They had escaped into a real and ordered freedom. But here in Indonesia their new freedom was just a word. How disappointing that they could not eat it.

At a street stall we were offered peanuts steamed in their shells and still attached to the plant. We passed two kinds of goats. We saw quite a few white geese that looked like Emdens. They were not Chinese in type. We saw some very big frangipani, some allamanda in bloom, and many of the

largest elephant's-ears I have ever seen. There was a lot of
water hyacinth about. I was told that it is used for stock feed.
We saw an old man carrying two big bundles of corn in
the flowering stage on a shoulder stick to feed cattle.

The import tax on cars is 400 per cent (it was 300 per cent
in the Argentine), but gas is cheap here. A lot of smuggling
goes on—gold, opium, carvings, batik, and currency. In the
bird market, which we did not visit owing to the rain coming
down suddenly in torrents, there are mynah birds for sale:
fifteen U.S. dollars for young birds.

We saw a number of very fine long-legged game fowl, one
splendid cock, white, with eccentric black and chestnut
blotches of feathers. Cockfighting, except in Bali, where it
is permitted as a tourist attraction, is against the law and
draws a three-month jail sentence. There is nothing humani-
tarian in this. It is simply an effort to control gambling. Poor
men lose more than they can afford betting on this sport.

I have seen a few fights in France in my boyhood and
though I do not regard it as elevating I do not think it particularly cruel or unpleasant. A good cock gets a run for his
money and may even die of old age in a breeding pen if he
has proved himself. Gamecocks cannot be stopped from fighting, and since every chicken ends in a pot anyway, the objection to the sport seems somewhat academic. This is where
I would take issue with the bullfighters. At least in cockfighting no one pretends it is as beautiful as a ballet, or an
education. A cockfight is simply a combat between two male
birds bred for centuries into an allergy to their own sex. They
are not tortured into attack by *banderillas* and, though armed
with spurs, the end is never a foregone conclusion. There is
no contest in a bullfight. The Brave Bull is as dead as a steer
in the race of a stockyard when he enters the arena.

Cockfighters are generally workingmen who breed their
own back-yard champions, not great landowners priding
themselves on their culture. Not women. For though lady
tourists, a breed apart, may go to bullfights they seldom
patronize a cockpit.

The diet of the poor appears to be dried fish and rice. We are bringing two thousand bags of rice from the U.S.A., which seems odd. This was once, I think, a rice-exporting country. Four crops a year can be grown here. Everything will grow—rice and bananas on the alluvial flats and apples and strawberries in the cool hills.

Few of the streets seem to be properly paved, but their wooden clogs keep people out of the mud. Some of the women wear trousers, others sarongs. We saw a few Indian women in saris. I have never understood why this garment is so admired, since no garment could be better designed to disguise the figure. There were flower sellers sitting in the rain. They had no problem about keeping the flowers fresh. The flowers were gladiolas and the same bright daisies we had seen in Bangkok.

What else did we discover in one way or another? There are several papers, only one in English, and all controlled. There is no free press. Girls marry young—at thirteen or fourteen. Many men who are Moslems have several wives and often desert them. This was the explanation given to us when we asked about a young girl whom we saw in the road talking and gesticulating. Apparently she had been abandoned by her husband and was crazy. This appeared to be a quite common occurrence.

To change money, Malay or U.S. dollars or traveler's checks, they must be declared at the customs, taken to the immigration building, and finally cashed at the bank. A three-hour affair in a steamy climate like this, even if everything goes well and the bank is open when you reach it. This does not encourage tourists. The necessity for these precautions appears to be in the amount of foreign currency being smuggled out of the country. Very high rates are offered for U.S. and Malay dollars. People, particularly the Chinese and Indians, do not have much faith in Indonesia. Many of them have had their businesses expropriated and have returned home to India or Red China.

Sukarno, the Prime Minister, is a spellbinder, but not as popular as is generally believed. There have been several attempts on his life. Clearing ground for the new stadium for the Asiatic games in 1962 has made thousands homeless, and what will the games do for Indonesia? What do Sukarno's around-the-world trips do for the country except cost it money? People complain of the taxes, as they do everywhere, but here the needs of the country are so obvious that these international junkets are most unpopular.

Sukarno is much liked, I understand, by the ambassadors of the free world in Jakarta. He is gay, friendly, fond of the ladies, and altogether an endearing character at the social get-togethers of the international elite. But I question the knowledge of most diplomats abroad, particularly in Africa and Asia. They do not mix. They live American lives, eat American PX food, draw hardship allowances for living in luxury, and associate only with the other diplomats or such rich landowners and businessmen who talk fluent English.

High-level diplomacy makes no sense at all in the countries where people are hungry and ill housed. Communism is making great headway in Indonesia. In the provincial elections the Communists got seven million more votes than any other party, and the only really anti-communist force in the republic is the rebels in the outer islands.

There are too many troops in town, sentries and guards, too many officials, and, with it all, little order or security. In fact in the *Indonesian Observer* of today, February 6, the chief prosecutor stated that no one "should be detained any longer than six months before he is tried. . . . There must be no more persons kept in detention for many months and even years . . . [before coming to trial]" So much for Justice, Freedom, and Brotherhood.

This is not a country in which it is safe to travel, or at least not one in which I should care to travel. The bureaucratic problems now are so great that several shipping lines have given up calling here. An example of the difficulties that deter them occurred just before sailing. The medical authorities had decided that the crew's vaccination certificates were invalid because, though officially stamped, they had not been signed. So, although accepted everywhere else in the world, they were refused here and a medical outfit came on board and vaccinated most of the crew. The bill was being sent to the company.

There was a Polish vessel in harbor and a Russian ship had just left. There is an uneasy feeling here. The country is definitely leaning toward Russia and Red China. Cargoes of rubber in the godowns are earmarked for the U.S.S.R. We did not get our quota. These are straws in the wind. The papers are anti-West and pro-communist. That is the way the news is slanted.

The trend for the undeveloped countries would seem to be toward Chinafication, a system by which vast numbers of people are coerced into doing the work of machines, thus avoiding the danger of becoming economically dominated by the West, and making use of the immense hereditary skills of these oriental people. The thought is expressed in this extract from the *Indonesian Observer:*

We cannot wait for the acquisition of technical know-how, technical equipment and other similar non-human resources. We must therefore plan in such a way that we turn the human factor from a liability into an asset. . . .

There is a lot more in the same tone, all plainly stated, and not hidden between the lines. There is a feeling that the expropriated Chinese will come back from Red China in force one day. No one knows the richness of the country or its vast possibilities better than they.

Our impression was one of a beautiful, disturbed, and unhappy land. We saw not a single smile or a happy face. I do not say this because no one smiled at us. Why should they? But they did not smile at each other, either. The children were not happy. There were no dogs. People were scavenging in the rotting garbage of the overflowing cans along the street and in the smoking dump that decorates the highway to the city. In this hot, humid climate putrefaction is almost immediate and still they hunted for edible scraps, for reclaimable rubbish that could be sold for a penny or two. And this in one of the potentially richest countries in the world, an agricultural and mineral bonanza needing only capital and know-how to explode into unbelievable prosperity. But so afraid are they of economic colonialism and exploitation that they are rotting slowly away—free to starve, to be exploited by their own corrupt leaders, free to lose business by default. To give an example: It sometimes takes more than three months to clear a shipment of carbon black through the customs. Ships come back with a second cargo and find the one they brought in on a previous trip still on the dock, in bags that are falling apart from exposure.

There were mountains of carbon black on the dock that had been waiting for months to be cleared through the customs. This was the last thing we saw as we put out to sea again.

A DUTCH WIFE

Sixteen

We sight land. There is always a feeling of excitement
with a landfall. We had been cruising along the coast and
now came slowly into an immense bay. Numbers of small
fishing boats flit like white butterflies over the water. There
are two sunken ships, further souvenirs of the Japanese bomb-
ing. Some small gray warships lie at anchor. A great stream
of muddy water from the river seems to cut the harbor in two.
A white heron, its neck folded back and legs extended behind its body, flies solemnly over us.

Our tugs, busy and self-important, arrived and began to
maneuver us into the dock. This is a near thing. There was
almost a collision with the stern of the next ship.

There are Indonesian flags by the score in the harbor, a
few British ships, one German, one Liberian, and two Panamanian. The longshoremen in Surabaja seem quite different from those in Jakarta, darker in color and wearing blue or
black Nehru-like caps instead of pointed hats. The dock
facilities seem much better.

In the evening more big white herons and flocks of white egrets flew into the red-streaked sunset toward the marshes across the water. After the last one had gone, as the sunset faded into the mystery of a crepuscular dusk, a big nightjar, large as a kite, appeared from the west and began his wide-mouthed pursuit of the insects attracted by the ship's lights.

The night as usual was hot. Sweat poured off my body, collecting first into drops on the skin, then forming small lakes in the body's depressions that finally overflowed in rivulets of acid water. It was in Indonesia that the "Dutch wife" was born, the long, linen-covered bolster that was clasped to the breast to drink up the sweat.

If it had not been for the German concentration camp atrocities I would feel that it is heat that engenders both cruelty and sensuality. These hot lands are the countries of deterioration—of exploitation in the collection of rubber, of ivory, and slavery; of ritual murder, cannibalism, head-hunting, and witchcraft. A white man alone, without the restraints of society, driven by fever and loneliness to drink and native women—enraged at the changes he feels taking place in his personality—may finally let go, and in an effort to escape from this tropical trap; to save his own life, he may drive his labor force brutally for more rapid gain. He may kill someone—or himself. The real tropics will find the Achilles' heel of any man who lives there without the discipline of service to God or country, corny as this may sound.

I do not believe that the undeveloped nations are going to succeed in their aims as things are going now. A slow development under colonial guidance for another thirty years, in some parts, and one hundred in others might have done the job. As it is, suffering from a corrupt and comic-opera version of parliamentary democracy, many will fail, and turn to communism and the use of force to attain the industrial ends they so ardently desire. We may be able to check this movement. But we must devise new methods and not try to buy trust with money.

The offloading of rice goes fast. It is hauled up from the hold in slings. The bags are dumped on large tarpaulins and loaded five to a two-wheeled dolly which is taken at a run into the godown.

By each tarpaulin there is a group of women with grass hand brooms and round flat baskets into which they sweep the rice from broken bags and run with it, before another load lands on top of them, to the godown, where they decant their gleanings into new bags. They have threaded sail needles stuck in their blouses ready to repair the bags that are damaged.

Many of the people in Java are almost red in color. As red as Gauguin's figures that I always thought to be an artistic exaggeration to make them more complementary to the green of his foliage. The women are beautiful, with superb carriage. They wear a sarong and a hip-length fitted jacket, collarless, and buttoning down the front. The material is generally batik and we saw no sign of designs "running." But naturally, if washed in a washing machine with detergents and hot water, some of the colors would be affected. In most hot countries, except in the dust of the dry season, clothes are more sweaty than dirty and sweat is perfectly soluble in cold water. On their heads the women wear bright, eccentrically draped turbans—all-anyhow and every which way but most artistic, with a loose end hanging over one ear at the back. They seem to have no system of tying them and each girl has her own style.

Last night we were up several times to look out at the lighted ships reflected in the basin. Their superstructures, lighted up like Christmas trees, outlined them against the dark bank and trees behind them. Another interesting thing was an insect, possibly attracted by the ships' lights, that made a noise like a kind of rather ineffective policeman's whistle and would then be answered by another, more distant policeman—some form of cricket or cicada, I think, or it might have been a frog.

We had arranged to hire a car to pick us up at 9 A.M. for some sight-seeing. At 10:15 it had not come. It may never come. Or perhaps it will come tomorrow.

The first thing the women on the dock did this morning was to sweep it. A hangover from the Dutch administration.

The ship is now surrounded by sections of floating banana leaf and big teak leaves that had been thrown down by the longshoremen on the dock when they had finished eating their rice, which is wrapped in them—the first disposable plates.

White-headed, chestnut kites sweep down, curling out of the sky, looking for scraps. Ashore on the dock the sparrows will have a feast day when the activity slows up. We stare over the side looking for sharks. No luck. We should have brought a couple of hand lines and hooks. I suddenly remembered a hand line I had bought in Hermanus, South

Africa—a long way from Surabaja. The chief engineer gave
us a hook. All we need now is a nut for a weight, some wire
for a leader, and some bait. I have made a float with a wine
cork.

It is amazing to think of the tall Dutch East Indiamen
sailing from here with spices for Europe. Of the British East
India Company, of the Portuguese and the French, all on
these seas—the Java Sea, the Indian Ocean, the Bay of Bengal, the China Seas. To think of the sea battles and the pirates
looking exactly like the men on the dock here, turbaned or
capped, stripped to the waist or naked, swarming up long
bamboo boat hooks as the money-changers did in the Saigon
River. A hundred men perhaps from a hundred small boats,
climbing up with their knives and krises between their teeth.

The same jade seas, the same red kites, the same women,
but bare-breasted then, awaiting the pirates' return in the
same reed, rattan, and bamboo houses. Wearing the same
batik. Eating the same fish, rice, and fruit. In the Far East
the veil between the present and the past is silk-muslin thin.
In Africa there is more past than present. There it is all past,
the present just smeared on here and there in dabs of literacy, trousers, dark glasses, cars, and ball-point pens. But all
these new countries are going to develop in their own way,
in a manner suited to their national temperaments and cultures. Nor is it easy to judge them, to say, "This is evil."
"This is bad." What is a little internal war, a little ritual cannibalism, a little female circumcision, a little polygamy, compared to some of the habits that we have and accept without
question as correct? What savages can compare for brutality
and sadism with the Germans of Hitler's Reich? Who but
the civilized West have atomized the innocent populations
—men, women, children, cats, dogs, birds, rats, and mice—
every living thing in two whole cities? How many Christians
practice Christianity? How many are really monogamous?
Why are multiple wives set in a row in time better than a
harem of wives at one time? Why are concubines worse than

call girls? How do our religions compare ethically with those of the East?

We excel in mechanics and in the organization of business, that is to say, materially. And it is materialism that is our greatest export with its by-product of discontent.

At 2 P.M. the agent, a young Indonesian of thirty, came on board and said he would drive us around the city himself. He told us to bring our passports but almost no money. This is the first place I have ever been where they don't want your money, where you may be searched on returning to the ship, and anything you have bought may be confiscated.

We showed our passports at the gate near the ship and again at the dock entrance to a tough-looking khaki-clad gang of men all armed to the teeth. The first thing we saw was the big gas tanks, spotted with camouflage against the rebels, who apparently once nearly took the place. The rebels are still active in the mountains and wilder parts of all the islands, particularly the Celebes, and even have set up a government of their own with representatives from the various areas in their sphere of influence.

The picture over the Far East, from China before the communists took over, to Indo-China, Indonesia, Burma, and Malaya, seems to be much the same. Bands of nationalists, rebels, patriots, bandits, and gangsters (operating separately or in alliance with each other), seizing power wherever there is a vacuum, creating panic, misery, and famine, and profiting by it to strengthen their forces by the promise of food and loot. Food is expensive and scarce, but in these countries a soldier always has a full belly, so there is no shortage of recruits.

Everyone is afraid of war with the Dutch about Dutch New Guinea, which they call West Irian. But everyone says it will not come till after the Asiatic games next year. Everyone is frightened of the communists, who are now in the ascendance, except perhaps the workingman, who, now he is free, doesn't even have his freedom to lose. Too much export is going to Russia. Rubber in particular. And they are getting little back except war material. We saw our first MIG today —short, squat, and ugly—and some Russian jeeps for which they can get no spares.

There has been no real peace here for a long time. First the Japanese. Then the revolution against the Dutch. And now the revolution against the revolution. There are wrecked ships in the harbor and wrecked and gutted buildings in the town that are still unrepaired. It reminds us of the Philippines, who had the Spaniards for centuries, then the Americans, and then the Japanese.

Great offices of shipping lines stand empty and have been taken over by the government. The vast dock installations, godowns, and warehouses are inactive. The town is big, with wide streets and low houses. Two stories are the exception. Everything is running down slowly. Nothing is being repaired.

This must, in the time of the Dutch, have been a most beautiful city. Streets, miles long, of neat houses with good gardens, once belonging to the Dutch and Eurasians, have now been taken over lock, stock, and barrel, furniture and all, and are falling apart. In one place where the river winds through the streets it is landscaped on both sides with wide grassy swards, once lawns, dotted with trees and great beds of flowering cannas. There are plenty of trees and shrubs in the town. Great rain trees, parasitic figs that drip long aerial roots like hair, mangoes, breadfruit, frangipani, and quantities of the most beautiful rose-pink oleander I have ever seen, a shade quite new to me. There were rows of flamboyants not out yet, casuarinas, palms, yellow cassias in full flower, very large elephant's-ears and patches of a big-leafed peanut that may be indigenous here. We saw some rice paddies with bananas growing on the raised banks that separated them.

Though four crops a year can be grown here food is dear, and people are on the verge of starvation. They are apparently improvident, and though they work hard they do so spasmodically and without a plan.

Java is overpopulated, but no one can be persuaded to take up land in Sumatra, which is underpopulated, even when offered free land and free seed by the government.

They really hate the Dutch, and, with the Dutch most white men. This seems to include Eurasians. The word *"Blonda"* means Dutchman. It also means white man in general. The Dutch are said to have been hard taskmasters and not to have encouraged education among the Indonesians, though there seems to be some confusion about their attitude toward color, since so many thousands of them married local girls. Like most colonials they appear to have been stupid. Too hard one day and too soft the next. And, like most colonial peoples, the Indonesians may have cut off their noses to spite their faces.

The problem in every underdeveloped colonial country that wishes to enter the modern industrial world is not getting rid of the white man (the Congo is the latest example of how easy it is) but how to get on without him.

Freedom is wonderful. But Indonesia is perhaps less free now than it was in the time of the hated Dutch. The press is controlled. Conversation has to be guarded. Businesses are taken over and nationalized without cause and people thrown into jail without trial. Freedom means a flag, a seat in the United Nations, and embassies in the capitals of the world. It means jobs for the elite few, but very little for the peasant mass—unless they are satisfied with slogans—with words.

Freedom has to grow like a plant from deep cultural roots. It cannot just arrive. It must be born of something more valid than discontent.

The streets are full of rickshaws with the riders in front facing the oncoming traffic. The pushers all wear conical straw hats with no brims, like inverted ice-cream cones. There are two-wheeled wagons, the wheels seven feet in diameter, drawn by pairs of beautiful, mild-eyed zebu bulls, or Brahmans, as we call them. Most of them were white or white shaded into mouse gray. They had short, stubby horns of two types—one going upward in the usual way, the other turned downward. The profile, forehead, eye socket, and expression were those of the Afrikander cattle in Africa. How this type of Eastern cattle reached the Hottentots at the Cape of Good Hope, via Egypt, the Sudan, and the coastal plain of East Africa, would make a fascinating story. We saw some sheep, also of the type we saw in the Sudan, and the kind of dog that I now call pure mongrel, smooth-coated, with wide prick ears, which can be found everywhere, if European breeds have not been introduced, from China to Nigeria.

The oxen were driven by rope reins strung through the septum of their noses, which had been pierced, and they wore shoes with soles of leather and a fiber binding that ran up between the cleft of their hoofs and tied at the fetlock. Besides these pale-colored heavy draft oxen there were pairs of smaller, faster oxen, also humped—colored chestnut, lemon, black, and gray—no broken colors.

There were a lot of goats about—loose in the streets; more goats than sheep, but there were both lambs and kids. Many of the sheep had twins. We saw numbers of game fowl, some pure white and all very beautiful. In fact we saw no other kind of poultry. There were quite a lot of little two-wheeled horse cabs and carts. The horses were small and the usual type, but many of them with very pretty harness, heavily decorated with shiny brass. The shafts, even shorter than those in Jakarta, were also decorated with brass and ended in short, sharp outward curves like tiny blunt horns that kept them from slipping out of the harness.

School was over and the children of the well-to-do were coming home in rickshaws, in pairs and alone. If children are brought up this way it must be impossible for them later to believe in the dignity of man. We saw few small babies and none were carried in slings.

Having passed through the better area of the town, we drove through the poorer section and slums, though not the worst, till we came to an immense market. What was once called, I imagine, the "native market" is something that I always want to see in any country, since this is where one can really see the products of the country—the clothes, furniture, food, and utensils of the poor. What we wanted to see was the bird section. We had passed several bird vendors, half trotting, with bundles of cages fastened to their shoulder poles. We had seen small houses with bird cages slung to the tip of thirty-foot bamboo poles. These, our friend told us, were very expensive birds and were kept that high up because of cats. The cages had roofs on them and appeared to be pulled up by a string on a pulley. The "expensive bird" intrigued us. Was the height due only to the cats or was this a form of status, a way of proving that you owned an expensive bird?

The bird market was in a section of the main market and there were literally thousands of wild birds in wicker cages. The "expensive" bird turned out to be a variety of dove; its neck and breast were gray, polka-dotted with white spots like the feathers of a guinea fowl. They must have some special significance, be sacred or lucky in some way. We fell in love with a small, half-naked parrot. It was mutual, and it refused to get off my finger. A tall, good-looking woman with gold teeth (many people here have gold teeth) offered us a bouquet of white mynah birds, holding them by their legs in her hand. Then she popped four small ducklings on the ground by her feet. They were very intelligent little ducks that did not try to run away but stood on tiptoe staring up at her. They were not ordinary ducklings, but purebred and aristocratic-looking. There was also a young white cockatoo that was most endearing. The Indonesians seem to have a special talent for handling birds. They were all so tame. There were dozens we should like to have bought.

In the afternoon we went to the zoo, a good one, though somewhat neglected, and filled with large and beautiful trees. Palms, teak trees with great hairy leaves like heart-shaped plates, and other forest trees, many of them orchid-covered.

The most exciting animal we saw here was a full grown male orangoutang—the wild man of the woods. Immense, with great bare black cheek pouches like goiters and another on his chest just below his chin. He had tiny eyes, a big slit of a mouth set in his black face and long arms, as thick as a man's thigh, that ended in bare black hands. His whole body, including the arms, was covered with long matted chestnut hair. It was coarse in quality and about the color of an Irish setter's coat. He was without exception the most impressive animal I have ever seen, more so than a big gorilla or a lion. I have never seen such a fine specimen before, not even stuffed in a museum.

The monkeys were beautifully kept, each kind on a separate island in a large circular enclosure surrounded by water. The water was grass green, covered with small, circular-leaved water plants. Algae such as we had seen in the zoo in Rio. On each island there was a small stone temple-like structure on which the monkeys sat and disported themselves. They also had caves cut into the outer walls. Many of the monkeys were paddling and bathing. Some leaped high in the air and landed in the water with a loud plop, like children playing in a swimming hole.

We saw two komado lizards, dragonlike reptiles that are found only in Indonesia, and several large crocodiles and alligators. The crocodiles cause some loss of life and are generally found in brackish water near the sea. The alligators live in fresh water and are smaller and less dangerous. We had seen this variety of marine crocodile in the Raffles Museum in Singapore.

The pythons were big. All seemed to have just changed their skins and were very pretty. They were in large, high-netted cages whose back was a rough stone wall like the walls of a ruin. Some were asleep on high ledges and we watched others climbing. They took what amounted to a turn around a projecting stone, snubbing themselves on it, and reached upward with swaying heads looking for a new hold on which to lever and chin themselves still higher.

There were the usual other exhibits: elephants, giraffes, zebras, lions, and tigers. There were some very attractive small wildcats the size of domestic cats and a larger, bushy-tailed black animal like an enormous mink with white whiskers. The aquarium—salt and fresh water—would have been more interesting had it been better kept, but it was outstanding anyway. It could have been marvelous.

After going to the zoo we went to a book and curio shop filled with Bali carvings. There must have been several thousand heads, figures, and animals, some traditional and some in modern style, with immensely elongated slim figures. Our hosts insisted on buying two pieces for us, a frog and a small head. It was an extraordinary sensation to be moneyless and a tourist in a place where one is not allowed to buy anything. It was also very embarrassing to be asked to choose something for ourselves.

All the heads, male and female, have different expressions. In the female figures the heads are too big and the mount of Venus extremely well defined. Some pieces were extraordinarily good, such as a pair of cockatoos and two fighting horses. There were also plaques in low-carved bas-relief reminding us of those we had seen in Nigeria. The books were a very catholic collection and ran from "whodunits" to the sex life of animals. What was particularly noticeable was the number of books and periodicals dealing with Russia and Red China—*New China, The U.S.S.R. Today,* and so on. These books are subsidized and very cheap—ten rupiahs— with comparable American books selling at one hundred rupiahs. This would seem an error on our part, as subsidized magazines and books would seem to be a very cheap and effective way of putting over our ideas.

The more we see the more confused we become. There are, for instance, four rates of exchange. The U.S. dollar is worth forty-five rupiahs officially, for export, and two hundred for import. Tourists, if they can manage to exchange it, get a rate of ninety rupiahs for a dollar, and on the black market the price is three hundred. In order to change traveler's checks it is necessary to get a customs clearance and then go to the bank to get the money. The banks appear to close at 11 A.M. Working hours are curious: 7 to 2 in business; 7 to 11 and 2 to 4 in government offices, as far as I can make out.

Having made purchases, or rather having been given our gifts, we had to show them to the two sets of guards (military and customs), who, if they had wanted to, could have prevented us from taking them on board, though as a rule they permit one or two small pieces to go through. It is illegal for batik to leave the country, and the shirts I bought in Singapore are made of smuggled material.

So, in a world where every country is doing all it can to encourage tourism and the sale of local textiles, art work, and curios, Indonesia alone does all it can to discourage visitors in every way. Each time we went out we had to show our passports and visas both coming and going. We had to declare that we had no money, be subjected to the possibility of search, confiscation, and the chance of being flung into jail if they had found money other than the legal one hundred rupiahs, the maximum amount one is allowed to spend, which would just about buy two bottles of beer or a rickshaw ride to town, and then no beer when you get there.

This country, which was once self-supporting in rice, now imports 700,000 tons P.A. The farmers no longer grow enough because they have to sell it at a controlled price and then buy the things they need at the import rate of two hundred rupiahs to the dollar.

The well off are called capitalists and are afraid of communism. The poor are hungry and short even of clothes. There is a great shortage of textiles, medicines, and paper—from wrapping paper to toilet paper. There are plenty of capital goods—refrigerators, radios, cars, etc.—whose prices are not controlled and on which a profit of from 100 to 200 per cent can be made.

The security is such that no one can even get onto a ship to visit it without a series of passes, all of which are hard to obtain.

In order to have the small party our friends gave for their six-year-old daughter's birthday a police permit was required. No one can have a party of more than ten people without one. All dancing is forbidden as imperialistic. There were seven nationalities at the party—Indonesian, Norwegian, Danish, German, Indian, American, and South African. The food was Indonesian, an excellent mild chicken curry, and a kind of rice dumpling. There was also Chinese and European food. Among other things we were given some prickly fruit—ramutan—that our hostess showed us how to eat. Inside its red prickly jacket the fruit is whitish, sweet, and rather like a lichee. Everyone in Indonesia had a bad time during the Japanese occupation, and two of the ladies —young girls then—had been hidden out in the jungle by their mothers for the whole period. It is difficult to imagine what two city-bred girls from well-off families went through in the bush, with bad food and water, with snakes and insects, and their ever-present fear of being discovered and raped by a Japanese patrol.

The second night here we dined at a real Chinese restaurant in Chinatown. It looked like a dump, not overclean to American eyes, but the food was excellent—a wonderful soup, frog's legs better than I have ever had in France, roasted squab cooked with head on (one to each person), Chinese mixed vegetables, and a delicious baked fish. I was now introduced to pigeon's brains that one sucked out of the decapitated bird. The Romans' eating peacock's brains as a delicacy now became explicable, and I regretted the peafowl I had eaten without sampling their brains. There were only chopsticks to eat with, but we did not mind at all, being glad to show off our skill.

We ended the evening at the International Seamen's Club, where there are never any seamen. It is too expensive for them, since they are allowed to take so little money ashore and there are no girls.

A solution to the exchange problem would be for the government to send a bank official on board with the immigration and health officer to effect the necessary exchange. Any money changed here must be spent. One is not allowed to bring any back, in this Alice Through the Looking-Glass economy.

The general idea seems to be that the more controls and forms there are, the more civilized and Western the setup. Ten copies of the passenger list (there were only two passengers—Tiny and myself) were required. The godowns are full of goods that the customs have not cleared, or of raw materials—rubber, copra, and tin—destined for the communist countries of the West.

We saw several short-tailed cats. There is little doubt that the Manx originated in the Orient and was brought to the Isle of Man by some sea captain coming from the East. I have seen Japanese prints with tailless cats. We also saw one crossbred Siamese, buff-colored, blotched with pale chocolate. As a rule Siamese crossbreds are black. I have seen only one—a half Persian, in New Orleans—that was pale yellow with black points.

I think our cargo of rice, two thousand tons, is a gift from the U.S. Such gifts as this are eaten and pass unnoticed, much of it getting into the black market, whereas the Russians are building an imposing stadium for the Asiatic games. In spite of the many homes and even small factories that have been bulldozed to make room for it, they will get credit for their generosity and leave a lasting monument, long after our gifts have been forgotten.

HOW TO KEEP
OFF DEVILS

Seventeen

We have sent singers and musicians over here who played American music, strange to all but the most sophisticated Asiatic ears. Again, the Russians went one better and sent artists who had learned national Indonesian songs and music which everyone was capable of enjoying, apart from being flattered by the compliment.

The women all wear their hair either short in the European fashion or oiled and pulled back into a bun at the back of the head. Many of them wear a switch. The national costume is a hip-length, tight-fitting one-button jacket with no collar, worn over a sleeveless blouse. The skirt is a sarong, often batik, and is held up by a cummerbund—which no doubt originated in the East and is a good protection to the kidneys if the temperature drops rapidly.

No building other than the new hotel, Japanese financed, the stadium, Russian financed, and a new building for the Indonesian Navy is going on.

The town at night is beautiful, dirty, and romantic, and I should say unsafe. There are no street lights. In the residential areas all the houses burn their lights and in the poorer areas the light comes from shops and the flares of the street vendors who squat beside their wares in the flickering shadows.

Passing through the town, we saw several illuminated fish tanks. Tropical fish are a hobby here, and many that we see in the pet shops at home, guppies among them, come from this area. A lot of chess is played, and every time we pass the guards at the gate a game is going on. This too originated in the East, I think.

We saw some white Chinese geese and some ducks, very attractive ducks, with a semivertical carriage like an Indian runner. There were game fowl everywhere, some with a kind of rose comb, all long-legged, wide-breasted Indian game type but very prettily marked.

The shortage of textiles is so great here that on a previous voyage the bags that contained a whole cargo were stolen and the flour left loose in the hold. No one wanted it. It was even taken back to the Philippines, where it was refused, and then dumped into the sea.

The whole business of nationalization, really expropriation or theft on a national scale, is interesting. At first when it was only the Dutch, it was fine. Next came Chinese farmers, who had bought their land and worked it for generations, and the shopkeepers. Now it is the Indonesians themselves. Whole businesses are being taken over, the compensation being government bonds repayable in forty years. Anyone leaving the country is allowed to take no money and only one watch, one bracelet, and one pair of earrings. No one may have a bank account in another country.

Our five-day visa having run out, we stayed on board and

watched the unloading of the ship; slept, ate, and did some painting and writing.

In the evening for the first time in Indonesia we saw the mountains clearly, a thousand feet high, black against the evening sky, rising out of a snow-white mist at their feet. The sun went down in a blaze of scarlet glory, fringing the top edges of the clouds with gold. Higher up the sky was lemon yellow that merged from pale veridian green into cerulean blue. The mountains became blacker, their edges more crisp, and every star, still pale, showed just faintly as a bright pin-prick in the sky.

Into the west a solitary heron flew majestically to bed.

Psychologically the fascinating experience has been to find oneself without money, without a nickel. I have never been without any money in my pocket since I was four years old. It is a most curious sensation to be utterly dependent on one's hosts, who are all but strangers, and we reverted to a kind of tacit barter system. Tiny found a pair of gold earrings she could spare for our hostess and some toiletries—face cream, a compact no longer new, Band-Aids and sticking plaster for the children's cuts. Even a partly used lipstick was welcome.

The old idea of a sailor's having a wife in every port is an illusion. The officers hardly get ashore anywhere for more than a couple of hours, and what they see of the world is simply a number of waterfronts which, though more interesting than airports, still resemble each other in a greater or lesser degree.

The more we travel the greater the disorder and uncertainty we find. Panama obsessed with its flag. A minor revolution in Costa Rica. The Philippines riddled with corruption, suffering from a vast unemployment problem with Huks and bandits still in the hills. Hong Kong a window into Red China filled to overflowing with refugees. Saigon unsafe away from the city with communist gangs active. Bangkok peaceful enough but still worried about what will happen in

Laos and South Vietnam. Singapore orderly and peaceful on the surface but with undertones of trouble. Indonesia apparently subsiding into a red morass with anti-communist rebels still active in many islands. Apart from Ceylon, the countries we shall pass through or near are all disturbed—Kenya, Somalia, Ethiopia, Saudi Arabia. Egypt and Algeria complete the picture. Rabid nationalists, fanatics, brigands, and communist agitators are all active in countries riddled with corruption, inefficiency, and xenophobia of every kind. Nasser and NKrumah playing for high stakes in Africa. The Congo back to the jungle, from which it had just begun to stagger, and the Russians and Chinese with a finger in every nationalist pie.

Their plans are unbelievably simple. First, playing on the xenophobia of the nationalists, they get rid of the white man, then the Eurasians, then the Indian and Chinese businessmen. The economy now fails. The fragile structure built upon the brains of these executive types collapses and unemployment and hunger are followed by chaos. They now step in and help. The help, whether it is in arms, machinery, or building projects, means technicians. And every technician is a propagandist who blames the imperialistic nations and the capitalists, that is to say, America, for every ill. So to sum up the communist policy, the plan is first to create a powder-barrel situation and then to light the fuse. To succeed, they need only create a state of chaos where the masses are hungry and then produce the scapegoat—the white man in general, and the U.S.A. in particular. How to defeat their machinations is the problem. In each country there seem to be strong parties that are for or against communism. In each there is always the possibility of civil war as tensions increase.

The Western policy is vague. We are still plagued by the echoes of Little Rock. This seems to be the best-known town in America in the Far East. We are anti-communist but this is negative. We are pro a freedom that often turns into li-

cense. We are for free enterprise, which, to peasants living
in a state of precarious subsistence farming, means exploitation and capitalism. We are for education that eventually
leads to sufficient literacy to read propaganda against us. We
are for happiness, for full bellies. We are against sin and for
God. We support some far-from-admirable leaders and cannot say, "Do this. Follow this plan, liquidate these people,
and your problems will be solved." The fact that this is not
true does not worry the communists.

Some interesting oddments of our stay in Surabaja occur
to me: The use of cooked papaya leaves as a specific against
malaria. The burning of a candle in the daytime to get rid of
flies. The flies here are very active and intelligent, not at all
like the sleepy friend we brought from San Pedro to Manila.
The man on the wharf with a kind of umbrella, a metal
circle with two crossbars and a handle festooned with crickets on strings and carried to ward off the evil spirits which
the longshoremen believe live in carbon black. The nearly
naked red-skinned blond half-caste boy working on the docks
whom we called Jock Strap because he needed one. What
was his story? Who was his father? The fact that there is a
mountain of solid sulphur nearby and that sulphur is imported. That there is a sugar shortage here and that once
they used to export it. How it is that a small illustrated
book titled *Arts and Crafts in Java* is published by the department of information, Republic of Indonesia, giving par-
ticulars of everything made and listing the shops where
things can be bought, despite the fact that nothing can be
bought.

We steamed out of harbor in the early evening past the
war-wrecked, half-submerged hulks, leaving a rainstorm behind us. The sky was almost navy blue and the mountains
again completely concealed. We woke up in the roads off
Semarang waiting for lighters to bring us more rubber in a

beautiful jade-green sea dotted with the tiny white butterfly sails of the fishing fleet.

In the past few years the only countries we have seen where there was no trace of war are the U.S.A., South Africa, and Switzerland and Thailand. England, Ireland, France, Italy, Spain, and now in the Orient Manila, Singapore, Saigon, Jakarta, and Surabaja all bear traces, more or less severe, of the Second World War and internal revolution. All are scarred, all bear unhealed wounds—a testament and a warning of the time in which we live.

At 11 A.M., after we had given up hope, a launch came to pick us up. It had called on every ship in the roads, some eleven others, to pick up Chinese crewmen who were going ashore to celebrate the Chinese New Year. The water was glass calm, and in the tremendous reflected heat and glare several medium-sized fish swam toward us at great speed, almost on the surface, attracted possibly by the vibration of our engine, and then veered off. We were again struck by the lack of sea birds. At the dock we were met by the agent with a car. He got us through the very tight security measures of the customs and immigration. Moored beside the customs house was a small, very beautiful one-masted ship which had no deck. The sides came up and turned inward, forming a neat house with a roof tree on which the boom lay. Lashed to the roof were some bright red forty-five-gallon drums, presumably for water.

The owner was bailing water out of the dock and washing his feet on the tiny deck astern. He probably led a life very little different from that of his ancestors three hundred or four hundred years ago. We wondered if happiness was a matter of material possessions, of refrigerators and sanitation, or of living as fully as this man, competent to deal with a natural environment. We have no natural environment left. We use nothing that we make or can repair ourselves. We are utterly dependent on technicians of one sort or another in every phase of our existence.

We drove to the agent's office in Semarang, which must once have been a very beautiful town, but is now falling into disrepair, even greater than Jakarta or Surabaja. Many of the houses reminded us of those in South Africa with the same voluptuous gables and red-tiled roofs. Certain things in Semarang differed from what we had seen in other towns. There were tiny wooden cabs, with wood roofs and two windows, drawn by tiny horses. Many of the men wore round conical reed hats such as the girls wore in Saigon. Women carried loads of produce in baskets slung on their back with a cloth strap over the right shoulder. We saw one baby carried in a sling in front of its mother in the same way.

All the larger buildings were occupied by soldiers, and we saw some road blocks. The rebels appear to be fairly near here. This is an army town (we saw the commander's house), as Surabaja is a naval town. We drove up the mountain which was covered with small, very attractive villas that had pretty trees and shrubs in their gardens—the usual allamanda, croton, palm, flamboyants, and frangipani. The flame trees were just beginning to flower. We saw one West African spathodea in bloom.

We passed several wire-enclosed pedicabs filled with garbage. They looked like rabbit hutches or bird cages on wheels. We saw some soldiers in spotted jungle camouflage uniforms. The army was well dressed and booted, though not smart. We saw one group of small houses with "expensive" birds hanging on the tops of bamboo poles. Why are they seemingly grouped like this?

We had beer and lunch at the Du Pavilion Hotel, a new and very fine building. The lunch consisted of a kind of cooked mixed vegetable salad followed by a big dish of fried rice mixed with shredded shrimp and chicken, a variety of pilaf. The meal ended with a very dry, hard-skinned papaya and Java coffee. It cost a dollar a head. After lunch we went back to the dock, had our passports examined by three different sets of soldiers all armed to the teeth. We passed an open shed filled with thousands of rolls of No. 6 galvanized wire, all rusting, and the lower rolls sinking into the muddy ground. No effort had been made to raise them on balks of wood. We saw two very pretty proas, or big sailing canoes, their bows shaped like sharks' heads, painted blue with eyes looking up out of the water as if they were looking at the sky. The sterns, also painted blue, looked like tails. We came back alone on the launch, a half-hour run. The sea had become quite rough, which made getting back onto the ship difficult. Half our crew were leaning over the side to watch. Captain Bergan came down the steps to catch us as we jumped, timing our leaps to the rise of the launch.

The agent had warned us to be careful of pickpockets on shore, and the impression we got was one of great poverty, and suspicion. As it was Chinese New Year, all the shops, which seem to be mostly Indian and Chinese (there still are some of them left), were closed. The streets were full of people but there was no gaiety.

I think these people, like many others, have a feeling of bewilderment and betrayal. The freedom for which they fought has fulfilled none of their expectations, nor do they see any possibility of improvement.

There are eleven other ships, four of them British, with blue funnels, lying in the roads. One of them has been here nearly three weeks waiting for cargo which is in the godown but not yet cleared by the customs for export.

Our lighter, a U.S. landing craft, brought out twenty tons of rubber in two-hundred-kilo bales. We are picking up two hundred tons and some goatskins for Boston.

There were five sharks near the ship this morning and after supper we baited the hook made by the chief engineer and tried to catch one, but they were too smart for us in spite of our chumming the water with a big pail of garbage.

Sometimes the mountains, symmetrical as if they were cut out of tin, are visible; at others they are hidden by clouds.

Every afternoon it rains in squalls. Sometimes there is thunder. We had one flash right on top of us. The steward saw the lightning strike the water beside us. There must be a lot of storms here, as every house in the mountains had one or more lightning rods.

The lighters are now run by the government, hence the delay. They used to be much more efficient, the captain said.

Our sailors, the officers included, are filthy with grease and the remains of the carbon black that has filtered into everything. In spite of Tiny's having washed her hair three times it is not clean yet.

Because the stevedores felt they had done enough for the day, at 4 P.M. the lighters returned to port in spite of not having discharged all their cargo. The chief engineer had his cigarette lighter stolen from his cabin while he was asleep after lunch. At lunch time a launch came out with food for the stevedores. Each man had a neat parcel tied up in a section of banana leaf.

There were large schools of a pretty silver fish about twelve inches long swimming around the ship very near the surface. We tried to catch them with some meat on a small hook, but they paid no attention to it and just swam by it.

We saw a frigate bird today, also a flat fish, perhaps a ray, that jumped out of the water and landed with a splash. It was about two feet in diameter. Later we saw a sea snake that looked like a white ribbon. They are very poisonous. We could see only its belly as it dived. Two smallish ash-tray-sized seagoing crabs were swimming about on the surface, doing a kind of labored breast stroke. The sea is shallow here and there is a lot of garbage in solution around a ship when she has been anchored several days.

So far the general picture of the Orient continues to be one of unbelievable poverty, of poverty beyond our concept of poverty. When people have literally nothing, no house, no clothes, no cook pot, no cup, no knife, the effect is astonishing. How can I love so many brothers? How can I share?

How well I understand that in their desperation they would destroy me just to live a few more hours.

Now we begin to look for answers. There are no answers. There is contraception. There is forced labor for necessary development in which hundreds may die today so that thousands may live tomorrow.

There is cold, calculating organization in which men and women cease to be human but are simply labor units requiring a minimum of care, just enough to keep them functioning. This is what is going to happen eventually. It is on its way. Chinafication. Where human labor replaces capital. When the means justify the ends, when even if they don't it does not matter.

If a million die through some miscalculation they are regarded as expendable.

It is this concept that it is difficult for us to grasp. People are cheaper than machines. It is better to destroy a thousand people than one factory. Once the concept of human life's being almost valueless is realized, the rest is simple. The Germans felt this way about the Jews. Perhaps we did when we bombed Nagasaki. The Romans felt this way about the Christians. Catholics have felt this way about Protestants and Protestants about Catholics. White men have felt like this about Negroes and Negroes about white men. There is nothing new in the idea, but it is hard to accept when divorced from the fanaticism of religion or racial emotion, when it is seen in terms of production alone.

Proceeding northward through a now glassy sea, we passed small islands off the coast of Sumatra and drove on toward the Gulf of Siam and Bangkok. Although a cargo of one hundred tons of rubber had been waiting for us in Jakarta the necessary export permits had not come through and the captain decided not to wait. A pity from our point of view, as we should have liked to see the Hendersons again and be shown something of life on the island.

It will be curious to be in touch with the world again. Not

to get letters, because none are being forwarded, but to see
the papers, *Time, Newsweek,* and so on. I gather that Lu-
mumba has been killed and that the Russians have got a
six-ton Sputnik into orbit, but have no idea how true these
stories are. In the past everyone must have lived like this, on
rumors, travelers' tales, each isolated enclave building up a
thought pattern, brick by brick, in which every premise
might be wrong. On the other hand, we may get too much
news. News every hour on the hour gives no time for thought.
There can be no perspective if everything is foreground.

The Gulf of Siam is very calm, a smooth, oily bottle blue.
We see several large jellyfish, pale, dirty cabbage green,
with sepia feelers. They look revolting, like bowels and innards floating in the sea, revolving gently in a kind of dance
just below the surface, like great obscene cauliflowers.

The wake of the ship is a straight line running from the
stern to the horizon on the south like a road. Like the track
of a wagon through the long grass of the veld, straight as
the flight of a bullet.

At dusk a bird about the size of a robin settled on the mast.
I do not know if it stayed. We are not too far from land—
thirty or forty miles from the Thailand coast. But why should
it come? There was no wind to drive it out to sea. And why
alone?

The sunset tonight is one of the most beautiful we have
seen, blood red to salmon pink behind a filigree of dark gray,
almost black, clouds. Above it is gold, then veridian green,
then cerulean blue, then a deeper blue, almost a pale indigo.
Small golden clouds highlit and twisted like sticks of barley
sugar hover over the horizon, break apart, and turn into multicolored fish. Dark gray clouds of all sizes now swim like fish
on the wind across the sky.

The falling sun shines like an eye out of the darkening
firmament below a bright half-moon. This has been a mirac-
ulous evening.

At dawn we anchor a few miles from land and await instructions. This is the charm of a freighter, the wonderful uncertainty as to destination, as to date, as to day. The anchor goes out with a roar of links. The chain lies on the bottom around the anchor that lies flat on the sand. The hook does not engage anything. It has taken me all this time to figure that out. The anchor is really little more than a weight that drags down and holds the chain centered. If it did catch in anything it would be impossible to haul it up again.

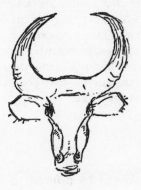

GIRLS AND WHISKEY

Eighteen

We were awakened by a hundred men beating on the cabin walls with sledges. Actually it was only five men. In order to fill in time while we were waiting for instructions the paint was being chipped off the whole ship, including our cabin. Three men attack it with heavy jackhammers, two men beat at it with sledges. The noise was unceasing and unbelievable. Driven out of the cabin, we went on deck. It was just as bad there. More men with more machines were getting off the paint here too, and the deck itself was being sanded down with a machine that made as much noise as a tank.

Two large moths in our cabin, when the noise began, flew around madly, frantically, then fell down dead on their backs. A noise like this would be a wonderful method of sending a man crazy, a form of third degree.

Koh Sichang is an alternative harbor for Bangkok. It has no regular docks, all goods being handled by lighters. The mainland lies about five miles away. Nearer to us is an island with a few buildings.

Some gulls, a hundred or so, rather like kittiwakes, sit in patterned groups on the water around the ship. When one comes in to join them it always tries to land in the middle. There are also a few bigger brown gulls and a few small schools of little fish near the ship. There are said to be a lot of sharks here—none visible today. And for the first time we saw cuttlefish bones, the kind you give canaries, floating in the water. Of course they have to float or they would not be washed up on the beach the way they are, but we have never seen them before. We saw six in the morning.

This island is supposed to be the birthplace of Buddha. He was also born in a number of other places, but there is one of his footprints here in the temple on the hill. At one time the king was going to build a summer palace here. It was begun but later abandoned for various reasons, one of them being a shortage of water. All the water has to be brought down from Bangkok. There is some talk of building wharves here so that ships could go alongside instead of lying out in the roads. In fact they appear to have been begun.

The captain is ill today and while we were having a drink with the officers the talk turned to sickness, accidents, and deaths at sea. A Siamese doctor came on board. It was lucky we were here. The doctor gave the captain some pills and injections, but since they had to speak English, a language neither the captain nor the doctor knew perfectly, no one knows what the trouble really was and the whole business was an act of faith.

English is the Swahili of the Orient and as spoken by Vietnamese, Thailanders, Chinese, Germans, and Scandinavians often sounds like an unknown tongue scattered with a few recognizable monosyllables. All the officers speak and read English, but with an accent that one had to get used to. We are the only people who seem to learn no foreign languages. I am fortunate to talk French by an accident of birth.

At dusk a small boat came from the shore with girls and whiskey. Thai girls and Thai whiskey—labeled Taai Tum.

The girls didn't need a label, as they climbed up the lines and dropped over the stern like pirates.

In the morning about 10:30 A.M. we watched two of them go home. They went down the steps into a biggish boat and flopped down on their backs utterly exhausted. One of them had a half bottle of Thai whiskey which she drained, and then, like children after a party, they examined their presents, the loot they had collected in plastic baskets or wrapped cloths. Soap, cigarettes, apples and oranges, and other undistinguishable oddments. One of the girls had on a man's silk shirt.

The interesting thing was the way they set up their gifts on the seat of the boat, as a girl might after a visit to Coney Island or a ten-cent store with her boy friend, as a woman in a different economic bracket might pour the jewels out of her jewel case onto her dressing table—gifts possibly gained in the same way—only the circumstances and the values being different.

In the evening there are always a lot of small swifts or big martins around the ship, their screaming reminding us of New Orleans, where we heard them last.

The Siamese seem much more energetic and intelligent than the Javanese. Everything they do is neat and precise. The way they keep their boats and throw a line. The men on the boats that came out to service the longshoremen with food and drink did not just sleep or do nothing. They fished —and caught fish, too, a lot of small silvery ones that looked as if they would be good eating.

We are loading tapioca (cassava) that comes up from the lighters fifteen bags to a sling. This is checked by two men on board by the hatch, one with a book and pen and the other with a box divided into partitions into which he sets white painted sticks, each indicating one sling unloaded in the hold. As it goes down he moves a stick into a partition. These lighters are large and well kept. Those in Java were all but sinking and had pumps lashed on their decks to keep them afloat.

I got some figures today. A ship like this costs about fifteen hundred dollars a day to run. We use thirty-five to fifty dollars' worth of paint every day. It costs a dollar and a half a day per man to feed the crew. The anchor weighs five tons. The big jumbo boom, though seldom used, will raise thirty tons. This ship cost five million dollars twelve years ago. At the age of twenty she will be sold to some other company. Statistics like this give one a sense of businesslike reality, something I lack almost completely. If we tie up for a day doing nothing I think it will be nice to fish, and not that fifteen hundred dollars in running expenses has gone down the drain.

There are sharks lying in the shade under the boat; they come out when garbage is thrown overboard. This may account for the way the gulls sit in groups on the water and all try to be in the middle. It may also account for there being so few young gulls, unless these particular birds have adult plumage at once instead of after the first molt. No gull settles in the water near the garbage and they pick up what they can on the wing with the greatest caution.

We have had a little passport trouble here, as my visa was for one visit only, so we are stuck on the ship till the agent gets back from Bangkok on Monday, where we hope he will have been able to fix things up. I gave him three extra signed passport photos. It is a good thing to always carry extra ones.

Two days of idleness, a kind of unreal gap in time. We read, we write, we fish with a borrowed hand line and catch one tiny pink fish, which we gave to the Chinese laundryman, who was delighted. The Chinese like odd things to flavor their rice. We do not have enough variety in our diet. There is no reason why fish and meat should not be cooked together. The Thai stevedores have their own cook on board.

The stove is a curved sheet of iron like a chimney, three feet across and three feet high, open on one side. On top of this they put a big iron basin for the rice water. To steam it, they cover it with a big metal lid shaped like a Chinese hat. They make a fire beside the stove of broken planks and then transfer the glowing coals to the stove. This would be a wonderful barbecue idea if the fireplace had holes bored into it to take some iron rods to form a grill.

Everyone out in the Far East is frightened of devils and evil spirits. To keep them off, they use pieces of red paper and ribbons. All our lighters have red cloths tied in the bow, and at night they set off firecrackers. This seems a good idea. I'm inclined to believe in the existence of the devil.

At last we sail up the river, past fishing villages, past little temples in the jungle, past small Thai warships with their big Siamese white elephant flags, past fishermen in sampans setting their nets like underwater tennis nets to poles in the river.

A big ship passes us with a deck cargo of fat buffalo and golden-colored zebus tied to the rails. Tame as kittens, they were contentedly eating hay as they went to their doom. Seeing cattle on their way to an abattoir is always an upsetting sight in spite of a fondness for steak.

A man on water skis flies past us. Dangerous with all the rubbish in the river from the inland floods. The monsoon has begun and we have had light squalls, showers, and mists for several days. Some children go by in a canoe using a palm frond for a sail. Lighters pass us in towed strings, many of them with tiny toy temples on the roofs of their deckhouses. We pass the docks and anchor upriver.

The immigration people and the agent came on board. We shall get our visa (mine, Tiny as an American does not need one) tomorrow and can go ashore then.

There are plenty of gulls here eating ships' garbage and

perched equidistantly on the horizontal bamboos that support the nets; each bird allows itself enough room to open its wings to take off. At one time there were nineteen kites in the air, darting down and picking stuff out of the water with their claws, and a solitary crow that picked something up in its beak like a gull.

Near us there was a big concrete lighter, a ship of stone that I had read about, never seen, and certainly would not like to travel in.

In the evening more girls came on board, brightly dressed as butterflies, some of them pretty, and all as well behaved as if they were coming to a tea party. Some passengers, it appears, object to this procedure, but it's better to have the girls on the ship than to let the crew go ashore to find them. This being the alternative. At least this way the men are all on board in the morning.

Certain regulations are made to be broken. Smoking, for instance, is forbidden in the hold, but if rigorously enforced cigarettes are thrown down still burning. So anyone who really wants a cigarette is allowed to come on deck to smoke it.

In the evening we fish with cheese bait. This is what the Chinese second cook told us to do, and Tiny catches five catfish, which we throw back.

The night is beautiful as fairyland, with the lights of the little houses in the jungle, the lights of the other ships at anchor, and the lines of tiny lanterns that mark the nets— one to every pole—reflected in the water. Sampans bright as fireflies flit up and down the river.

In the morning we are awakened by the song of birds. The tall palm frieze borders the dawn with black feather dusters. The river flows in a liquid pewter stream against a sepia bank.

We had just finished breakfast when the Barber Fernville launch arrived to take us ashore. Their bus took us to town, about a half hour's run, through banana-planted gardens, small villages, and isolated houses, to the Rama Hotel. The staff welcomed us like old friends, smiling and bowing. The boys are very good-looking in their high-necked white jackets and dark blue sarongs that are twisted into tails between their legs and tucked in at the back. The Thai are a small people, small-boned, neat, graceful, and unbelievably deft and quiet in everything they do. Nothing is ever put down with a bang. Their voices are never raised. In color they vary from a beautiful white gold to golden brown. Their necks are thin, their hair strong and vital, springing up in a mane from the forehead. Their eyes are almond-shaped—oriental—showing the white on the inside near the nose. Their eyebrows are heavy.

Being here again, we recognized all these characteristics once more. It was like recognizing the features of a friend. All the strangeness was gone. We had been here before and met before.

We were now able to see Ayudhya, the old capital that was sacked and destroyed by an invading Burmese army two hundred years ago. We drove through Bangkok and out into a flat country of paddy fields and villages. We saw ducks in flocks of several hundred watched over by a child or woman. We saw at least a thousand being driven by three men who controlled them with blue flags on the ends of long, thin bamboos. In some villages rice was being threshed by three buffalo that were tied together and were being led around and around on a heap of straw. In several places there were large, pot-shaped baskets placed over gamecocks to prevent them from fighting.

For miles the road was flanked by canals, or *klongs*, that were filled with lotus, the sacred flower of the Buddhists. In some places the rice stubble was being burned off, and, as in Africa when the veld is burned, the air was full of birds—white egrets, small hawks, black shrikes and crows, all looking for the insects damaged by the fire or fleeing before it.

The stacks of rice straw built around a vertical bamboo pole looked like native huts in Africa. Indeed the whole scene was reminiscent of the veld—a flat, khaki-colored plain broken by clumps of feathery bamboos that concealed the buildings of a tiny farm. The houses as usual were mounted on stilts. The road, which was a raised causeway, was lined with trees that had been planted at an angle and leaned outward over the *klongs*. There was, according to one's personal taste, a lot—or nothing—to see. To us the buffalo that were now almost always in sight were a pleasure. They were at once both dignified and comic, looking like big game, a kind of cross between African buffalo, hippo, rhino, and elephant—a sort of composite animal. They grazed, they bathed, they wallowed. They soaked underwater with only their faces showing above the surface. They went skidding down steep banks into the water. They climbed out of the wallows shiny as eels, gleaming with mud. As they caught the sun they shone like silver. Children lay asleep on the backs of the dry ones, on their sides, on their bellies. A fascinating thing was the number of pink buffalo we now saw. More here than ever before. They were really a pale beige, but in the evening, when we came back in the early sunset, they were even pinker, rosy as a Renoir nude. We must, during the day, have seen well over a thousand buffalo. We saw more geese, all Chinese. They were either white with orange knob-nosed bills, or dark brown and buff with black bills. The ducks were large, buff-colored, and I think probably the progenitors of such laying breeds as Khaki Campbells.

A lot of kapok is grown here, but we saw no plantations, just odd trees and groups of trees in the villages. Bare of leaves, the long seed pods hang like green bats from every twig. We saw one large white heron fishing and two king-fishers of medium size, not brightly colored.

We visited the king's Summer Palace. It was built with Chinese labor in the 1880's, probably by Anna's King of Siam. It is a curious mixture of beautiful craftsmanship and splendid color and design, yet it remains somehow in principle rather vulgar. Or is it that I have no taste for Chinese taste? Each object, every vase, every inlaid mother-of-pearl screen, every tile, every scarlet, gold-decorated beam was individually beautiful, but the general effect did nothing to me. Like all such places the palace compound was a complex of buildings—the palace itself, a little temple, some Victorian buildings, Chinese arches, bridges over the water, more nondescript vaguely Chinese buildings, dwellings, offices, and so on, all in different styles and none related in any way to the next.

The palace itself was extremely uncomfortable, as all palaces are, but it was cool. Instead of doors there were screens that had mirrors on the outside placed just inside each room so that anyone coming in to visit the king could check his appearance in the glass before he entered.

In the garden, which was somewhat neglected though repairs are going on, was a blue lotus in a large china basin. This is very rare and not really blue but mauve. The most interesting thing to us was the fish near the temple. We bought a little paper horn of popcorn from a little girl at the palace gate who ran up to us crying, "Feedafish, feedafish," which at first we did not realize was an English phrase. They were from twelve inches to eighteen inches long and exactly like the fish one sees in Chinese pictures—pop-eyed, vari-colored, pink, green, and silver, they came by the dozen, shouldering one another aside for the crumbs we threw.

We now drove on toward Ayudhya. In the wide ditches—they were no longer canals, though they were as wide—lines of women were fishing with wicker fish traps. These were shaped like wide-bottom pitchers, but they had neither top nor bottom. Moving in a line, the women banged their baskets into the water and sank them in the muddy bottom. Then they reached in through the top and scrabbled around to see if they felt a fish. If they did, and they did sometimes, they popped it in the creel slung on their backs. But the real idea was to drive the fish before them into a dam, a foot or so high, which they had built across the ditch in front of them. It was in fact a fish drive.

Thailand must be the worst place in the world to be a fish. Everywhere, in every *klong*, there are permanent fish traps and weirs. Almost every house along the waterfront has a large square lift net fastened to two long sticks bent in a bow that cross it diagonally. These are let down at night, presumably baited, and raised in the morning. Then there are the lady fishers with their baskets and old men and children with rods and lines, all after fish.

We now saw some ruins in the bush about us between some ordinary houses, a curious blending of old brick buildings, still bleeding from the sack, and new little jerry-built houses of today. We passed small open sheds containing cement Buddhas that were exactly like the juju houses of West Africa. Another confirmation of my theory that the Chinese were once there. The orange toga worn by the priests might also have come to West Africa this way, and not from Rome, along with the royal umbrellas and sacred stools. We saw a number of the small-flowered wild red cannas which are also found in villages and in juju houses in West Africa and Central Africa. True or not, this is an interesting idea and not at all impossible. I even think the West African dogs, including the basenji, may be of oriental origin—a form of degenerate chow.

We had a picnic lunch in an open shed facing the *klong* near a temple. Hard-boiled eggs, chicken and ham sandwiches, coffee, and a most excellent fruit—a pomelo. This is a big citrus fruit that can weigh several pounds and looks rather like a papaya in shape and color. Inside it is like an enormous orange, but each separate segment is covered with a thick, kidlike membrane that has to be stripped off before the fruit can be eaten, but it is very sweet and juicy, and I wonder why we do not grow them.

After lunch we drove on a few miles to the place where they used to capture wild elephants. Our guide called it the "crayal" but spelled it "kraal," so that is probably where the

African word came from, via the Portuguese and the Dutch in Batavia, together with the little flat *klompie* bricks, ornate gables, and furniture styles of South Africa.

The kraal was an enormous circular enclosure of stone with an inner ring of very large round-topped red-painted teak logs set two feet apart. In the center is another ring of tall red posts from which the men operated and to which the captured elephants were tied. The kraal is made along an old path that the elephants used on their annual migrations. They were led into it by tame Judas elephants as sheep are led to slaughter by a goat. Opposite the gate was a large concrete platform reached by stone steps where the king and his court stood to watch the proceedings—an elephant rodeo. It was easy to imagine the milling, screaming elephants, the shouting men, the king and his courtiers in their golden robes and finery, the women, the servants, slaves, and guards. The land all around that was now more or less tamed and cultivated must have been jungle then. From it would have come the cries of wild birds and the crash of the escaping elephant herd. There would be smells, smells of cooking food, of perfume, of elephants, of sweat, of dust, and burning wood.

We returned to the ruined city, ruined but still inhabited. The houses were shacks compared to the ruins of this old capital that had pink brick walls six to ten feet thick. Tottering pedis and prangs pointed accusing fingers skyward as if blaming God for their destruction. A half-dozen had been restored a few years ago by the Burmese, who apparently offered to rebuild the whole city. The offer was turned down. The Thai did not want to lose their grievance. They wanted to go on hating the Burmese. In one of the restored temples there were three similar Buddhas. The two outside were solid gold and said to weigh five tons each. No one knew about the middle one. Under his concrete coat he may be gold too, but nobody dared take a chip out of him to see. We went past other ruins in the bush, houses, temples, and shops all mixed

up with second-growth jungle, to see the famous great concrete reclining Buddha. It had once been covered, and we
found the bases of the immense pillars that had supported
his roof. Tiny stood by his elbow and did not reach the top
of it.

SPIRIT HOUSES
AND THE JUNGLE

Nineteen

BANGKOK—ELEPHANTS—SALT PANS—MUDSKIPPERS
—TAPIOCALAND—SMELLS LIKE COLORS—A NOISY
LITTLE TRAIN—A ONE-LEGGED GIRL—PINEAPPLES
AND BANANAS—JACK FRUIT—A BABY GIBBON—A
SHORT-TAILED TOM— BULLFROGS—BREAKDOWN—
CICADAS — MORE BUTTERFLIES — LITTLE BLACK
BEES—ELEPHANTS AT WORK—THE JUNGLE—CHAR-
COAL OVENS—NIELLO WORK—THE NAKHOM PATHOM
CHEDI, AN ALTAR WITH HORNS—A SUCCESSFUL
BUDDHA—BUFFALO RELAXING—SPIRIT HOUSES—CO-
LONIALISM — CHINESE CEMETERY — DUCK FARMS
AND HOUSEBOATS—NAKED BABIES

There was a "see elephants at work" tour that we had
wanted to do the last time we were here and now had time
to take.

We left the hotel at 1 P.M. and arrived at Sriraja at 3 P.M.,
110 kilometers along a road running roughly parallel to the
coast. We drove past a number of salt pans, several miles
of them, where the sea water was being evaporated. The pans
were drained by windmills operating very simple water
wheels. The mill turned a wheel connected to it by a pulley
that in turn operated an axle that worked a belt to which
were attached a series of wooden flanges that lifted the water
from one level to another. The shore is covered with mangrove which in some places has been clipped into neat triangular forms and in others sculptured into hedges. Where it

had been cleared there were plantations of palm growing right into the salt or brackish water. This turned out to be the nipa palm, which likes a mixture of fresh and salt water, and so grows in tidal areas. The trunk grows horizontally in the mud and is not visible. We saw some mudskippers here. These fish hop about in the mangrove swamps, spend much of their time out of water, and have air-breathing organs as well as gills. We saw similar fish sitting on mangrove roots in Nigeria, so here we have another tropical parallel.

We were now in tapiocaland. There were neat, cordwood-like stacks of tapioca roots resembling thin sweet potatoes the length of a man's forearm, waiting to be picked up. There were concrete tapioca floors where the broken-up tapioca was waiting to be milled. There were platforms of tapioca being fermented and mills where it was ground. Tapioca (cassava in West Africa, manioc in the Congo) is a root that is used for making the edible tapioca we buy in the supermarket. But its main purpose is commercial, as a basis for glues and gums of various kinds, and other, mysterious purposes.

At this moment, going through this small town of Tapioca-ville, there were some remarkable smells, smells as bright and clear as colors. Fermenting tapioca blended into night soil, shaded off into curry, and was topped off by the perfume of wood smoke, frangipani, and tuberose. Add fish, urine, sweat, roses, stagnant water, the smell of buffalo and pig with a touch of drying fish, and you have it—"The Bouquet de l'Orient"—never to be forgotten—each odor pungent, each isolated, each perfectly dreadful or beautiful, yet blending and breaking away only to merge again in some new and interesting combination.

We are stupidly allergic to smells, not realizing the way we have been conditioned. There would be no problem in training a child to think that violets stink and garlic smells wonderful. The Italians think garlic smells good and it never worries me, having been brought up in Europe. Nor do I understand why women are afraid of the smell of their own sweat, which, outside America, is considered an aphrodisiac. Why should we stifle our sense of smell and want everything deodorized? Today we neither see, smell, nor hear properly.

At Sriraja we got into a little train. Just one open car on a two-foot-six track that made so much noise we could not speak to each other. Going out of town, we passed a number of shops and houses and here I saw a pretty girl of eleven or twelve with long black hair. She was hopping on one leg, with no crutches, and a beautiful expression on her smiling face. Her accident was no doubt the result of living along the line as a small child. No one had told her she had a problem. They probably just told her she was lucky, lucky to have one leg instead of none, and to be alive.

We rode noisily through tapioca plantations, through pineapple plantations interplanted with bananas. There were only two patches of corn, a lot of peanuts, and more tapioca, and, as we advanced into the semi-cleared forest, the sugar cane began. This seems to be the first crop grown once the land is cleared. Here and there there was an odd castor-oil plant. What we were going through was a scene of devastation, rather like a battlefield, that is called progress. The timber companies' exploitation was followed by that of the farmers—the jackals that follow the lion. Of course it was logical, essential even, but it was also sad. To us the felling of a great tree is always a tragedy. Somehow the hundreds of years it has taken to grow should not end like this.

The little train rattled over log bridges. We passed patches of tall elephant grass, more bush, and jungle. At one place we stopped there were several naked little boys and three very pretty little girls, also naked except for a tiny leaf-shaped piece of cotton suspended strategically on a piece of invisible string around their bellies. They did nothing but laugh and wave at us in a most endearing and natural fashion. It is difficult for me to believe that children of our race at that age (they were between three and six) are as happy or even as healthy. If, as must happen, there is an enormous infant mortality, such survivors as these have qualities that we do not recognize. Any more than we really understand the relationship between sickness and happiness, having lost our concept of either real health or real contentment.

There was a lot of orange-flowered lantana that, originating here, has spread over the world and is, in some places such as Hawaii, regarded as noxious weed. I saw what looked like a blue-flowered bignonia, but not much else of interest, as I am not a botanist. A botanist would go crazy here with the variety of plant life about him.

We stopped at a siding to wait for a train and made friends with a very nice, rather long, short-legged yellow dog with prick ears. The usual type but longer, lower, and more corgi-like, very loving and friendly. The chickens were all Rhode Island crossbreds, which confirmed my opinion of this breed's being the hardiest and most suitable for underdeveloped areas, whether they are in the Orient or Africa. Everywhere along the road we had seen jack fruit for sale, some as large as small watermelons, but pale green in color and covered with small warts.

When the train came down the line from the forest some of the logs—they were thirty feet long and over four feet thick—were smoldering from the chafing of the chains that held them. The logs had slots at one end so that they could be dragged out of the forest. The engine loaded up chunks of wood fuel and when the line was clear we went on, and arrived at the logging camp in time for beer and a wash-up before dinner. On the train we had had a basket of bananas, and tangerines, both excellent, and at Sriraja the offer of a toilet room.

The resthouse in camp was comfortable enough if you are used to resthouses. We had an excellent dinner of Siamese curry and Siamese soup, which is served last in the Chinese fashion. Before dinner the light effects on the edge of the forest were magnificent. Many of the great trees, which went up a hundred feet or more before branching, were white-trunked and buttressed. Illuminated by the setting sun, they turned to gold against the blackness of the jungle behind them.

The wife of the caretaker brought in a beautiful young short-tailed thickset tabby tomcat. He was very bold and friendly. There is a tremendous percentage of short- and broken-tailed cats here. We are beginning to count them up.

There was another animal at the resthouse, a baby gibbon, three months or so old, off white in color with a black face and hands. This dark-handed gibbon is not so common as the wak-wak or white-handed kind. Both species vary in fur color from almost white to almost black, just as people vary from blond to brunette. These anthropoid apes are our fairly close relations. This one liked to have the hair of her head parted as if one were looking for fleas, though monkeys do not have fleas. What they are really doing in this so-called flea search is getting out scurf.

The beds were hard plank beds with a foam-rubber mattress over them and had one sheet, the lower one, and a blanket to pull up if one needed it. A blanket is, of course, much cooler than a sheet, as it allows the heat of the body out. The toilet facilities were primitive but convenient.

A lovely big frog woke us in the night. It began in a slow way singing some high notes like a bird that ended sharply with a series of deep-pitched cries like the cry of a cock pheasant roused from cover.

Before dawn I was awakened by the songbirds. The early birds getting ready to hunt the early worms. This kind of well-watered, sparsely populated forest country, such as one finds in Venezuela, in Surinam, Ghana, or the Congo, is always full of insect life, and therefore full of the birds that live on them.

The cocks now began to crow, answering and challenging each other, and we got up. Tiny repacked everything as she always does so as to be ready for any emergency, and after breakfast we set off in a jeep to see the tree-felling in the jungle. When we had gone about ten miles and crossed a number of crude bridges, over deep chasms, the driver discovered that the shackle that controlled the steering rods of the front wheels was broken. We pulled to the side of the road and waited for another vehicle to come and pick us up. A truck carrying logs from the felling area passed us and our driver, mounting it, set off to get relief.

It was three hours before it came, but the experience while waiting was memorable, more interesting than seeing some big trees felled, which inevitably we missed by this delay.

Sitting quite still in the primeval, untouched forest was a strange sensation. Leaves fell from the high trees, butterflies flew in the treetops, and it was hard to distinguish the one from the other. Small, star-shaped flowers and seed pods fell, twisting and spiraling like pinwheels in their flight. In the distance gibbons called to each other—Whoo hoo. Whoo hoo. Birds sang and called. The cicadas at times were deafening. They broke the silence of the forest with a wave of sound like the sudden switching on of a hundred tiny buzz saws. There were several kinds. The buzz-saw kind, the dynamo kind, the kind that worked themselves up, winding themselves up like a toy, and then went off, and a marvelous kind that was very menacing and went "Aar aar."

We saw a chestnut squirrel climb a tree quite close to us and jump into another as it searched for food. Great lianas, some as thick as my wrist and others as thin as wire, hung from the trees. There are only three ways lianas can get onto a tree. They are brought by birds and grow down from the treetops, they are the same age as a tree and grow with it, or they climb it by clinging to its trunk. Anyway, there they are, like the rigging of a ship, attached to every tree. On each tree or almost each tree there were orchids like aerial ferns or cabbages stuck to the bark. They do not kill the trees, but there always seem to be more orchids on dead trees than live ones. There were innumerable butterflies, more than I have seen anywhere except in Central Africa. They were here in the hundreds. The commonest were white, like cabbage whites, and plain brown ones. I saw some sulphur-yellows, a lot of orange tips, and one small tortoise-shell, all resembling those of Europe. There is a question here that has not, as far as I know, been answered. Are these a local variety, locally arrived at? Or do they all have a common ancestor? Will the African python breed with the Asiatic and produce fertile young? Will the Eastern leopard breed with African?

How is it that we find all over the world animals that are almost identical. Birds such as nightjars, bee eaters, hawks, swallows, pelicans, and herons. Mammals such as deer, antelope, wild cattle, wolves, otters, mice, and rats. Did they evolve on their own, or are they mutations of common ancestors? If so, why the change? The law of natural selection is valid only just so far. It explains neither beauty nor unnecessary complexity in any organism. Why should a hen pheasant prefer the cock with the longest tail and thus induce cocks to grow longer and longer tails?

Certainly protective coloration helps animals to escape their enemies, but when did the first moth resemble the bark of a tree or the first stoat put on its ermine winter coat?

These are things we think and talk about. Things that make us wish we knew more and had more time to read and learn.

God comes into this somewhere. The mystery of God, the mystery of life—the quality that is subtracted from a man or a mouse at the moment of death—the soul in a man. But does a mouse have a soul? I don't see why not.

It was extremely hot waiting in the jungle, and I was covered with a kind of rather nice small black bee that liked to drink sweat, presumably for the salt. This was a stingless bee, genus Trigona, a very abundant and social bee, according to the books. Luckily Tiny does not sweat, as twenty or so bees all over her face, chest, and arms would have upset her. Even if they could not sting. Insects are not her cup of tea. In fact she was almost knocked off the back of the jeep by a big butterfly that struck her in the face. There were some very big butterflies in the jungle, one large velvety black one, and a bright, almost morpho-blue one marbled with black. Where there was water, and there were puddles here and there from showers, the butterflies were clustered in hundreds and rose in a multicolored cloud as we drove by.

One tree had a waxy flower like a yellow magnolia. From another a liana hung decorated with fruits shaped like red apples that we were told were poisonous. They must have been or the monkeys would have eaten them.

At last the relief car came. It was of course too late to see the tree felling and we went back to camp for lunch. First we had beer, the local Singha, and cleaned our faces and arms with cold wet towels that had been kept in the refrigerator, and sprinkled with eau de Cologne. This was real luxury.

On the way we had stopped to see the elephants at work. There were three of them. The oldest was thirty and not very big. In fact they were all very small by African elephant standards. They all understood the orders given them by their mahouts and seemed able to do everything but talk. They could do things no bulldozer could do. They rolled logs with their foreheads. They climbed logs to push others down. They dragged logs. They carried their own chains and small trees in their mouths, something I had never known before, putting them in with their trunks and holding them with their teeth. They were tuskless and, like all Indian elephants, have only a single tip to their trunk. They wore permanent shackles on their forelegs which had rubbed their fetlocks smooth, indenting them without breaking the skin. The chains leading from the shackles went up behind the forelegs over the shoulders, where they hung like crossed stirrups. The harness—a chain breastplate—was padded with sacking to prevent chafing. The chain that went over the back to support the traces had a small wooden saddle to keep the pressure from the spine and skin. These elephants' eyes were amber-colored, quite expressionless, and much larger than those of the African elephant. The flies were bothering them. So they scraped up dirt with their front feet, as a man would, picked it up with their trunk tips folded like the palm of a man's hand, and flung it up under their bellies. Last year they had to kill an elephant that went mad. Being as intelligent as they are, they must suffer from boredom and sexual frustration. In Burma I believe they now breed elephants, which, if true, seems a good idea.

At last when lunch was over it was time to go. But the glow of the golden sunset on the tree trunks will remain with us, as will the dawn song of the birds, the great trees rising out of the forest mist, the slow blue smoke of the cooking fires, and the sound of the dew dripping from the roof of the guesthouse. Our clothes, when we put them on, were quite damp from the moisture in the air.

What else was remarkable? The horrible fecundity of the forest, the thoughts of the war in Burma and Malaya, of fighting and trekking through this savage bush. The great parasitic fig trees that grew around their hosts and throttled them with their gray filigree trunks epitomized the jungle. Beautiful, horrible, and dangerous.

Coming back, we saw a leopard trap in a path in the forest. We saw some long-tailed birds that looked like widow birds, a small kingfisher, and one chestnut kite, with a white face and neck, similar to those we had seen in Java. We passed some large clay ovens that a man could get into and that were used for burning charcoal. They are probably better than pits. While we were in the little open train, which had only a roof, there was a terrific tropical downpour. If we had not brought our slickers we should have been drenched. Nothing else of much interest occurred. We were tired now, and wanted to get back to the Rama for a drink and a bath.

The Rama Hotel is really beautifully decorated. There are two lovely murals of Thai life in the dining room and we certainly appreciated everything very much more after having been in the bush. Just as one appreciates the bush after having lived in the city. People who have a bath every day and never get really dirty don't appreciate baths.

Great use is made of basketwork—lamp shades, lamps, chair seats and sofa backs—in the familiar crisscross pattern of Western chairs, whose design probably came from the East. The shadows thrown on the walls by the pierced-brass hanging lamps, in the shape of bells, are beautiful. In the coffee shop there were room dividers made of screens only a quarter of which were eccentrically filled in with lacquer panels, but the illusion of privacy was complete. There were flowers everywhere—orchids and other flowers we had never seen before. I found later that the Thai are great flower breeders and have perfected many varieties, such as the double Barberton daisies we had seen everywhere.

Some screens were ornamented with solid raised designs in niello. This has been made in Siam for eight centuries and consists of a design in gold or silver *repoussé* which is filled in with a mixture of lead, copper, silver, and sulphur and fused into place. It is then highly polished and surrounded by many layers of lacquer. I had often seen this work but thought it to be Chinese. It still may be, in origin, because it was the Chinese who taught the Thai to make pottery and the Vietnam people to use lacquer, so that in the final analysis most of the Far Eastern arts, including those of Japan and Korea, are probably of Chinese origin.

Not that the Chinese were then, or are now, one people. In fact, it would seem as if one could regard all these Mongolian peoples, from the Tartars of the Steppes to the Japanese, as tribes among whom the Chinese were by far the most advanced. These tribes, as in Africa, were continuously at war with each other. Their rulers and boundaries changed with victory or defeat, each ebb and flow leaving its traces on the culture and in the blood of the conquered.

Petchaburi, sixty miles from Bangkok, was once the eastern terminus of the overland routes from Europe and India, just as Ayudhya, on the river, was the seaport where the goods from the West—England, France and Italy—were exchanged for those of Japan and China in the East. The merchants were Arabs who did their purchasing in Venice, brought their goods down the Red Sea, and sailed to and from the Far East on the monsoons from their colonies on the East African coast.

We now went to see the Nakhon Pathom Chedi, which rises several hundred feet into the sky. This is the oldest and largest monument of its kind in Thailand. Not that one sees the original Chedi. It has been enclosed in the new and beautiful structure that has been built over it to preserve it.

The wat was beautiful. There were ancient frangipanis, twenty feet in height, with gnarled trunks six feet in diameter. Old clipped trees tortured into knobs and humps. Seats carved in the rock and stairs cut in caves through the solid rock, so that this temple may have been the origin of the Tiger Balm garden idea. Statues of gods and devils in the courtyards. Open temples. Big bells by the dozen to be rung by worshipers to call Buddha's attention to their virtue. One big one was five feet tall. There was a stone gong, a slab three feet square, that hung from a hole pierced in the top that was used before metal or even Buddha was known. This seemed particularly interesting and important to us. And the usual beautiful pagoda-like incinerator where the symbolic paper gifts to the dead could be burned.

There were circular cloisters lined with Buddhas. The oldest, with long-lobed ears to denote longevity, had no hair-do. The next oldest had a little chignon and the later ones wore high pointed hats. There were also, mounted on pedestals, various ancient carvings found in the vicinity, including one small statue of a sitting woman (as if she were seated on a chair). The others were seated in the conventional lotus position. A bas-relief, in which the arms were foreshortened in the modern manner, made perhaps two thousand years ago. There were a large phallus and a number of other fragments of various kinds.

Inside this outer ring of cloisters was a hall where the kings went after or during the coronation ceremony to kneel facing the ancient Chedi. Here there were a marble altar and *prie-*

dieu which had stone stags' heads with large real horns affixed to them on either side. A study of horns and their mystery would be interesting. Their use by witch doctors, their use in houses and huts to keep away evil spirits, their employment on helmets such as those of the vikings, all might have some common denominator.

Among the trees in the temple wat was a pink flowering tree that looked like a cherry or an apple and was a solid mass of blossom. There were other big and ancient trees, each with a seat or bed where people could sit and meditate and stare at the great yellow dome of the Chedi. It looked like an immense pudding bowl that had been covered with shiny yellow-ocher tiles. It was spotted with mynah birds that popped in and out of the structure.

In the king's altar hall there was a painted dado of Buddhists who all looked out of their picture toward the Chedi. They varied in skin pigmentation from the palest gold to almost black with Negroid lips, presumably Melanesians.

We looked at an enormous gold reclining Buddha with mother-of-pearl eyes. In another open room were two big pale gray roots that looked like driftwood magnified a thousand times. They rose in great twisted whorls and stretched out for yards from the corners of the room.

Among the stone statues was a Chinese lion dog, rather like a Pekinese, whose tongue was a round stone nine inches in diameter that you could roll about inside its mouth. It had been carved there.

Here we once again watched women telling their fortunes by means of numbered sticks, like giant toothpicks, in a container of bamboo. They are rattled together with an upward movement until one falls out. Its number is then looked up in a book held by the priest. The answers appear to be somewhat cryptic, as they have to be checked by throwing three eight-inch banana-shaped bits of wood that are round one side and flat the other. If they all fall round side up it is bad, and vice versa. They are thrown quite high and fall with a clatter.

The Buddhas, and each person seems to have a favorite, are rewarded with a bit of gold leaf or a silken scarf if a particularly important prayer is successful. Many of the Buddhas are plastered with gold-leaf sheets about the size of a cigarette paper, others have only a few—so a god or a statue can also be a success or failure. In some the gold leaf, adhering only partially, flutters and shines in the breeze as it blows through the temple. Statues are rewarded when a lottery is won or a son is born. That is to say, as it is with us, the Thai thanks God for his help when something he prayed for has been achieved. The whole temple wall was lined with small flatiron-shaped recesses that almost touched each other. There must have been several thousand of them, and in each in the old days (before electricity) a candle burned. To watch the robed priests lighting them, to see the walls take fire and the fire reflected on the great shape of the Golden Buddha must have been something to see.

At lunch time we saw teak logs, previously dried by the sun to make them float, drifting past us down the river. We also saw a beautiful bird, a blue-throated bee eater, which resembled almost exactly the African blue jay.

Much of the paddy stubble had been burned off, and very high dust devils, two hundred or three hundred feet at least, swirled up into a cloudless sky.

We saw many buffalo, but they were handled differently here and they all had summer houses, open sheds with roofs, where, as we passed, they lay or stood at ease in the shade. We saw one light sleigh that must be used in the mud of the rainy season. The road was lined much of the way with tamarind trees, and children with long bamboos were poking at the fruits. In many of the gardens the tree convolvulus was in flower.

We stopped to buy a pomelo. This is where they are supposed to grow best, and we got one weighing three pounds at least. There were some bigger ones. This must be the world's biggest and least appreciated citrus fruit. In the same market there were baskets of a pear-shaped pink, luminous,

and shiny fruit that was quite beautiful, growing in clusters
of two or three on a twig with dark, shiny, mango-like leaves.
This was the Laos apple, and it tasted of nothing at all except
faintly like the cotton candy on sticks one buys at the circus.
We saw some purplish-colored bananas in baskets and a few
cultivated koko yams. There were what appeared to be guava
trees. I have an idea they are an Eastern fruit. We also saw
tamarisk trees, which I have not noticed before, Kaffir boom,
or erythrina, again, the usual casuarinas, palms, and other
large local trees whose names I do not know, and more red
water lilies. We saw spider lilies everywhere in the East and
crinums, or Java lilies, several times.

Our guide, Mr. Leck, was most helpful, explaining everything to us. The small temples on sticks we saw by so many
houses and on ships are spirit houses. Candles and joss sticks
are lit in them, food is put into them at feast times, and when-
ever a new house is built they are dedicated by a priest. A
rather nice idea. We passed a small roadside factory where
they made them of concrete. There were three or four designs, some more gaily painted and fancier than others. The
tall pinnacles that stand up like pencils in the temple wats
are pedis. The squarish ones are prangs. They are the result
of a Cambodian influence. Cambodian, Indian, and Chinese
influence in architecture and custom has been superimposed
upon other older cultures in some of these countries, seldom
destroying them but modifying them, blurring the sharpness
of their edges.

The white man has done this in the East too—changed
very little really, but added things. Buildings, roads, docks,
and so on. His greatest contribution, apart from the buildings, communications systems, ideas of hygiene and government, all of which are subject to great and rapid deterioration, has been the introduction of food and cash crops: and
a metropolitan language by means of which immense groups
of people who, only a century ago, were unable to communicate with each other, can now not only do so but also can
converse with the whole Western world.

One of the reasons colonialism is so hated is the knowledge that without it these countries could have progressed no further than they had done when it overtook them. The colonial period is the link between a static past and an unknown future, in a world that becomes daily more technologically advanced and more morally confused.

We passed a Chinese graveyard that made me think of the one above the sampan town of Aberdeen. It seems a pity that cemeteries should take up so much room. It would be nice if these were turned into parks and planted with fruit trees. When I am dead I should like to be an apple to be eaten by a little boy, and if he ate me green I'd give him a bellyache. Bodies buried in blankets would produce fine fruit, blossoms in spring, shade in summer, and fruit in the fall. A playground for children and retreat for lovers. What more could anyone ask for?

Returning, we saw more duck farms and one where there were a great number of geese. The ducks are now incubated, but these duck farms are older than incubators and I have a feeling that the duck eggs were once hatched by the use of fermenting manure. Certainly hens could not have been used because hens are relatively scarce, and would have been utterly at a loss when the ducklings they had hatched swam away across a flooded rice paddy. We have seen three or four Muscovy ducks, another Portuguese importation from Brazil. These ducks do sit and hatch their own eggs but do not seem as popular as the ordinary brownish duck that one sees by the hundred. We have seen only one small flock of white, or Pekin, ducks. They must be exclusively Chinese and thrive better in the north.

Coming back into town, we saw a number of very prettily painted house boats in one of the *klongs*. These are real floating houses and can be moved anywhere. They looked a bit like Swiss chalets.

We ran right into the worst traffic hour, but everyone was very good-tempered. The policemen in khaki, with large, rather flattened white plastic helmets, directed the traffic without excitement. There were hundreds of schoolgirls in white blouses and navy tunics on bicycles and on foot. Men, women, pedicabs, motorcars. People moving, people waiting to move. None of the babies wear anything but a short shirt and are held every which way, but they look contented and happy and never cry.

Mr. Leck, our guide, was charming—a thickset, powerful man in his forties, who said as a boy he had served Somerset Maugham when he lived at the Oriental Hotel, and was writing *The Moon and Sixpence*.

A tourist is very dependent on his guide. Most of them are good. They have to be to put up with some of their patrons and not get ulcers. But Leck was wonderful, not merely in his historical knowledge but in pointing out things we might otherwise have missed on the way to the Nakhon Chedi. He showed us how the tall palms, rather like the vegetable ivory palms in Africa, were climbed. Each tree had bamboo poles attached to it and the climber ignored the tree and just went up the bamboo. It was Leck who told us we should see the kite flying and took us to see it. This is the kite-flying season. Clubs and individuals compete. There are male and female kites. The female kites have tails and are allowed to be flown in pairs. They attempt to entangle the male and bring it down, while the male tries to knock the female out of the air. A lot of betting goes on and the whole affair was fascinating to watch, though the details and techniques remain obscure to me. The male and female contest was interesting psychologically. The crowds were enormous—several thousand people—hundreds of kites were in the air and a dozen kite fights must have been going on in different parts of the park. There were also people flying kites for fun, and some of the more competitive kite flyers had snake kites, which are very hard to operate, difficult even to get off the ground. They were generally green, snake-shaped, with heads and eyes. They appeared to swim through the air. Since the Philippines we have seen children with kites everywhere. Homemade kites on thin bamboo frames. The kite is another Eastern invention.

They were also playing the rattan ball game in the park and we watched it for a while. The ball, about the size of a soccer ball, is made of wickerwork and very light. The game seems to consist of getting it into a basket and resembled the American game of basketball, but they used only their heads and feet, often kicking it in a kind of backward kick with the heel from behind.

We should like to have seen some Thai boxing, which is very formal in some ways—with ceremonial prayers and gestures. Kicking is usual and it seems likely that the *savate*, what used to be called French boxing, originated in Indo-China and was brought back to France by the troops.

We visited the zoo, which like most zoos in the East is partly an amusement park. There was some remarkable topiary here—trees trimmed into men, into peacocks with spread tails, into monkeys and Walt Disney dwarfs. This is another art that must have come to Europe from the East. By now I was getting a little tired of discovering that so many things I had regarded as products of our Western culture were not ours at all. There is little doubt that until the industrial revolution most races in Asia surpassed us in many ways. In culture, in luxury, in manners, and cleanliness. In the seventeenth century almost everyone in Europe appears to have had lice and fleas. There were no bathrooms or toilets in such palaces as Versailles. Our strength is our ability to develop natural resources and make gadgets of every kind, from automatic can openers to atomic bombs. I am not at all sure if this is good or bad in terms of world happiness or content. People may have been better off in the Middle Ages, when they believed in God and knew nothing.

We saw the sacred white elephant. He was very disappointing—not white at all. He differed, as far as we could see, from the other elephants only in having a few pink spots. One of the working elephants we had seen up country was far pinker than he, having very pretty spotted ears that looked like rosy freckles on her gray skin. The zoo was pleasant and well kept, with a quite large lake where we fed buns to the fish. They were very big, two or three feet long, and dark in color. They had no teeth, so they charged the buns, bashing them about like a football team with a ball till they disintegrated.

These fish were carp, one of the kinds that are kept all over Southeast Asia and fattened for the table. In commercial ponds several varieties are kept together. The grass carp, which has teeth, can eat grass and leaves. The mud carp lives in the mud on the bottom, and the big-head and silver carp eat the plankton that grows on the ponds, the former eating the larger organisms, and the latter those barely visible to the naked eye. This division of the food resources permits fish to thrive in what could otherwise constitute serious overcrowding.

Most carp are bred in Chinese rivers and imported as fry. Until recently they came from Hong Kong in wooden tanks as deck cargo, but now they are flown, which cuts the loss in life. The water in the tanks used to be aerated by the splashing of an attendant—one to each tub.

The origin of carp farming in China is lost in antiquity, but has existed there for thousands of years, and up to four thousand pounds of fish have been produced per acre.

These fish at the zoo did not compare in looks with the royal multicolored carp at the Summer Palace, nor did they in manners, either. But there is always something fascinating about feeding anything in the water—ducks and swans with bits of bread as a child in the park, seals with fish at the zoo in Rome, carp and turtles in the Orient.

Actually it is not only in the water. Most people like to feed anything anyway—to feed monkeys nuts, to feed elephants, to feed pigeons and chickens, to give horses lumps of sugar. It is this instinct that may have led to the domestication of our farmyard animals.

THE AMERICAN INVASION

Twenty

WEDNESDAY, BANGKOK

We were called early and telephoned to the agents at eight-thirty. They had no news of the ship's sailing time but asked us to call again at one-thirty, which we did and made an appointment to go with Mr. Udom to complete the immigration papers and get our exit permit. It was a good thing I had given him my extra passport photos so that when we went there everything was ready. But having received our exit papers, we now discovered that our ship was not sailing after all. She was held up another day. To cap it, in the meantime we had been thrown out of the Rama as six hundred American tourists had just come in and all the rooms were booked. We went to the agent's office and called every hotel, and by every we mean *every* hotel. Every first-class, second-class, and third-class hotel. The *Gripsholm* had come in too. That meant twelve hundred tourists, not six hundred, as we had thought, and there was not a bed in Bangkok. So we went back to the Rama and hoped someone would figure out something.

We filled in time by eating and drinking beer and coffee at the coffee shop, and once again were impressed by the charm and gentleness of the waitresses. They put everything down quite soundlessly. There was no rattle of crockery or silver. Then when they had put something down—a salt cellar for instance—they would look at it with lovely, reflective al-mond eyes and decide it should be moved an inch to the left. Then the flowers were too close to the salt cellar and they had to be moved. Satisfied, they would look at us to see if we were as pleased as they with the arrangement—and we were. It was delightful.

We decided we should buy a couple of charms for Tiny's sister-in-law and niece, and bought them at a jeweler's across the street. One was a lucky gold coin and the other one was an abacus no bigger than a nickel with little balls on it that really moved on golden wires.

Everyone uses an abacus in the East. The first one we saw was in Manila and we have seen them in every shop and restaurant ever since. Why don't we use them? They are much simpler and cheaper than our calculating machines.

Our other method of passing the time was to look at one of the receptionists. She was probably about nineteen, a really beautiful girl, with long black hair, lovely eyes, and a magnificent carriage. She wore Western clothes with a won-derful clothes sense, style, and chic. We had seen her before but now had time to appreciate her. We told her how pretty she was and that we liked her clothes, and she seemed pleased.

By now we were tired. Nothing is more tiring than sitting about in a hotel lobby all packed up, from 7 A.M. to 4 P.M. Then someone had a brain wave and suggested some bungalows. Did we mind bungalows? We said, "Not if they're clean," meaning no bedbugs. So we got back into the company bus and went to the bungalows. Ours was No. 15. They were arranged like loose boxes in a racing stable and approached through a gate guarded by a bunch of toughs.

But No. 15 seemed clean and we paid in advance, one hundred ticals (five dollars). For anyone who has read *Suzie Wong* this was quite obviously a long-time, short-time job. And they really seemed surprised that we wanted it all night and had brought our luggage. The room was a large square box, with a big bed, eight feet by nine feet, in the middle of the floor. On the wall was a notice to beware of fire, printed in English, Chinese, and Thai. The toilet was Eastern, a china pan with a hole in it and two foot rests set in the floor, flushed by a rubber pipe attached to a brass tap in the wall. There was also a square tiled tank for water served by another tap and a small aluminum basin to use as a dipper when showering. This is done in the East by filling the little basin and pouring the water over oneself with the dipper. Beside the washbasin was a blue plastic comb and some baby powder, both I imagine by courtesy of the management.

There was a radio in the room, which was air-conditioned. There was one sheet on the bed over the mattress and a loose blanket, and next to the bed on the floor an enamel spittoon half filled with water. It might have been much worse, but Tiny did not think so.

Dumping our luggage, we took a taxi to the Oriental Hotel, where we had an excellent dinner sitting by the river, and watching the boats go by. The colored neon lights came on across the water, painting the waves in the wake of the boats red and green and yellow.

After dinner we returned to the bungalow, where Tiny catalogued some of the more outstanding examples of my inefficiency. I should have called up the U.S. Ambassador, the British Ambassador, and any available consuls, newspaper editors, and so on and informed them of our plight. The only trouble was that I was not really aware of our plight. It was not the Ritz, but our quarters had a roof, seemed clean, and were air-conditioned. The uses to which the immense bed had been put and would be put again seemed irrelevant. It was the squat-down toilet that worried Tiny, though I pointed out that this was a natural position and recommended by the medical profession, and reminded her that she had seen them in Europe a couple of years ago.

The night passed without adventure. There was considerable activity among our neighbors, a great slamming of car doors and girlish laughter, but nothing else.

We packed up in the morning and took our gear back to the Rama, where we had breakfast. The bellboys were used to us now and laughed when they saw us. After breakfast we took a walk around the block. Nothing of interest was seen, but we speculated about what there was, what rabbit warrens existed, in the center of these big blocks. We did see some bad coarse batik in a dressmaker's shop and a white squirrel in a cage. We wondered what would happen if there were a serious fire in Bangkok. The wooden, palm-thatched houses, the shops all filled with combustible merchandise, all crowded together, presented about as bad a fire hazard as we had ever seen.

Tiny had found that there was a cancellation at the Oriental, and when our friend Mr. Udom proved to be still vague about the time of departure we decided to take the room and to hell with the expense. It was a lovely room overlooking the river, air-conditioned, with one wall blue, one yellow, and two rose. Very modern. The furniture was comfortable rattan.

We sat in the garden for a while watching the river traffic that moved up and down in endless variety. Small steamers, launches, junks, sampans, and lighters all busy as water bugs going about their affairs. There were two Victorian statues holding lights in front of the hotel, which was being renovated. The men were working on bamboo scaffolding that was as pretty as lace. The crosspieces were fastened by loops of rope twisted tight with a stick that was then tied to an upright. We had first noticed this scaffolding in Hong Kong.

We had a wonderful lunch in the air-conditioned Normandie Grill overlooking the city. I had a baked fish stuffed
with fragrant herbs, with mashed potatoes, and Tiny had a
steak. We drank a half bottle of dry white Chianti and con-
gratulated ourselves on having a bedroom if we were not going to get away today. After lunch we slept, had tea in our
room, and called the office again at 4:30 P.M. Now we were
really off, they said. The car would pick us up at 7:30 P.M. We
had drinks in comfort, dined early, and waited, all packed
up again, for the car. In the meantime we had met Robert
Fasson, the manager, a most charming man, and we passed
the time very pleasantly. He suggested if we came back,
and we said we might, that we should like it upcountry on
the Burmese border. December is the best month, or, for a
longer period, October to March.

While we were waiting in the open-air lobby a bullfrog
in one of the drains opened up, making a really terrific din
and sounding more like a bird than a frog. This is the same
animal that we heard in the elephant camp upcountry, and
I am told it is no bigger than an ordinary toad. In the open
court where we sat there was a fountain and pool in which
several large black goldfish—they were too superior to call
them carp—swam round and round.

The drive, in the dark once we left the city, was along
the road we had taken when we went into the jungle to see
the elephants at work. We passed the salt pans glimmering
faintly. We passed the smells—fomenting tapioca that
smelled like pig swill, the night soil and a smell that was like
that of a tannery. We smelled curry again, sweet flowers,
and incense. But at night the smells were sharper, clearer,
better defined. They did not blend and merge but appeared
to be separated by slices of darkness.

Several times little white frogs hopped across the road
in the lights of the car. Dogs lay sleeping on the side of the
road near dark cottages. I never heard one of these dogs bark

at any time, another characteristic they have in common with the basenji and East African native dogs. The driver, since he was a Buddhist, was most careful of all animals including the frogs. It took two and a half hours to make the trip. A launch was to meet us at eleven to take us and the ship's papers out to the *Pleasantville*. She was due to sail at twelve. But at twelve there was no launch and we decided to go to bed in a bungalow here till dawn, when the launch would probably appear. At 11 P.M., when we arrived, there was a great deal of activity in the town. Cooks had set up their charcoal grills and tables on the sidewalk. Restaurants were open. Children of all ages were up. There was no drinking or shouting. Everyone was quiet and good-tempered, eating what seemed to us the most delectable food, but stuff that we dared not touch since this was no moment to get even a touch of dysentery. Actually, I am sure it was safe enough.

While wandering about waiting for the launch we saw one short-tailed cat, one broken-tailed cat, and one Siamese with a white triangular mark on his chest with the point of the triangle pointing down. We also made friends with a very pretty young white cat marked in almost Thai lettering, with gray. In character and shape of head he showed a lot of Siamese. Of course all the cats we have seen are Siamese since we are in Siam, so I suppose what we call a Siamese is here described as a temple cat, which is still, on the whole, I think, owned only by the nobility and priests.

These bungalows we went to here, the Grand Hotel Bungalows, I think they were called, were really guesthouses rather than a brothel, being too far away from the bright lights of the wicked city. Brothel is the wrong term anyway even for the other place. Such places are really Houses of Assignation on the do-it-yourself plan—bring your own girl. They were built out over the water. We walked at least a hundred yards between rooms, along passages over miniature docks, through a big central hall to a lovely suite of two bedrooms, a tiny sitting room, and bathroom set right out in a kind of cottage peninsula with a balcony over the water, which was as black as a pool of ink. Twenty yards away the light in a Thai cottage was reflected in a solid golden bar. Three sampans, blacker even than the water, were tied to the posts that supported the house. A great red half-moon lay on her back midway up in the indigo sky.

What had interested us most in our walk to our quarters were the great Ali Baba earthenware pots full of rain water. At the corners of the roofs were down pipes that could be swiveled so that with the addition of a piece of guttering all the pots could be filled from one place or another. There were four bottles of water on the table in our little sitting room, each topped by a glass. The Chinese owner or manager said the water was all good, as it was rain water. Then he brought us a bottle of Chinese tea, pale-colored, lukewarm, without sugar and milk, to which we had become accustomed, said good night, and left us.

When I closed the door of the bedroom two large roaches ran up the wall, to Tiny's horror. I killed them with my shoe and they made a kind of gray porridgy smear on the brown wood. When I moved the pillows on the bed—they were snow-white clean—two more roaches even bigger than the last ran down behind the mattress.

Now things became really interesting. Tiny was paralyzed with fright and horror. Though she is undeterred by snakes, elephants, or lions, insects produce in her a state of cataleptic shock. I said, "They've gone now." "Yes," she said, "under the mattress."

"They'll stay there," I said.

"How do you know? How can you know what a roach will do?"

"I know," I said. "They don't like people." Of course I had no idea what they would do.

She said, "What about your father? Didn't you tell me that once on a ship they ate off all his toenails?" She has a terrific memory for things like this.

I said, "Yes, but it was a different kind of roach. Those were black beetles. These are American roaches," I said, appealing to her patriotism. "Just like the ones in Louisiana with those big beautiful sweeping antennae."

"Bigger," she said. She was still standing frozen in the middle of the room.

"Let's go to bed," I said, and began to undress.

In a kind of zombie reflex she took off her clothes and we lay down.

"I'll turn off the light," I said. "We shan't be able to see them then. You don't want to see them, do you?" I thought this was rather humorous. Laugh it off with a combination of patriotism and humor, I said to myself.

She lay stiff as a little poker. After ten minutes in the dark, when she showed no signs of relaxing, I turned on the light again and said, "I'll pull down the mosquito net." It was reefed like a sail above us.

"No," Tiny said, jumping out of bed. "It may be full of them."

"Oh no, there won't be any up there," I assured her. At least I hoped there wouldn't. And there weren't. When I got it all tucked in under the mattress I persuaded her to get back into the bed. She went in diffidently as if it were a trap, ready to jump back.

"They're all outside," I said, hoping it was true, and we went to sleep. The sleep of the exhausted tourist, which is 100 per cent deeper than that of the just.

At three o'clock we were awakened by the shouts of the agent and dressed again. The launch had been found. It took us an hour to reach the ship and that made it about forty-two hours since our first alert. This is one of the difficulties but also one of the interests of freighter travel. The sailing date depends on the delivery of cargo, on the weather —cargo cannot be loaded in the rain—on the stevedores and longshoremen. These impalpables may hold one up for days and add to the expense. But this time at least we did not have the worry we had had in San Pedro. The ship could not sail without us. We had her clearance papers.

We now had only one full day to do our notes, laundry, and repack for Singapore, which we reached on Saturday morning. The ship dropped anchor in the roads just outside the city. The dawn came in a Kiplingesque manner like thunder outer China 'crost the Bay, the bay being the Gulf of Siam, presumably, and the thunder literally a big thunderhead of monsoon cloud to the east, through which the sun emerged, a ball as red and round as that on the Japanese flag.

This part of the harbor reminded us of Hong Kong in the mass of ships that lay at anchor, but was much less lively, and there were no sampans, junks, or ferries. It was just a lot of ships lying waiting at anchor.

The immigration cleared us and by ten we were on shore, having taken the agent's launch, passed the customs without their opening anything, and then took a taxi to the Raffles Hotel, where we checked in. Lucky to get in, as they had just had a cancellation—this in spite of our supposed registration by cable to the agent, who said he had booked a room.

After a gin sling each and leaving our luggage, we took a taxi to the Bank of America and cabled for three hundred dollars, as we had run short. Next time we will take a letter of credit as well as traveler's checks. We had a good lunch at the hotel and slept till dinner. We dined in the Elizabethan Grill, on chicken and prawn curry, fruit, and a half bottle of Pommard. Later I got the barman to give me the recipe for a Singapore gin sling, which is certainly one of the best drinks I have ever had.

SINGAPORE GIN SLING

½ jigger gin
½ lemon squash or fresh lime
¼ cherry brandy
¼ orange curaçao
4 drops maraschino
2 drops Angostura bitters
   (Ice only. Not soda or water.)

In the early afternoon it had poured with rain, a real tropical shower, and, coming back to our room from lunch, we found a very fine young rat, about full grown but in beautiful condition, with bright black button eyes, trying to get in at our door out of the rain. In the afternoon we went to the Indian shop in the arcade where I ordered three more batik shirts and Tiny bought three pieces of batik material and took them to a dressmaker to have them made up.

I changed some Bangkok money and got two and a half Malay dollars for twenty bahts. The money-changers and moneylenders—the bankers of the poor—are the same everywhere, cold-eyed as snakes, quick as monkeys. It is not surprising that Christ chased them out of the temple. Now I can see why they were there, with Jews coming in from all over the world to Jerusalem with every kind of currency in their purses.

At night there was a special dance mostly for Chinese. The ballroom was reserved, but there were some Indians, Malays, and white people as well. It is amazing how clumsy white people appear beside the slimmer, small-boned men and women of the East.

When telephoning or giving a room number here the word zero is used. A great many of the women wear pajama suits, many of them silk, but the coats are longer than in Hong Kong and the necks higher. In Hong Kong many of the cotton pajama suits worn by working girls do not have a high collar. The cheong sams here are split higher, to the very top of the thigh, so that the bottom of the panties sometimes shows when the girls sit down. Their long bare legs look beautiful as they walk in their brilliant silk dresses. I was told that the higher the slit in the skirt the less inhibited the young lady was likely to be. We show our bosoms —they show their legs. The result is the same. Our dinner table had a vase of orchids rather like corsage orchids—only a quarter the size. Other tables had small bunches of gladiola a few inches high.

Sunday we got up late and lunched at the Cathay—a

Chinese restaurant. We had shark-fin and crab-meat soup (good, but not as good as at Aberdeen), bird's-nest and shredded-chicken soup that tasted of very little, prawns and vegetables, minced pigeon—excellent but very rich, and "old eggs." They were very good, cut into slivers so that they looked like a strange, orange-like fruit, divided into sections. They were served like the petals of a flower on a dish in the center of which was an arrangement of white raw sliced ginger that was not too hot. The yolks of the eggs were olive green, the whites a bright, dark, shiny chestnut that looked almost like aspic. Bird's-nest soup is made from the saliva of the swiftlet, small sooty-brown swallow-like birds that nest in colonies in caves. They use their saliva to cement together the moss from which they make their nests. In Sarawak and North Borneo considerable revenue is derived from their nest collections by the inhabitants who farm the nests and have a closed season during which they may not be touched. Shark-fin soup is made from the fins of several kinds of shark, guitar rays, and sawfish. The whole meal, and we could eat less than half of it, cost 15.50 Malay dollars or about $6.00 U.S., including the tip. We ate it all with chopsticks and china spoons and were pleased we had had so much practice on the ship, where we had taught ourselves to pick up peanuts in the privacy of our cabin.

When one looks at the Chinese women's eyes again, several more things become apparent. There is no tear duct at the corner near the nose, or if there is it does not show. The lids end neatly, even sharply, which is very pretty. On the outer side of the face the upper lids project beyond the eyebrows and more of the eye is visible in full profile than in a Caucasian face. The jawbone also seems to be a little farther behind the ear. Perhaps oriental women really cannot cry with the readiness of the occidental woman, which is why, in the old days, they treasured their tears in teardrop bottles.

Our room, No. 71, is on the ground floor and opens onto the cloister that runs around three sides of the building and gives onto a lawn where there are tables and seats. The lawn is planted with some very tall palms I do not know, traveler's palms, and frangipani. The frangipani bushes are about as tall as they grow—twenty feet or so. As they age the trunks thicken tremendously. But the white flowers of these trees, though not so numerous as others I have seen, are enormous, the four petals of a single blossom fully four inches in diameter, filled the whole palm of my hand.

This is the first time we have been able to see fan or traveler's palms in every stage of development. They grow as suckers with three or four shoots coming out from the parent. Transplanted, they grow into real fans of fifteen or so banana-like leaves at ground level. Then they come up on a single stem. The tallest here, outside the ballroom, must be fifteen feet high with a fan of twenty leaves eight feet or so from tip to stem. They appear to grow slowly but are worth growing, as they are so attractive by both day and night. Climbing up their trunks are big, arum-like golden-leaved creepers known as aroids. This one—Scindapsus aureus—lived fully up to its name when floodlit.

The Raffles Hotel features the traveler's palm in the neon light over the entrance. In fact now we can't see a traveler's palm without thinking of the hotel. If allowed to grow naturally and sucker they form big banana-like clumps that are without distinction.

One of the architectural features that have impressed us in the Orient is the beauty of the roof tiles, which look like shagreen or lizard skin, having the effect of scales. First U-shaped tiles are laid upside down side by side and overlapping in the row. Then the joints are cemented and capped with a similar tile upside down. These too overlap, starting naturally from the bottom, and produce a most picturesque effect in their ordered irregularity.

The hotel barber, a Chinese of course, gave me a wonderful haircut and the same kind of neck and shoulder massage I got in Saigon, forcing his hands together with a kind of click as he rubs and strikes the shoulders. Outside the barber's shop, on the opposite side of the street inside a compound, a fine breadfruit tree shows its leaves silhouetted against the sky above a sway-back roof of red-brown Chinese tiles.

We went to see the Hindu temple, garish and untidy, with men (presumably monks) asleep on camp beds in every piece of shade. From here we went to the aquarium, which was only a couple of hundred yards away, but we failed to get in, as there were a hundred or so school children lined up waiting to buy tickets. In the park on the way to the entrance we found a small kitten dying under a stone seat. It was a very remarkable color and resembled an Abyssinian cat—rabbit-colored with two little black streaks on its cheeks that were paler than the rest of the body. It was in a coma and we could do nothing for it, which depressed us terribly. During the course of the day we saw several more short-tailed and broken-tailed cats. The cats of the Orient are the most interesting we have ever seen. The wide concrete street drains and canals were running with floodwater,

stained a rich red ocher from erosion in the hills, the result of yesterday's rain. The street drains are narrow but at least three feet deep.

We now visited the Jade Collection. This was housed in another residence of the late Tiger Balm King, and is now inhabited by his heirs, who throw the collection open to the public during some hours of the day. The Sikh-guarded iron gates were flanked by pillars surmounted by a large China tiger and a leopard in full color. On the short drive there are several stone statues, two of them wearing shoes that are like chickens—little hens with heads and combs covered the toes.

There are seven hundred and two pieces of jade in the collection, many of them priceless; some are quite small, others are almost two feet high. The cabinets are unfortunately not lighted and the heat in the house was so intolerable that I did not appreciate the pieces fully. Moreover, to really understand them, one would have to be a specialist not only in oriental art but also in jade. The thing that surprised us most was the number of colors there are: green, white, smoky black, amethyst, mauve, golden chestnut, yellow, pink, and, best of all, imperial green that was a real emerald color. There were some pieces of crystal and some of lapis lazuli from Russia. This was a bright Ricketts blue spotted with white—the matrix—which looked like limestone.

The big thing in Singapore for Tiny was of course her clothes. She had three dresses made of batik and one black satin cheong sam. These had to be fitted but when done were perfect. She also bought three beautiful pairs of embroidered Chinese satin shoes, two at six dollars U.S. each and one pair decorated with pearls for ten dollars.

The shoe merchant, Mr. Liew, took us to Chinatown in the evening, to the immense People's Market, which must cover several acres, and where everything imaginable is for sale, but all of it, that we could see, was either of Western origin, Japanese, or a Chinese copy of the Western. There were numbers of open-air and semi-open-air restaurants where Chinese food of every kind was for sale. People swarmed. The girls, and I have never seen more really pretty girls at one time, were neatly dressed in pajama suits. The population of Singapore is a million and a half and most of them seemed to be shopping here.

The hair-dos of the little girls all over the East were very amusing. Many of them had pony-tails like scalp locks set anywhere on their heads—on the very top or over one ear. Sikhs never cut their hair, and we saw young Sikhs with little topknots the size of a tennis ball on the tops of their heads; some even had them covered with tiny pink turbans that looked like icing.

In the streets many doors were open because of the heat, and we saw the so-called cubicles in which the poor people live, or rather sleep. They are not cubicles in our sense, that is to say, fenced-off areas divided by partitions. They are simply bunks set one over the other.

Mr. Liew showed us a shop where they sold snake wine, chicken wine, and frog wine. Exposed in the windows were big jars containing skinned snakes and frogs in spirits—rice wine probably. These wines are considered very healthful.

We ended the evening in a large night club and dance hall, the "Great World," where there were five hundred most beautiful hostesses, taxi dancers and B-girls, all dressed in cheong sams. The band was very good and said to be the best in the Far East. Our waitress, a handsome woman though on the fat side, pressed herself most amiably against me every time she filled up my beer.

These clubs were once very gay and wicked. But they have been emasculated by Freedom. Freedom and sex being considered incompatible and girl shows a by-product of decadent Imperialism.

The cheong sam is a most seductive garment when well made and properly worn. Most of the girls are small but some are very tall, five feet six inches at least. All are slim and graceful. Sixteen inches is an average waist measure, though some are only thirteen inches. They have small bosoms but beautiful hips and legs. Their slimness is most apparent side view. From behind they have a well-defined, rounded, almost hourglass shape. All the male tourists on the ship agreed about their beauty. But the women, except for Tiny, insisted that they had no shapes, nothing in front or behind, compared to the figures of European ladies in late middle age. They were correct. But the comparison was not apt—after all, one cannot compare a daffodil to a cabbage.

It is not surprising that many white men, soldiers in particular, marry these girls, and the marriages are on the whole said to be successful, particularly if the couple remain in the East. The girls do not transplant well and become ill on Western food and from nostalgia.

There is no way to describe Chinatown except by using the ant-heap simile again—a dirty but curiously contented ant heap. This is the superficial view. Underneath a content born of Chinese philosophy, there is an uneasiness which can flare up into trouble at any time as it did in 1956, when the trade unions and students rose and rioted spontaneously. A lot of damage was done and several white people killed. Only the presence of British troops prevented a really serious flare-up. Fifty per cent of the population is under nineteen. Students everywhere all over the world are uneasy, worried about their future. This is particularly true here. Singapore is a small island already overpopulated by its million and a half inhabitants, whose favorite amusement is the procreation of children in spite of the government's enthusiastic planned parenthood campaigns. The Chinese like children, which is not surprising when they are so attractive. But the unrest of the young people is explicable. There is not likely to be work of the kind they want on an island whose future is most uncertain. Several things can take place here. Singapore can continue as it is—a great free port, but with the collapse of the British Empire its importance is so reduced that this seems unlikely. The status quo is over. There is the possibility that Singapore, whose population is 78 per cent Chinese, may return to the Chinese womb, or that China may absorb it. The historic influence of China in all these areas cannot be ignored. Finally, Singapore might join Malaya. Nothing could suit the island better. But Malaya knows that the addition of so many more Chinese could tilt the already precarious racial balance of Chinese and Malays in their favor. Some Chinese from Singapore have gone back to Red China, despairing of a future here. Others stay, those who have been thrown out of Indonesia, and some who, seeing what was going to happen, left there while the going was still good. All these people remain in touch with their friends and relatives. The Chinese everywhere, even in Hong Kong, while they are glad to be out of it, are still proud of the achievements of the communists in their homeland.

So under the peaceful exterior of the crowded streets there is a latent ferocity that comes out in murders, people tortured, and kidnapings. There is extortion everywhere. Every storekeeper, street hawker, or shoeblack pays some form of protection.

Last year I was told twenty prominent businessmen had been kidnaped and ransomed. All this is the work of organized gangs that began in China centuries ago as political movements, whose members tried to rectify the injustice of the Manchus by intimidation and murder. They helped the poor, negotiated jobs, and kept order among their own people under the administration of elected elders and leaders.

This is all changed now. The original societies have gone, and numbered gangs remain—24, 969, 309, triple 8, and so on. The money they exact is always in multiples of their own number—$2.04, $24, $240, $2400—according to what the traffic will bear for the 24 gang.

In time of trouble, such as student riot, they really cash in. Despite their smiling faces, the beauty of the women and children, and charm, the Chinese are a cruel race. I was told that had they been in the position of the Japanese they would have been much more brutal, something the reports coming out of Thibet confirm. The Chinese have always had the reputation of being the world's most skillful torturers, and I heard numerous stories of children torturing puppies and kittens till they died.

Our concept of cruelty, charity, kindness, and mercy is peculiar to us—something inculcated in childhood when we are punished for pulling the legs off grasshoppers. I am much affected by cruelty of any kind, but I wasn't once. I was much more careless about inflicting pain. But I do not think our psychiatrists have found the real cause of pleasure induced by torture. It differs in a savage, who probably likes to see his victim scream and dance, and the S.S. trooper who is sexually stimulated by the sight of blood.

In Thailand we were twice offered bunches of ducklings, tied together by the legs as if they were flowers, by boys who evidently felt nothing, in spite of the waving necks and desperate quacks of their living bouquet. Cruel? How do I know? How cruel should I be if I were hungry? It is easy to have high moral views with a full belly.

Next day we drove to Johore with our new friends, the Chiolis. We passed the bridge by the Y.M.C.A. where the Japanese used to expose the severed heads of thieves and pilferers. For the first offense they chopped off a hand. Their cruelty seems so unbelievable, as does that of the Germans, that it is hard for the human mind to take it in, even though one knows it to be true. However, their drastic measures did stop crime and is something to be considered by those people who maintain that capital punishment is no deterrent. It is no deterrent as long as it is not certain. As long as murderers get off through technicalities, the intimidation of witnesses, or, having been condemned, have their sentences remitted, the death penalty is ineffective. But when retribution is certain it must have an effect, horrible as this is. Where witnesses have been intimidated it might be a good idea to accept purely circumstantial evidence, beginning with the silence of the witness.

We drove past the site of Japanese concentration camps where hundreds of people had been mowed down in cold blood when it became impossible to procure food for them.

We passed several Chinese cemeteries, some very fancy ones with the tombs painted a pale turquoise blue. They are always on hillsides and are built like dugouts, just wide enough for the body to be slid in through the narrow entrance in the masonry, which is then closed by a stone slab that runs through slots.

An interesting feature of the drive was the poles imbedded in the water along the shore—they were some fifteen feet high—on which fishermen sat perched to fish at high tide. They had no supports and no seat. Unfortunately, as it was low tide, none were in use when we went by.

The island of Singapore is joined to the mainland of Malaya by a causeway three quarters of a mile long. At the Johore end there is a section twenty feet long that was blown up when the Japanese attacked, and it did not delay them for more than an hour or two. A demolition of this kind could have been repaired by boy scouts and was completely useless against an efficient modern army. Had the whole causeway been destroyed several days would have been gained, but, even if the Japanese had never been able to reach the island, it would have fallen, since all their water came in a pipe line from the mountains of Johore.

We visited the sultan's mosque, a splendid building magnificently carpeted and hung with chandeliers of Venetian glass and Czechoslovakian crystal. As usual we left our shoes outside. The walls and floors were marble and the whole effect calm, beautiful, and smelled of incense. The floors felt blissfully cool to our tired, tourist-worn feet.

In the gardens there were several groups of sealing-wax palms, the first we had seen. Their slim trunks were patched with scarlet. Terry Chioli said Malay gardeners, when they knock off work in the heat of the day, take their birds out and hang the cages on a branch and lie down to watch them. They say it is relaxing and it seems a charming idea, like that of the Chinese who take their birds to the teahouses when they go there.

Most people in the East, but not everyone, seem to have a caged bird or fish, and plants in pots. The flowerpots everywhere are attractive. Some are expensive colored and decorated ceramics, others are plain red or brown earthenware, but no two are exactly the same shape or size, and all are wider and flatter than those we use. I have the feeling that these are probably the best tranquilizers, that people who have plants watch birds and fish and do not get ulcers. I have another theory, too, after wrestling with a roll of Scotch Tape, that ulcers have become much more common since the invention of cellophane. Whatever you buy is there, visible in your hand, but you can't get at it, so efficiently is it protected.

Coming back, we stopped at the Kranji Cemetery on a hilltop on the Johore Road in Singapore. A great number of soldiers were killed by shellfire here as they lay down to rest, exhausted by the fighting. The graves were symmetrically arranged on the contours. Each had a man's name and above it, carved in the stone, the crest of his regiment. Each, that is, of those who were known. Some were marked, "An Australian soldier known only to God," or where there had been no identification at all, "A soldier of the 39/45 war." Curiously, to me, the graves were planted with South African flowers— Barberton daisies and plumbago.

At the top of the cemetery were walls like the pages of a book, similar to those in the American cemetery in Manila, with names of twenty-four thousand men whose bodies had not been recovered—"soldiers and airmen of many races who died in the service of the crown."

We saw two more short-tailed cats on the trip but no birds. The Chiolis told us that the area in which they live, once inhabited by the British and now taken over by the Chinese, is almost denuded of the trees which shaded all the gardens. The Chinese are great people for conspicuous spending and if they buy a house they want everyone to see it, and no nonsense about shade.

We ended the day with tea at the Dutch Club, a very nice country club a few miles out of town. Coming back to Raffles Hotel, we had gin slings in the big open ballroom. It has a bar at each end and is decorated with a dado of Chinese hats. After a bath we dined in the oak-paneled Elizabethan Grill under a picture of Elizabeth I. They had very fine artificial flowers against the paneled walls and small bowls of orchids and African daisies on the tables. Many of these Barberton daisies were new to me in color, shape, and number of petals, and are apparently varieties produced in Bangkok.

Next day we watched the snake charmers who came to the entrance of the hotel every morning. They had the snakes in small flat wicker baskets like sewing baskets. Their lids were tied down with string.

There was a medium-sized yellowish cobra with its question-mark, omega-like design on the back of its hood. It did nothing except sit up in its basket, its head about a foot from the edge, and extend its hood when the charmer poked it with his finger. It seemed to pay no attention to the pipe—a gourd with a mouthpiece at one end and a kind of flute at the other. Only the Indian cobra has marks on its hood, but all cobras have hoods. The cervical ribs are elongated so that when they open they flatten the neck and expand it into a hood.

He also had a very nice fat little "short brown python." These are thickset pythons that never exceed nine feet in length. It was very happy in my hand and had a blunt nose and blue eyes. The third snake was more spectacular, being black with brilliant canary-yellow markings—half rings that extended to the middle of the back. Despite its appearance the yellow-ringed cat snake or mangrove snake is not poisonous.

When he had done with the snakes the charmer put them back in their baskets, where they curled up comfortably. He then did some simple conjuring tricks, making balls and eggs disappear and picking them out of unexpected places. All old tricks, but interesting in so much as magic and conjuring probably originated in the Orient. There is something fascinating anyway in being tricked by a hand that is quicker than the eye.

This is another art that is being lost with the other ancient vaudeville skills—tumbling, juggling, trapeze work, skills that have been passed on in families from father to son since the Middle Ages. Gone with the ballad singers and dance teams and comedians.

PIGTAILS, ANTS, AND LEECHES

*Twenty-
one*

We were awakened by a phone call at 7:30 A.M. and told that we were sailing at 10:00. It was a good thing we were almost fully packed, as we had not expected to leave till midday. The office where we had to get a pass for the taxi to get onto the dock was very congested. At least two hundred Indians were lined up, so I went to the head office and showed our passports and said as we were sailing in half an hour, could they push us through. Everyone was most helpful.

In the dock area we passed a number of Chinese women with pigtails that reached to the backs of their knees. We had first noticed this very long hair in the female lead in the Cantonese opera in Hong Kong but thought it could not be real. Such hair is evidently a national trait. We got on board about nine forty-five and we actually sailed at ten-thirty, going past a ship filled with Pakistanis bound for Mecca, all camped on the hatches among their packages and bundles under black umbrellas.

And so out through this magnificent harbor with its scattered islands, into the Strait of Malacca, passing more islands anchored like a fleet of ships, each with a fairy, dreamlike quality of its own. But islands have begun to bore us. Like the cathedrals of Europe and temples of Bangkok, the time comes when one has had enough—the last one indistinguishable emotionally from the first. The sea, as it has been ever since we came into the Gulf of Siam, was calm as watered silk.

Tiny did laundry, ironed, and packed again, as we would be going ashore at Port Swettenham next day. We dropped anchor in the roads about midnight and went ashore with the agent in his launch.

There was great congestion in the roads with several dozen ships of all kinds lying at anchor waiting to be discharged or for cargo. Some have been here eight days already with a loss of from $1200 to $1500 a day. It took almost half an hour to get to the wharf, and on the way we were attacked by the largest horsefly I have ever seen. The tide was an extra-low spring tide and we climbed over several small boats that lay almost aground in the thick, glutinous, steel-gray mud to reach the dock. Coming in there was a sharp line that might have been ruled with a ruler, dividing the jade-green water of the estuary from the thick yellow floodwater of the river.

The docks were crowded with hundreds of Indians. Some of the young women were very beautiful. In their saris they were as gay as tropical birds, purple and citron, blue, mauve, and pink, worn over white undershirts and blouses. The clothes disguise the figures of the women, drawing the eye away from them, so that they are lost in the blaze of color that envelops them. The saris themselves are lovely, but as a garment they are not designed to show off the wearer unless they are of very thin and sheer material.

The drive to Kuala Lumpur took about an hour. Our driver was an enormous Sikh, complete with beard and turban, a very handsome man, like all his race. The road runs uphill from the coast, a great deal of it past rubber plantations and oil palms—Lever Brothers. These palms were dwarf, the kind they were hoping to get in the Congo when we were there in '53, as they were finding difficulty in getting men to climb the taller trees. They told us then that there were two palms in the Far East, Java, I think, that were dwarfs but that they thought the Japanese had destroyed them. Evidently they did not do so, or else some seedlings of this dwarf mutation were saved. They do not seem to use palm oil here for cooking or to bleed the crown of the palm for its delicious wine. It is curious how the same crops and trees are used in different parts of the world.

We saw some very dark red erythrinas in flower. We have seen this tree everywhere, from the Cape to the Congo and from Brazil to Thailand. There was a big yellow cassia in full bloom—the last we had seen were on the borders of Lake Kivu, in Central Africa. Numbers of the big trees we drove by were encrusted with orchids. They seem to prefer certain trees and need a rough bark and the protection of heavy foliage to grow at their best.

We passed a big dredge in an open-faced tin mine, sitting like a duck in the small lake it had dug, surrounded with its white muddy sludge. These dredges are similar to those used in the forest marshes of Ghana for gold. Then quite suddenly we came to the city, which on first appearance is as lovely a place as we have seen. We expected to be disillusioned later, but we weren't. Full of big trees with government buildings in the style of oriental palaces, almost Moorish in their arches and cloisters, with lovely corkscrew outside staircases.

The Merlin Hotel is the last word in modern comfort, air-conditioned, with a radio in the room and the decoration a mixture—a delicate blend of the East and the West. (We certainly do not have the last word in hotel design in America or Europe.) Our large room, with big cupboards and a fine bathroom, is partly wood-paneled and part dark bluebell paint. There are two armchairs, two straight chairs, a small table, a bed, side table, a big dressing table and writing desk the whole length of the window, which covers one wall. There are plenty of lights and it could not have been more comfortable. The price is thirty-four dollars a day, which is about eleven dollars U.S., with early-morning tea and laundry (this is a service we had never had before) thrown in.

We had lunch in the Chinese restaurant of the hotel— shark-fin soup and a dish of vegetables. Then after a rest we drove down to see the Sunday Market before dinner. This is the last day of the month-long daytime fast of Ramadzan, and is known as Hari Raya day. This is a world-wide Moslem festival. In Nigeria, Ramadzan is called Ramadan and we saw its proud finale in Bida at a festival there known as Sala. Sartorially this is a kind of Moslem Easter Sunday with everyone parading in their best clothes and having a good time.

We saw men in pink, rather bright-colored, pajamalike jackets with sarongs about their hips that reached to their knees. All wore small round velvet caps called *songkoks*. The women wore short, richly embroidered muslin jackets with pointed ends, and long, very fancy sarongs. The straps of their brassières were visible through the thin material of the *kabayas,* as these jackets are called. The Sunday Market was in Kampong Bahru. It was crowded with people buying food, eating it, and just milling about. We bought some imitation orchids from a stall for three Malay dollars. They were quite beautiful. And we gave silver to the beggars squatting in the road, in the Moslem tradition of charity, and as a reward Allah permitted us to see two wonderful cats, one with a tail that curled upward like a scimitar and the other with a short tail held straight up that ended in a kind of shaving brush. We left in a haze of acrid smoke which made us cough. Later we discovered that these fires were made from coconut shells, which smoke heavily enough to drive the swarming mosquitoes away.

We dined Chinese and had the best creamed corn soup we have ever eaten, followed by Drunken Chicken. This was cold with a sort of wine sauce and not very good in spite of its intriguing name. It tasted rather like calf's foot vinaigrette. We also had vegetables, fried rice and stewed chicken. The dinner cost five dollars U.S. and was beautifully served in a lovely dining room decorated with red Chinese lanterns. Around the wall there was a dado of golden dragons on a red ground. These dragons were most attractive and looked like dachshunds wearing high-heeled shoes. Some had luminous green eyes, some red. I took the red to be males.

After dinner a party of Indians, three men and two girls, one of them quite lovely, asked us to join them and we all had drinks together and watched the floor show for which they had booked a table.

The show consisted of two Danish lady acrobats, again very exotic to the almost exclusively Chinese and Indian audience. As it was Saturday, and a festival day at that, the clothes were lovely. Cheong sams in every color, beautifully worn by slim, proud-looking girls who moved with the grace of queens. Of course it is impossible to slouch in a cheong sam with a three-inch collar. But the carriage and grace and charm of these young ladies are remarkable. So is their behavior. There must have been three hundred people in the room and there was no noisiness. Just a hum of talk. Whole families were together, old and young, all getting along most happily. Most of them were in large parties, because in order to get a balanced meal at least ten people are required. There was a good orchestra, a dance band, and several Chinese lady singers who sang in English with strong deep voices. We met and talked to the manager, Mr. Neil Walsh, for some time about our plans, and he told us about Cuba, where, until recently, he had managed a hotel in Havana. He hopes to go back and seemed optimistic about the future.

The sunset which we watched in the market was wonderful, great piled clouds tipped with gold as a backdrop for the tall coconut palms, with the moon and stars just visible in a sky of the palest indigo. All about us the swifts were screaming as they flew, catching the first insects in the dusk, and people, bright from the shop flares, moved into and out of the smoke of the smudge fires.

Malacca was not to be missed, so, leaving early, we drove there, arriving just in time for lunch and able to go sightseeing in the hottest time of the day. This happens everywhere—it is the fate of the tourist. The drive was chiefly through rubber estates, some so dark that it was black under the closely planted trees with an occasional fleck of bright sunlight spotlighting through the foliage. Plantations have to be dark, as the sunlight, if the trees are too widely spaced, dries out the flow of the rubber. Plantations are called estates here, and the trees, owing to there being no really dry season, are a much prettier green than in Liberia. There are always young leaves on the branches and they do not have the drab, half-dead look of their African counterparts. But the rubber is an uninteresting tree from the naturalist's point of view. Few insects seem to eat the leaves and since there are no bugs there are no birds or other animal life. We passed whole areas of dead trees, big ones thirty or more years old, that had passed their prime and been bled to death, not only to extract the last latex from their blood but presumably to make them fit to burn as firewood. The smell of burning latex would certainly flavor the food cooked over it if any were left in. A lot of trucks laden with chopped-up trees passed us. So did big lumber trucks with enormous forest trees destined for the sawmills along the road. There are quite a lot of panthers about, we were told. They are not called leopards here, and more of them are black than spotted—both colors appearing in the same litter of cubs. There are wild elephants and tigers, too—both protected. While we were at Kuala Lumpur some elephants damaged a group of buildings only six miles out of town. There are few orchids on the rubber trees. They grow too straight and the bark is too smooth for them, though we did see a few in the crotches of trees that branched fairly low. We saw two very large Chinese knob-nosed geese and one monitor lizard about three feet long trying to cross the road. As we approached Malacca, not only did the houses change, becoming more decorative, their roof trees bent like bows, but there were little bullock carts that looked like tiny temples with their sway-backed roofs projecting quite a long way in front of and behind the body of the vehicle.

We entered the town, passing the old Portuguese gate that resembled that of the Spanish fort at Manila. All this early Iberian architecture looks much the same to the ordinary, untrained observer. The old town was rather like Bahia, in Brazil, or Manila. The government buildings were painted a dull red like the fort at Charlotte Amalie in the Virgin Islands. We drove up to see one of the smaller forts—on what seemed to be the only hill—past a big old Chinese cemetery that was much neglected. Some women wore hats as big as umbrellas, but others wore cloths over their heads which, when they wanted to, they turned into sunbonnets of the South African *kappei* type, by inserting a piece of cardboard or similar stiffening under it, like a bridge over the head to shade their eyes. Since the South African sunbonnet differs from all the others I have ever seen it may have originated here.

The fort on the hill reminded us very much of one we saw last year in Tobago. There were these definite styles of mansions and fortifications in the sixteenth and seventeenth centuries, just as there were the later British colonial styles —forts and houses such as those in Nassau, Jamaica, or Cape Town. The monoliths we build today, from New York to Singapore and São Paulo to Durban, looking like narrow boxes set on end, appear to express our love of the purely functional.

The older part of Malacca, the Chinese part, was wonderful—squalid, colorful, perfumed as usual with every odor from frangipani, joss sticks, curry, and cinnamon to rotting fish, dead dogs, and urine. The streets were arcades, therefore shaded, with the shops extending beyond their fronts into the pavement. Between the pillars there were great roller shades of every kind. The pillars decorated with slogans in Chinese letters that always look like lace.

We lunched adequately at the Rest House, an old house of great character overlooking a wide lawn and an avenue of royal palms leading to the sea, which lay spread like a blue cloth beyond the green cloth of the lawn. Some mynah birds pecked at the grass and we made friends with a very nice orange long-tailed cat who ate most of the fish we had ordered for lunch. There were some fine shade trees in the town —the big Eastern almonds being the only ones we recognized.

The Malayan flag of red and white stripes, like ours, with a blue corner ornamented with a yellow crescent and a yellow star, fluttered on the staff in front of us. The riders of the pedicabs or tricabs all wore khaki topees and looked very pukka sahibish and dignified as they pedaled along.

Few white people live here now, or indeed in Malaya at all, except in such places as Singapore, Kuala Lumpur, and Penang, where a residue of business people remained stranded on the sands of the empire when the sea of Britain's power went out in the most tremendous historic neap the world has seen since the fall of Rome.

At the entrance of the guesthouse and on the veranda were the usual curio vendors, squatting on their heels, endlessly patient, waiting like fishermen beside a stream, for a tourist fish to bite. We bought some beads for some children in Africa and looked at the Malacca sticks, which were not of good quality, having a hardly perceptible central vein. Malacca is a rotan or rattan—a cane—and the sticks consist of single internodes, or lengths between one leaf and the next. To get them long enough to make a stick, they have to come from the high, end parts of the cane and they are rare enough to make them expensive.

On the way back we passed a hot spring I had not noticed and we saw that much of the rubber was planted on contours in the hilly country. We saw lots of cattle. They were small and humped, rather like those of the Masai in Kenya. Later we did see one clump of buffalo standing by some tall bamboos. They always look like game and are more interesting to watch than domestic cattle.

Some interesting events now occurred. The first was a lunch with Mr. Lim, his wife, and little boy Willie, at the Coq d'Or, a club-*cum*-restaurant that he owns in the converted mansion of a Chinese millionaire. It has everything— wide, marble-floored verandas, sentimental marble statues of partially draped young ladies, Victorian pictures, chandeliers, carpets, old French furniture, ancient bathrooms with bidets—the works in fact, and an atmosphere to correspond.

Lunch was an experience. It began with fried shrimp with a special sauce accompanied by a tempting salad. Then came crisp ravioli, an invention of Mr. Lim's, made of half wheat and half rice flour, wafer thin, fried in deep fat. Then came strips of chicken, marinated in wine, bread-crumbed, and fried in butter over which liqueur brandy was poured and ignited. A wonderful dish that I named Chicken Suzette. The chicken was followed by a sweet—mixed fruit salad served with ice cream flavored with maraschino, over which another flaming sauce was poured. We drank a wonderful German wine and ended the meal with coffee and *crème de menthe*.

After lunch Tiny, who is quite a serious palmist, read everyone's palm to their satisfaction. Then we met Mr. Lim's second cook, who had had a remarkable experience. Two days before he had seen a snake in his garden and just as he was about to kill it it turned into a white butterfly and flew away. This event was witnessed by the cook's wife and her father. I said I thought it was a good omen. If a butterfly turned into a snake it would be bad, but snake into butterfly obviously was good. Mr. Lim also agreed it was good and that white was a particularly good color, as it is the color of silver and therefore means money. We now all went with the second cook to consult a soothsayer, a kind of unorthodox Buddhist priest who had a little temple of his own on the outskirts of town. It had been previously arranged anyway that he should tell our fortunes. His method was remarkable. He told it entirely by the face and by just looking at a person. But first we went into a small, hot room, partially cooled by fans, and talked Buddhist philosophy for two hours with Mr. Lim translating.

There are, it appears, five kinds of people—earth, air, fire, water, and wood people. These people get on or do not get on according to their natures. Fire and wood do not get on. The wood gets burned. Fire and water do not get on. The fire is put out by the water. Water and earth get on, wood and earth get on, and so do wood and water if there is not too much water. The whole discussion was a wonderful mixture of platitudes and wisdom. The priest, I call him that, was obviously a good man. About forty, emaciated, stripped to the waist, he exuded virtue and kindness. We drank beer and smoked cigarettes, the priest included.

Then finally he began on me and was in many instances amazingly correct. He knew I was a writer and well known—known, he said, to the world and beyond my village. He said I wanted to be a painter and that I could have been successful but had left it until too late. There was not enough time left and if I pushed it I might succeed but it would kill me. I might also fall between two stools. He said when I was sixty-seven (or sixty-six really, since the Chinese count a child's age from the time of conception) I should come to a gate and might die of a fall. I like the idea of a gate, a period when one is in danger of death. I have been through a number already.

Then we discussed the snake incident and he agreed that it was a good omen. The explanation to me is, of course, that the cook took his eye from the snake for a moment and when he looked again there was the butterfly on the grass. That is the Western approach, because we demand logical explanations for everything. The Chinese take snakes very seriously, as they regard them as a kind of dragon, and I like the other version much better. There may not be fairies and angels and dragons and devils all around us, but it makes life much more interesting to half believe in these things.

The afternoon ended with much shaking of hands and

good will all around and Mr. Lim drove us back into the modern, chromium-plated world of the Merlin Hotel.

Our next adventure was with Dr. and Mrs. Duguid, the government pathologist who took us into the jungle. We drove about ten miles and stopped at a ruined house whose walls were adorned with Eastern graffiti, very like our own except that the ladies had almond-shaped eyes and no body hair. Infuriated house swifts—infuriated at being disturbed—swept over our heads darting in and out through the empty windows. Leading from the house downhill was a small, overgrown path which we took somewhat hesitantly because of the possibility of stepping on a snake.

There were no snakes but there were ants—large red ants—the most savage I have ever encountered. Their bite was so sharp that it made one jump, almost sick with pain. They hung on like bulldogs and had to be killed individually. When squashed between the fingers the heads stayed put and had to be pulled off. From the point of view of natural history these red ants, or *kerenggas,* are most interesting. They make their nests by joining the leaves of a tree together with silken strands and savagely attack anyone who brushes against it. They have no sting but bite with their jaws and eject an acrid burning fluid over the wound. The ants have no means of producing silk, but their larvae have such a provision; no doubt it once enabled them to spin cocoons when they pupated. The ants make use of this infant talent, and when a new leaf requires to be joined to the nest or a rent repaired some workers hold the edges together while others fetch out some larvae from the nest and pass them to and fro from one to the other like the shuttle of a loom until a web is spun across the space. Not that we appreciated any of this at the time. We only found it out later when we made some inquiries about these beasts. Tiny does not share my entomological interests and failed to understand that these ants were only acting in self-defense when we barged into their home.

The next thing of interest we encountered was a large, very graceful, green, long-horned grasshopper sitting under a big leaf about two feet from the ground. These grasshoppers are predatory and live on other insects.

The path now went down steeply and we could hear the rush of water from an abandoned weir. A few yards ahead of us I heard a rustle and saw a quite large fern move violently as a big reticulated python moved out of our way. I just caught a glimpse of its tail. The situation, as we discovered a few minutes later, was ideal for a python. There was this old path, little more than a track now, but certainly one that animals, deer and so on, used to get to the water. There was the water, a deep pool ideal for the snake to bathe in, and a flat abutment of stone on which it could sun-bathe.

This was where we had intended to have our lunch—beside the waterfall—but the heat was so intense that after sitting there a while we gave it up. Tiny, who never sweats, had big drops like tears running down from her eyes and I was soaked, my shirt black with moisture. This made us think of the hardships of the war when women and children trekked for days through the jungle to escape the Japanese. It also made us think of "Elephant Bill" and realize the importance of having elephants to break down the bush and make a path.

Sitting by the water, we pulled off the leeches that we had picked up in this short, quarter-mile walk, in spite of tucking our trousers into our socks. The doctor had two bites. The leeches, satiated, had dropped off, but he continued to bleed. I had none, nor did Mrs. Duguid. Tiny had two but spotted them and pulled them off before they bit her. These leeches are one of the curses of the jungle. The leech is an elongated, active, dark-colored creature with a sucker at each end of the body by means of which it progresses by rapid looping movements. They are able to anticipate their victim's arrival, probably by vibrations, and rush to meet it. Their bodies are elastic and can be stretched like a bootlace or contract to a small blob. They are too tough to be pinched to death between the fingers. Burning with a match or cigarette end is about the only thing that will make them let go. The bite is inflicted with minute sharp teeth of the anterior sucker, and they inject, with their bite, saliva containing an anti-coagulant, which is why, even after the leech has fallen off or been removed, the blood continues to flow. There is an even worse leech, a much bigger one, known as the buffalo leech, that will attack anyone wading in the water and will even climb into boats. Of all the animal kingdom leeches seem to me the most revolting. This was, however, a most successful afternoon, as, while sitting below the waterfall, we saw at least six gigantic Rajah Brooke's Birdwing butter-flies. They are black, beautifully marked with brilliant green, and larger than a sparrow.

This butterfly was first discovered in Borneo but is found in several other places where there is primary jungle. The ones we saw were all males, the sex ratio being estimated at a thousand males to one female.

A plant of interest, growing near the road before we turned off, was the sensitive plant, a low-growing, thorny ground cover with small flowers like little mauve shaving brushes. The leaves are strung along a central rib and collapse when touched. This plant seemed to be identical with one we saw in a botanical garden in the Congo. I had an idea it was wild there too but am uncertain about it now.

Opposite, across the water about twenty yards away, there was a tiny spit of flat, pebble-covered land. Here dozens of yellow butterflies were congregated. It was the only place where the jungle shelved down to the water and must have been a drinking place for the animals of the forest and con-sequently soaked in urine, which, curiously enough, is most attractive to the butterflies—the prettiest of insects. The bait for most butterflies and moths is always of a somewhat re-volting nature—rotting papaya, banana, or pineapples, even rotting meat or fish. Tiger and leopard dung is said to be the best of all, but its collection presents certain difficulties.

At last having decided that nothing more was to be gained

at the weir, we went back to the car, getting bitten again by ants on the way, and drove on through really beautiful liana-hung and orchid-decorated jungle, past forest dells filled with the most beautiful tree ferns, to the top of a hill known as the Gap, where, at a small Chinese restaurant that was a bus stop, we ate our sandwiches and had two bottles of warm beer, the last two bottles in the establishment.

It was curious to remember that the last tree ferns we had seen were not in Natal or the Congo but at Kells in County Kerry in Ireland. These in Malaya were no finer.

There was a vendor of some kind of spinach at the diner who was making string, with the aid of an old woman, to tie up the bundles, which she first wrapped in a big leaf. The process was interesting, the raw product being the sheath of a large palm, that is to say the outer covering of the young central shoot. This was split down into strips about an inch wide. The strips were then turned sideways and split into thin sheets like ribbons. These again were torn into the string-like fibers that the girl used for her parcels.

As we went through the jungle we passed areas where the cicadas were making so much noise one could hardly hear oneself speak. The cicada is an attractive insect and almost impossible to see or to catch. The only ones I have ever caught came onto the ship at night when we were going up the Congo. They were an inch or so long, a pretty *eau-de-Nil* green, and had round blunt faces rather like a bulldog's. There is one here that I think we may have heard in Thailand called the empress cicada, which has a wingspread of eight inches. Cicadas do not sing by rubbing one surface against another, like most insects, such as crickets. They have membranes within a cavity of their bodies that acts like a sound box.

There were two dogs at the little restaurant, neither of which appeared ever to have been fed, since we had a lot of trouble persuading them to eat chicken sandwiches. They were probably unused to anything except garbage. One was a crossbred Irish terrier. We have seen several dogs with

Irish-terrier blood and that may indicate that of all Western dogs they are the toughest and best able to survive. We saw another interesting cat. We have now found out a great deal about cats, thanks to Mrs. Christian Olsen. She said she has never seen a tailless cat such as we saw in a Japanese print, but that there are more short-tailed than long-tailed cats, and they come in many odd shapes and are known as bobtails, pug's tails, pig's tails, pothook tails, and lightning tails. Short-tailed cats are higher in the rump than at the shoulder and sudden and jerky in their movements. They are very active and quick, jumping incredible heights to catch bats and birds on the wing. These are all Manx characteristics. There are many cats very like Abyssinians, long, lean, long-tailed, the color of a wild rabbit with ticked hairs. They have cream or almost apricot bellies and yellow-green eyes. They were probably brought to the East by Arab traders on their dhows. There are white cats with colored tails and ears, as if the Siamese pattern had been transposed to other colors, and self-colored cats with striped legs. Everything she said, and she judges cats at shows here, confirmed our opinion about the cats here being the most interesting and beautiful in the world.

We now went for a long walk up the drive of a tea estate, like "mad dogs and Englishmen" in the midday sun. We saw some wild hibiscus, which is the national flower of Malaya, and a wild poinsettia with a single white large bract which we had seen in the forest before, and which was exactly like one we found in Ghana some years ago. I picked a couple of ground-growing orchids, saw groups of a splendid bamboo I had never seen before with large pendulous leaves. We passed several erythrinas in flower. Two, some distance away, had orange flowers, so they may not have been erythrinas. We saw a lot of butterflies, many of them remarkably like those of Europe, chalk blues and orange tips, and one beauty —a big rich dark blue one, the color of the queen's cloak in the Annigoni portrait, that I think was a "dark blue jungle glory." Looking at the plates of a Malayan butterfly book,

I have found insects that are almost exactly like the chalk blues, red admirals, peacocks, and tortoise-shells we know in Europe. These similarities of plants and animals intrigue me.

At the end of the twisting drive we came to a house set on a hill with a magnificent, though neglected, garden in a dell at its foot. A garden with a waterfall and a bathing pool, old trees, a pagodalike summer house, and lovely flowering shrubs: bougainvillaea, poinsettia, acalyphas, and numerous crotons, one of them with large flesh-pink leaves. Nothing could have been more beautiful or romantic. Only the nymphs were missing, slim Chinese nymphs. But I am sure they had once been here, for the place still echoed with the sweet notes of Pan's pipe.

The waterfall was a gentle one that rippled like laughter over the rocks as it tumbled into the bathing pool the size of a double bed cut into living stone.

There are two abominations, to my mind, in a garden—a tennis court and a swimming pool. Both belong in clubs. A bathing pool is something else. It is not practical. You can get no exercise in it. It is simply something beautiful and a place to get cool in on a hot day.

So ended our last day in K.L., as they call Kuala Lumpur, the capital city of Malaya. What a wonderful day it had been.

One thing remained to be done. We had to find a home for our white clock. We had been going to wrap it up in a flag and bury it at sea. But Tiny couldn't stand it. She could not even throw an empty chocolate box overboard because it was so irrevocable. So after some argument we had decided to give it to a Chinese who no doubt would find some means of repairing it or using its inward parts. And this was the place and now was the time. Malaya. We would give it away when we got to Penang. In the meantime we got it out to say good-by to, in our animistic fashion.

"Good-by, little clock, good-by," Tiny sang to the Western tune of "Old Paint," as I dug it out of the luggage.

"My God," I said, "it's going!"

And it's gone ever since, so we now have a "his" clock and a "hers" clock. The little white one never stops now, but it is not reliable, so we don't really trust it. But it gives us a good idea of the time. We always know about what time it is within an hour or so, and can check with the other clock if it's important.

THE CAVE TEMPLES
OF IPOH

GECKOS—FRESH EGGS FOR BREAKFAST—A TROPICAL
STORM—BUFFALO AND WHITE LOTUS—TWO POR-
TUGUESE HENS—LIMESTONE HILLS—THE CAVE
TEMPLES—A SMILING BUDDHA—PRICKLY HEAT
AND ITS CURE—AN AIR-CONDITIONED COLD—PE-
NANG—THE KHOOS QUARTER—MONKEYS IN THE
BOTANICAL GARDEN—STEAMED PEANUTS—CASHEW
NUTS — SEA SNAKES — COCONUT MILK — NUTMEGS
AND MACE—THE SNAKE TEMPLE—THE CABLE
RAILWAYS—PITCHER PLANTS AND FERNS—HUN-
DREDS OF TURTLES—A TAXI DRIVER'S COMPLAINT
—A CHINESE WEDDING—GODS AND DEVILS—BLAN-
KETS ARE COOL—RATTANS—KAPOK—BANANAS AND
ORCHIDS

Twenty-two

Our room looked out over the mountains that we had
explored with the doctor and his wife. "Explore" is a lovely
word. We had just touched the fringes of this great green
mantle of jungle that covers so much of Malaya and, in those
few yards, had discovered swifts, ants, grasshoppers, pythons, and butterflies galore. Twice in a week there had been
articles in the paper about an equatorial version of the
Abominable Snowman called the Ourang Jarang Gigi by the
aborigines. They are described as shaggy creatures, ten feet
tall. A game warden has obtained leave to go and hunt one.

This news did not surprise us. There may be other wild
things there, other mysteries, in forest that is so thick that
it is an element like air or water. It is no use thinking of the

jungle as trees or a mixture of trees, lianas, ferns, and shrubs. It is a live thing, a virgin thing filled with hatred for those who do not belong to it.

This would be our last night here and we wondered about the fate of our roommates, two house geckos, or chichaks, as they are called, or rather one chichack and one tokay, a bigger, rarer, and noisier kind of gecko. We had seen geckos all over Central Africa and enjoyed watching them catch the insects attracted to the lights. During the day we hardly saw them, but at night they came out from behind the lamp fixtures like tiny, transparent dinosaurs, and attacked anything in reach, even moths twice their own size. We once saw one fall from the ceiling with a big moth in his mouth and continue his battle with it on the floor. I used to think geckos had suckers on their toes like tree toads, but later found that their toes are divided into layers of little flaps of extendable skin that are covered with small hairs. It is the clinging action of these hairs that enables them to run upside down on even smooth surfaces.

Geckos, with rats, mice, and some insects and birds, belong to the small group of animals who find life easier with man, and live in association with him more easily than they did before his arrival. I never heard African geckos make a sound, but these Eastern cousins were so noisy that they woke me up. The tokay in particular. He began with a cackle that sounded like a bird. I woke up thinking, "The birds here start before dawn." Then, before I could carry this thought any further, he began to bark—tok-kaa tok-kaa—quite loudly, though not loudly enough to wake Tiny. Even lions roaring don't do that and, by the time I had her up and told her to listen to this remarkable sound, he had stopped. Her protests may have frightened him.

THURSDAY, THE TWENTY-THIRD. KUALA LUMPUR

After a breakfast of two very nice fresh soft-boiled eggs— fresh eggs when one has been at sea for some months assume a new significance—I paid my bill and said good-by to everyone. The bill was 461 Malay dollars, plus 10 per cent for tips. This included postage, quite a few things at the drugstore, and sixty dollars' worth of books on which I paid the 10 per cent for tips, not realizing it till afterward. However, the service had been so good that we did not mind. We had eaten everything we wanted and had quite a few drinks, bought cigarettes, and had wine with every meal. We had made some nice friends, seen some wonderful sights, and been altogether very happy, satisfied, and sorry to leave.

We had contracted for a taxi, a good new Mercedes, to take us to Penang for seventy-five dollars Malay, and left at 9 A.M. There had been a big storm the evening before, unbelievably dramatic, the mountains hidden by navy-blue clouds, the branches of the trees outside our window writhing like the tentacles of a green octopus, and the tall palms whipping down before the gusts and springing back into position again. The squalls of a tropical storm come in drumbeats, striking first one thing, then another. A tattoo on the roof is followed by a blow that bends the trees double and whips the long fronds of the palms over their heads as if they were skirts. Then, striking a new note, the wind lashes out at a wall with the fist of its rain. There is a madness about it all, an irregularity that makes it hard to face. The darkening sky was riven with vertical jags of lightning and the rain came down in buckets. We were afraid there might be some wash-aways on the road, as the morning paper reported serious damage at Klang, to the south, but we were going north and all the rain had done was to wash everything clean and leave the trees looking beautiful and fresh. We drove out of town on the Ipoh Road, one that we had not been on before, that was quite lovely, with immense old rain trees mossy with orchid plants. We saw orchids, the tall mauve kind, growing in many gardens and one yellow-brown spotted spider variety with a similar habit of growth. Leaving the town, we went through the forest reserve, untouched, primeval, and at once both grand and terrifying. The road was good all the way, but eight hours of it were tiring because it hardly ever ran more than a few hundred yards without a turn, as it writhed like a snake through the lush country. To begin with, it was mostly rubber estates planted with trees of all ages, from young clones a few feet high to old trees that had about finished their useful lives. There were a few plantations of dwarf oil palm and the usual other crops— tapioca, bananas, and a few patches of taro or koko yam.

Then the character of the land and cultivation changed and we came to rice paddies where buffalo were being herded. This was a different type of animal with short blunt horns. We also passed a large pond filled with white lotus, the first we had seen, and then came the ugliness of the dredged strip-mining tin mines, great floating factories scooping out their own ponds amid the untidy scars of sludge and destruction that accompanies any mining operation. The only thing that can be said for them is that eventually, as an area is worked out, small lakes heal the scars and attractive sheets of water are left to commemorate their passing.

There was quite a lot of traffic on the road—cars, busses, trucks loaded with great logs destined for the sawmills along the road, motorcycles, bicycles, and a scattering of bullock carts, drawn by pairs of white, pale gray or buff Jersey-colored beasts with beautiful mild eyes and long sad faces. Some of these bullocks—though only the white ones—had one horn painted red and one green. One had a yellow horn and a green one. The significance of this decoration remains obscure. We saw no wild life, no birds or reptiles. We did, however, see one mongrel dog wearing a red tag, showing that he had been inoculated for rabies, and two more short-tailed cats, both as usual higher at the loins than shoulder, like all Manx cats. We also saw two hens with bare necks, a certain sign of Portuguese occupation and influence wherever it is seen.

We now came to some very curious limestone hills rising sheer out of the plain and covered with very heavy bush. It is in these hills that the Cave Temples have been carved, with stairs and rooms and balconies all cut out of the living rock. These very steep limestone hills are a dominant feature of the landscape in some parts of Malaya and their forest covering that is like a thick green fur is quite different from that of the lowland jungles. Beneath the hills, when they are undercut, there are stalactites and stalagmites, adding to the peculiarity of the formation.

There was a big fat smiling Buddha in one temple chamber and a dozen smaller gold Buddhas in recessed niches. The whole effect was most impressive and reminded us of the pictures we had seen of Lhasa and Thibet on a much smaller scale. There was a pond full of terrapin that we fed, and a rather shaggy garden between the cliffs and the road. We had lunch at the Eastern Hotel in Ipoh, a rather sad place, staffed by depressed Chinese—the first uncheerful Chinese we have seen. But this town appears to be a center for the Malay gangsters. Two men were killed here the following week and no doubt our depressed Chinese were paying protection and had plenty to be depressed about.

After lunch we drove on and arrived at Butterworth at about five-thirty, crossed to the island of Penang in the ferry, and reached the Eastern & Oriental Hotel soon after six, pretty well exhausted by the sight-seeing in the heat and the twisting drive.

At eight Terry Chioli called. He had just flown in from Singapore and was returning at once. He told us he had some of Dr. Whitfield's ointment for my prickly heat and was sending it down to the hotel. I don't know what I would have done without it, as I was going crazy with irritation. This was the only thing either of us was troubled with on the whole trip.

We had a fine room overlooking the sea and after a bath, an application of ointment, and a drink I felt much better.

We had a good dinner in the air-conditioned grill, where I caught an air-conditioned cold. The sunset was beautiful and from our room, facing due north, we could see both the sunrise and the sunset.

Tiny woke me at dawn to see a junk in full sail quite close by, outlined in silhouette against the rosy sky. I suppose this would annoy some people, but we always wake each other if there is anything to see.

There were three quite big guns dated 1797 and one culverin on the lawn in the garden below us pointing out to the sea, which came right up to lap the garden wall twenty yards from the hotel.

The lobby was very big, with a vast domed ceiling. Plants and palms in pots stood grouped about on the floor between the tables, and there were the usual offices—reception desk, tourist desk, post office, book and gift shops and bar, all strategically arranged for the exhausted tourist.

In the evening the house swifts screamed in the dusk and bats, a dozen at least, fluttered through the sky.

MARCH 24

The first thing we did today was to find out where the nearest Federal Dispensary was and go there to get some more of Dr. Whitfield's prescription for prickly heat made up, as I did not want to be without a reserve in case I ran out in the Red Sea. We found they had it all made up and I bought two bottles, being attended in the drug department— the Federal is a kind of supermarket—by a beautiful young woman, tall and shapely, with enormous almond eyes. It is very satisfactory to be married and middle-aged when in the Orient, and to be satisfied to look at lovely girls, the way one looks at flowers and birds.

Coming back to the hotel, we stopped to talk to a West African parrot hanging in front of a tailor's shop. The young man who owned it asked us in to see his other birds. They belonged to his father. There was a Malayan dove, a small dove with a guinea-fowl-like black and white spotted patch on the neck; this is the "expensive bird" we had seen hanging in cages from tall bamboos in Bangkok. Besides a green Mexican parrot, and two very handsome mynah birds from Java that were as big as small hens, he had two tanks of tropical fish—and a big Siamese cat. This was a young man after our own hearts.

At eleven we began a six-hour tour around the island. We drove past the old Cornwallis fort, Chinatown, and through a milling mob of ten thousand Indians, who were seeing relatives and friends off on a hadji ship bound for Mecca.

We went to the family temple of the Khoo family first. This was the shrine of all Khoos, rich or poor, in Penang. It was lost in the depths of a series of blocks, some of which we should call slums, inhabited only by Khoos or relations of Khoos, one of whom, the guardian, unlocked the golden gate and took us in.

The temple veranda was guarded by two painted stone sepoys with muskets. The whole place was heavily carved, decorated, and brilliant with gold leaf. The pillars were surrounded by carved bas-relief dragons. The doors were guarded by stone lions that looked like giant Pekinese dogs. One had a cub at her feet to indicate her sex. All dragons are differentiated, the males being much larger and more noble-looking. Overhead, from the gold and Chinese red beams, enormous paper lanterns swayed at the ends of their cords, some of red paper, others with painted glass sides and silken tassels. The walls of the veranda were carved and painted in the traditional manner. Inside there was more gold, gold leaf, red paint, frescoes, statues, and big vases filled with sand containing the stubs of burned-out joss sticks. The atmosphere was in no way tawdry. One felt that here, as in the cathedrals built in the Middle Ages, people had done their best to glorify their gods.

There was a magnificent lantern here made of dark wood

with mother-of-pearl designs that were lit by electricity and through which the light shone. At the back of the temple was a long room evidently used for feasts and ceremonies, the walls of which were covered with large religious frescoes. In the temple there were, apart from the altar, three ceramic statues representing the three qualities needed for complete happiness—health, wealth, and many children. Outside, in the balustrade were two carved monks, one with his mouth turned down because he had received no alms, and the other smiling because he had. This struck us as a strong hint. In one anteroom there were golden plaques commemorating famous Khoos—judges, barristers, and so on. On the other side of the courtyard, facing the temple, was a small theatrical stage where the family could watch plays. The whole impression was one of clan solidarity and ancestor worship, an ancient cult preserved in the aspic of tradition and guarded from progress by its situation in this old quarter of the town.

We now drove through a beautiful residential area where the houses stood isolated in big compounds amid lawns and flowering shrubs. The road was cool, shaded by great rain trees that linked branches like hands overhead. A quiet suburban haven for the rich. It was difficult to believe that Chinatown, where people were swarming like bees, was only a few miles away.

From here we went uphill to the Guillemard reservoir, one of the many that supply Penang with water. It was surrounded by a beautifully kept lawn, trees, and flowering shrubs. Everything was whitewashed, pruned, clipped, and neat enough for a general's inspection. We have seen nothing to equal it anywhere.

At the botanical garden entrance we bought steamed peanuts for the monkeys, which are said to be dangerous, but seemed very quiet, almost timid, and took food from the hand. There were several mothers with babies under their bellies that were shy and the young monkeys had a tendency to snatch, scream, and fight each other. But an old male with a crippled foreleg was very quiet and responsible. He took nuts in a very restrained and respectable manner without snatching. All monkeys seem very serious to me, much less humorous than either dogs or cats. They always act worried, as if surprised to be what they are—upset at having dreams and projects that they are unable to carry out. Near the top of the mammalian tree, they seem to feel underprivileged and have a chip on their shoulder. These are the same species of monkey that we saw in Hong Kong, and they have a kind of flat-faced oriental look. They are long-tailed macaques, known here as *keras*.

A curious thing about the steamed peanuts is that their shells change color, becoming almost a canary-*cum*-ocher yellow. We were told it takes four hours to cook them. The other steamed nuts we have seen, sold still attached to the bunch, in Hong Kong and elsewhere, did not change color and may not have been cooked for so long. They are very nice to eat and I ate almost as many as I gave to the monkeys. We did not walk too far, as it was very hot and we had so much to do, but we did see a very fine pink cassia in full bloom and a yellow laburnum dripping gold—this is also a cassia (fistula) and it was interesting to see this English suburban favorite in its native land.

We now turned toward the sea and went up to a small hotel on a hill where we had a cool drink and watched some children swimming in the pool. I got a chance here to look at the tall, common mauve orchids that are grown as hedges in some of the gardens. This is the vanda, Miss Joaquim, commonest and most easily grown orchid, much employed as cut flowers. Also in ceramic pots, around the pool, were the lovely pink-flowered small succulent bushes we had first seen at the Raffles Hotel garden, but better developed and full of flowers, resembling somewhat the Star of Sabi that we found in Portuguese East Africa north of the Limpopo River.

At the bottom of the hill our driver picked us some cashew

nuts. These look like large brown beans and are attached to the bottom of a long yellow fleshy fruit about the size and shape of a chili. The nuts must be roasted before they can be eaten and are not, as far as I can make out, the commercial cashew nut, which grows on a thick-foliaged tree that looks rather like a mango. The fleshy fruit was very refreshing and juicy. It had a sweet and at the same time acid taste. We saw these nuts in Trinidad and were told there that the flesh was poisonous. The different approaches to various vegetables and fruits in different parts of the world are fascinating. In the Congo the leaves of tapioca plants, there called manioc, are eaten as greens and fed to talapia in the fishponds. Here it is never eaten. The best example of this nature is the ordinary tomato, which until a hundred years ago was thought to be poisonous.

We now went along the sea road and passed a lovely little beach where there were some big rounded rocks standing out of the water. An ideal bathing spot, but abandoned now because this is where there had been at least one fatal accident with sea snakes.

The common sea snake is about three or four feet long when full grown. It bears its young alive and lives on fish. Its bite appears to be fatal, causing death in under fifteen minutes. There is a large sea snake in these waters that is very rare but may have given rise to some sea monster stories. It grows to a length of nine feet, is as thick as a man's thigh, and covered with bands of black and orange. It must be a fine sight.

We had an excellent lunch on a lawn under palm trees facing the sea at the Lone Pine Hotel at Batu Ferringhi. This would be a nice place to stay, and it reminded us very much of the West Indies—the way they used to be.

We drove through a fishing village and saw a big flat fish—three feet both ways—a pink skate or a ray. They have sting rays here as they do in the West Indies, and also the giant ray, or manta, a surface-feeding variety that may span twenty feet from edge to edge.

This village was purely Malay. Everyone seemed very happy and relaxed. No one tried to sell us anything. There is a great difference in temperament between the Chinese and Malay fisherman. The Malay lives his life for what it is. He lives as an artist. A Chinese lives for what he can make.

We came to a small coconut plantation with attap-roofed houses on stilts and bought a half-dozen coconuts for a dollar. One of the men climbed a tall palm by tying his ankles together and then, putting both hands around the trunk and arching his back, he went up in a series of leg and arm movements—a succession of loops like a caterpillar. Reaching the top, he slashed the nuts, which fell with a terrific thud. Cutting away fronds that were in his way, he harvested all that were ripe. Then, coming down, he slashed and opened them for us to drink in glasses that his wife brought from the house. The fluid was excellent, not as sweet as it is sometimes, but cool from its natural insulation of shell and fiber, and was almost aerated or carbonated, fizzing a little in the mouth. Many old Malays do not know their age but, if asked, will point to a palm that their fathers planted when they were born and say, "That is how old I am." By every house there was a heap of husks that each evening were lighted. Slow-burning, they smolder, making a smudge of smoke to deter the mosquitoes. In almost every village there was a Moslem cemetery, a series of low stone phallus-like markers, some of which were painted blue. They were not very well kept.

We passed a small native rubber factory where the rubber sheets almost the size of towels and, like towels, flattened by the rollers of a rubber mangle, were hung out to dry. I imagine it is smoked here as it is in West Africa, as it is organic matter and goes bad if not preserved. It looks rather like tripe in this stage, and a rubber factory smells like a tannery.

This was where we saw the only bird of interest on the trip—a white-breasted kingfisher that flew over the road in a dazzling flash of blue.

On the drive we saw some interesting fruits that the driver pointed out and explained to us. First there had been the cashew, then came a betel-nut palm, a small single-stemmed palm from which the fruit hung in bunches; the oil palm that we knew from the Congo, the big-leaved teaks, jack fruit in fruit (very large green globular fruits resembling a coarse warty papaya in form), breadfruit trees that brought Captain Bligh and the *Bounty* to mind. He took the seedlings from the East to the West Indies to supplement the diet of the slaves on the plantations. Lemon grass that is sometimes used in curries and to flavor puddings and is, I think, the basis of citronella. The driver picked us some wild nutmegs. They come out of a nutlike shell that looks rather like an apricot. When opened the pip is black, wrapped about in an artistic and eccentric fashion by crimson-lake membrane. This membrane is a sort of pulp that develops around the fruit as it grows and is called an aril. Birds see the bright red pulp, which they like to eat, and in so doing scatter the seed. This pulp is mace, itself a spice. And the outer covering of the nut can be preserved, sliced, and made into a sweet. There were no ripe cloves, but we picked some leaves; they had a delightful fragrance when crushed.

We are very fortunate in being interested in animals and crops, trees and flowers and, as we have traveled so much, it is fascinating to remember where we have seen them or a near relative before.

Seeing people chew betel nut is something of a shock at first. They look as if they had been beaten up, their mouths and lips dripping with dark bruised blood.

Some domestic plants and animals have been carried along by people as they migrated or have been carried by birds. Many wild species have traveled tremendous distances in floods and storms. There are enthralling mysteries here, botanical and zoological "whodunits" that still remain to be solved.

This road wound about through the forest like a demented eel. The road we had thought so twisting between Kuala

Lumpur and Penang was straight as a bamboo by comparison. During the day we had made a complete tour of the
island and reached the Snake Temple on the way home. This
was the thing we most wanted to see in Penang. The temple
itself was very ordinary, with a grubby approach past the
vendors' stalls of Sungei Kulang village. Nor was it much
better inside. No gold, no scarlet, but on branches set in two
big vases there were dozens of snakes asleep. And that was
only the beginning. As one's eyes became accustomed to the
gloom and one's nostrils to perfume of the burning joss sticks,
more and more snakes became visible. Some were asleep on
the tops of picture frames, a head stuck out over one rafter,
a tail hung down from another. There must have been a
hundred snakes distributed over this central chamber of the
temple. In an alcove we were shown a small pagoda that was
used as a maternity ward for their pregnant charges by the
priests. These snakes, Wagler's pit vipers, are viviparous—
live bearing—and the young are a beautiful pale green with
tiny white spots along their sides. I handled one no longer
than a worm that curled around my fingers and held on to
them as if they were branches. The adults are far from pretty,
being a dull greenish black, speckled and barred with dirty
yellow. They are called pit vipers because of a deep pit on
each side of the head between the eye and the nostril that
is a thermosensitive organ which enables the snake to find its
warm-blooded prey in complete darkness. In the temple they
give them eggs to eat, which they are said to perforate and
suck. This seems unlikely and they probably live on the rats
and mice that come into the temple at night or even on each
other, and no doubt the priests eat the eggs the peasants
bring. In the compound there is a strong wire enclosure containing a big python. There was a dead chicken in the cage.
Whether it had been put in dead or had been killed by the
python and left I could not discover. I always thought they
would eat only live food.

We now went up Penang Hill by the cable railway, an
exciting experience, as the slope is very steep—up to a height

of 2070 feet through jungly forest, broken here and there by small farms and summer villas, to the hotel at the top where we had tea. The view is magnificent—Georgetown roofs a splash of color among the greens of the trees that surround it. The ships lie like cigars in the roads. The islands offshore look like Japanese prints in the dull mirror of the sea. The largest one had been a leper colony, till the Japanese, during the occupation, mowed them down with machine guns, thus solving the problem of feeding them. It is now used to isolate T.B. patients.

When the railway was laid in 1922 a leopard was killed on the track, and until comparatively recent times there have been tigers on the island of Penang. Coming up, we passed caves that were ideal haunts for either. We saw some monkeys; one sitting up on a tall bamboo eating the young shoots paid no attention to us at all.

There was a creeper with pitcher-like flowers that the driver said were called monkey cups, as the monkeys are believed to drink the water in them. Its correct name is *Nepenthe albomarginata* and it is, as I had thought, a regular pitcher plant—having a built-in device for capturing the insects lured over the rim of the flower by its perfume. They fall into a liquid digestive ferment and are consumed. Penang Hill is famous for these plants, and the monkeys may well drink the contents for their medicinal value. It might be interesting to taste it. I have always heard that we can eat anything that monkeys do with complete safety. I also learned that the lotus is exclusively Asiatic in origin and that both the roots and seeds—or is it seed pods?—are edible.

There was an immense variety of ferns on the hill: giant bracken, a branching fern that grew four feet high; staghorns, giant maidenhair-like ferns; and a big variety of palms. We saw one large fig, the kind that is a parasite on trees, growing over a large rock. Actually it does not prey on the tree. It simply uses it for support but ends by crushing it, so the same purpose is served by a rock support. It needs help only in its young stages before it develops a strong trunk of its own.

The tour ended with a visit to the Ayer Itam Temple, built on a hillside and crowned by a pagoda. Here there was another large fat smiling Buddha. The Buddhas in Malaya are so different from those of Thailand that it is difficult to reconcile the two in one's mind. This is the Buddha that we of the West are used to seeing.

The most interesting thing to us in the temple was the turtle pool where five hundred turtles swarmed about and, looking up expectantly, waited to be fed. We bought ten cents' worth of arrow-shaped leaves that looked like small arum leaves, and threw them into the water. They lasted only a few minutes, as the turtles climbed over each other to get at them. The majority of these turtles were, as far as I could make out, box tortoises, and the larger ones mud turtles, recognizable by a sort of knob on the end of their noses. There was another pool full of small carp. We fed them biscuits that they fell upon with the greatest avidity. Tortoises and turtles are symbolic of longevity and the presentation of a turtle to the temple regarded as a good act. In the turtle pool there is a big black carved stone turtle, about four feet high and six feet long, on which the live turtles climb to bask in the sun.

These arum-like leaves that are fed to the turtles are, I found, Pistia, and do belong to the arum family. We have seen them often on the borders of *klongs* and canals. Other waterweeds—duckweed and water lettuce—appear to be exactly like those that we saw at the zoo in Rio, where water lettuce was growing on the back of a crocodile. Water hyacinth is grown here as a crop for pig food. It does better in muddy soil—muck—rather than in water. If pigs in Southeast Asia will eat it, why don't ours? Has it been tried in Florida? Could it be dried into concentrate, ensilaged, or even composted?

We had two taxi drivers in Malaya who were very bitter

about having had no education. They had had none during
the Japanese occupation and when liberation came were told
there was no room for them in the schools, that they were
too old. This was one of the things that drove so many young
men into the jungle to join the communists.

The Chinese jungle fighters who continued to fight after
the Japanese defeat might have been lured out if a thousand
dollars instead of three hundred had been paid for every rifle
brought in. Millions of pounds and thousands of lives might
have been saved in this way. Just as the Mau Mau troubles
might have been checked by strong measures in the beginning and thousands of African lives saved. Or the ground-nut
experiment might have come off if the money had been spent
in Nigeria, where ground nuts grow to perfection, instead of
Tanganyika, where they hardly grow at all. All governments
appear to be mad to the simple observer.

Still no news of the ship and she should have sailed yesterday. We are delighted to spend a few more days here, but
some people, accustomed to regular schedules, apparently
become annoyed at such delays, not realizing that a freighter's main interest is freight and the passengers are of only
very minor interest.

Sitting in the lounge before lunch, we were fortunate
enough to see a Chinese wedding party. At least five hundred
people, the women beautifully dressed in Western clothes,
cheong sams, kabayas, and sarongs, went past us, accompanied by men in Western clothes—some in suits, others with
white shirts worn outside the trousers in the fashion of the
Philippines. The bride, a tall and beautiful girl, wore a regular Western-style wedding dress, complete with veil; the
groom had on a navy-blue suit and wore an orchid bouton-
niere. Behind them came the bride's amah in green trousers
and a black jumper. The group was followed by one brides-
maid in white, and what looked like a dozen best men. They
all moved very slowly toward the big room that had been

prepared for the festivity, where an enormous silver paper
bell hung over a many-tiered wedding cake. The orchestra
struck up "Here Comes the Bride." We followed the party,
only to be greeted by a volley of firecrackers to frighten off
the evil spirits. Speeches were made in Chinese, and bits of
cake, individually wrapped, were distributed from inside the
big cake, which was a prop and used at all important wed-
dings. The waiters carried around ices and soft drinks, while
the orchestra played "Never on Sunday," a very appropriate
air. In half an hour it was over and we watched everyone
leave again.

We did not have lunch in the grillroom. In fact we shall
not go into it again, having caught cold last night. The regular dining room was cool enough and we sat near the window
looking out over the water. The lunch was excellent: soup,
curry, with a wonderful vegetable—four-angled beans, an
Eastern green bean. Among the condiments there were
tiny dried fried whole fish that I think were anchovies. They
catch a lot of them here.

The pudding was tapioca, also a local product, with two
sauces—one caramel and the other hot coconut milk. Nothing
could have been more delicious.

In the evening Tiny wore her off-white satin brocade
cheong sam again and looked as if she had been poured into
it. She was lucky in being small enough to buy one off the
peg, as, not knowing when we sail, she would not have had
time to have had one made. The price was thirty Malay dollars, or ten dollars U.S., which in our terms is absurd. The
material alone in New York would cost as many dollars a yard.

MARCH 27

We called up the agents at 9 A.M. and the sailing date is
now the thirty-first! Last night we met some fellow passengers who were very tired of waiting and longing to get home.

Talking to a doctor who is a public health expert did
nothing to allay my worst fears about Southeast Asia. Given

unlimited funds, one still would not know where to begin. The problem is overpopulation, an unbelievable and horrifying fecundity. Birth control is the answer, but even that, if practiced at once, would show no effect for years to come. Nor is it possible to envisage birth control among the unindoctrinated peasant mass even if it is as simple as taking a pill. The pattern would probably be that of Europe and America, where the most intelligent and advanced people practice birth control and the indigent breed at their haphazard will.

How does one change the beliefs and practices of hundreds of millions of people? At what point does one begin? Improved medical services only aggravate the problem and humanity finds itself at odds with logic. In Singapore, already overpopulated, a child is born every seven minutes. In India, China, and Egypt the figure is much higher.

Infant mortality must be related to contraceptive practices. The principle of fewer and better children must be explained to potential parents, but in the long run it seems probable that there will be enforced sterilization under totalitarian rule. Democracy may be brought to an end by uncontrollable masses who will submit only to force. Our way of life and ideals are precariously balanced on the knife blade of the population explosion.

Nothing bar actual war could be more depressing than the world situation at this hour.

Force, except when used by the Russians and Chinese, is now outlawed. Persuasion remains. But how does one persuade the recalcitrant, the uneducated, and the illogical?

The Africans, for instance, who in the thousands of years of their tribal existence (to which they appear to be returning) have domesticated no edible plants nor tamed a single animal for use as food or transport, while the Asians who had a very highly developed culture thousands of years before we did are buried like flies in the amber of their hereditary customs.

Are we even sure of our own superiority? What is the relation, the ratio, between mechanization, flush toilets, electric lights, and happiness? Are we as happy as we think?

This is not a matter of Western scientific materialism's being balanced against Eastern esoteric philosophy. It is a spiritual question, a matter of fulfillment, of a man's life being complete instead of fragmented.

Only nominally Christian—most white men believing in neither God nor the devil—we live suspended on the string of status, of material possessions: harassed by Freudian complexes, regrets, and the scapegoat of Oedipus traumas, by means of which we try to pin the blame of our failures onto the coattails of our parents.

Perhaps people may be happier who honor their ancestors and scare away devils with firecrackers and pieces of red cloth.

Unfortunately, happiness and unhappiness, love and hate, are not scientific terms. They can be neither weighed nor measured, yet these abstracts are the only things a man will risk his life for.

It seems possible that each of us has a destiny, that each life is governed by the stars or genes, chromosomes, and opportunity. That we can only be what we are. That what we are depends upon our heredity, our environment and time in history. There have been a thousand Churchills, Roosevelts, Stalins, Hitlers and Ghandis, and De Gaulles misplaced in time. Our Lord, had he lived today, would probably have been incarcerated as a communist; had he lived in the Middle Ages, burned as a wizard by the priests of the religion he founded. Some men succeed, some horses win races, some women are beautiful, but our culture teaches us to resent success and envy those whose fortunes are better than our own, as being both unjust and undemocratic. Today we are all equal, the worst as good as the best.

Instead of having an upper sheet the beds here have a very thin flannelette blanket that is both warmer and cooler than a sheet. In Africa I used always to sleep with a blanket in hot weather. A sheet retains the body heat, whereas a blanket lets it out. Coming from lunch today, we found a beautiful, very large, swallowtailed brown moth dead on the floor, its body empty and dry.

In the passage, on the walls and ceiling, there are always a few geckos that add interest to our lives.

I have now found some books on plants and animals that clear up some mysteries:

It is owing to the lack of seasonal change, no real change in temperature or well-defined wet or dry season, that the flame trees or flamboyants do not ever come into full flower as they do in the West Indies. On every tree here at all times there are some flowers. On no tree at any time is there a solid mass of bloom.

The kapok that we have seen is the Indian silk-cotton, which flowers and fruits when it is completely bare of leaves, the long fruits looking like bats as they hang from the branches.

The rattan is a whiplike forest climber whose usual length is two hundred feet, but it has been known to reach six hundred feet. There are many varieties with different thicknesses. They are used for making furniture—chairs and tables —and basketwork. They also make canes for beating little boys. It was interesting to me, who had been beaten so often at school, to see them actually growing in the jungle and point them out to Tiny. Telling her of my hardships as a child sometimes makes her very sympathetic and charming.

Tapioca will grow into a small tree in eighteen months. At this stage its roots are too large and fibrous to eat and are used for the extraction of starch, which, when washed and dried, is the tapioca of commerce. Tapioca comes from tropical America and was brought to the East and to Africa by the Portuguese in the eighteenth century. When young the roots are edible and are a basic food in the Congo, but they contain little besides starch and an exclusive diet of tapioca will produce beriberi, as the people of Malaya discovered during the Japanese occupation when they had to use it as a rice substitute.

The tuber is not planted like a yam or a potato. Nine-inch lengths of stem are planted, half in and half out of the soil, and soon produce roots that turn into tubers.

The koko yam, or taro, is known here as *keladi*. It is elephant's-ear, or colocasia, of Asiatic origin and was known in the Eastern Mediterranean two thousand years ago.

The pineapple also comes from tropical America, another Portuguese importation. Insufficient credit seems to have been given to the Portuguese for the introduction of fruits and vegetables to their old colonies.

The pendulous male tip of the banana flower is edible and gives off a strong sour-sweet perfume soon after dark that attracts the bats which fertilize it. There are wild bananas whose inflorescence is vertical; one variety has bright lilac flowers. We have seen this plant in a botanical garden in Brazil. All bananas are Asiatic or Australian in origin. The Philippine variety, from which Manila hemp is made, is called *Musa textilis*, or abacá.

The orchids that grow on trees are known as epiphytes, that is to say, a plant that grows on another plant and has become so adapted that it cannot grow on the ground. They are not parasites and the only substance they absorb from the tree is taken from the dead and decaying bark, which is why old and dying trees are so often covered with orchids. There are 780 species of orchid in Malaya. They are divided into three groups. Terrestrial, that is to say, garden, orchids. Climbing orchids, having long stems to hold them to their host, whose roots may reach to the ground. The epiphytic orchids are those that live quite unattached to the soil.

It is interesting for us who are used to thinking of orchids as the last word in sophisticated floral luxury to find them among the commonest flowers here. But in these exotic lands of silk, brocades, satin, lacquer, junks, and temples, they belong. The violet and the daisy have no place in the Orient.

JEWELS AND SPICES

On Good Friday after a breakfast of hot cross buns we
sailed for Ceylon, three days and eight hours away in time.
We were on our way home now—to letters (we have had no
mail for four months except from Tiny's people), to telephones, to friends and acquaintances, to pick up in May
what we had put down in December. But we should not be
the same people. In a few months we had lived a lifetime.

We had done far more than join the hundreds of thousands who have circumnavigated the globe. We had been
deeply and psychologically affected by the Orient, by history, by the thousands and thousands of people we had seen,
by the cities and the jungles. Names that had once been only
romantic-sounding words—Hong Kong, Bangkok, Malacca,
Java—were now places like New York and Paris. We had a
new sense of wonder and an understanding of the limitations
of pity. For pity is limited. It turns from the particularized
pity for an individual in distress into abstract sorrow for the

mass. It is like the ocean. It is hard to believe the ocean is water, there is so much of it. It looks more like a prairie.

Many tourists seem to travel for reasons of status, or to get out of the winter, or to buy things cheap. Many only see the sights, see what they are shown. Very few appear to observe anything. Very few indeed seem to really enjoy travel.

In order to enjoy travel certain things are essential. Reasonable health, enough money not to penny-pinch on a budget, and above all an immense curiosity. Since there are long periods at sea with nothing to look at, one should like reading. We are extra fortunate in having so many interests. We are amateur anthropologists, zoologists, and botanists. We are both writers and painters. We like strange foods and strange smells, the good with the bad. I was a farmer for many years and can recognize most breeds of livestock and crops I see. Above all, there is our companionship and the fact that all our interests are mutual.

A lot of nonsense is talked about the impassive Oriental. I have met no people with a better sense of humor or more gaiety, none with greater vivacity than the Chinese. They are impassive only when annoyed. Face is important to them as it is to us. All that is required in dealing with Orientals is politeness and consideration. They abhor crudity and familiarity. By and large they have no chip on their shoulders, nor any reason for it, since they were civilized thousands of years before we were. In this they differ from the Africans. The Chinese culture is very deep, much deeper than ours. We tend to confuse civilization with mechanization. Civilization is a lot more than flush toilets and jet planes. They are only conveniences.

Orientals' concept of time differs from ours. They have a tendency to think in terms of seasons, of monsoons, and cherry-blossom time, of the length of time it takes to make a baby or grow a crop of rice. They believe in evil spirits and devils, but since we gave up the devil we have lost our confidence in God.

In all the time we have been in the Orient we have seen no one quarreling, no one drunk, nor heard raised voices. People seem to accept life and live it. We accept nothing and try to force all issues, losing today in our hopes for a better tomorrow, however good today may be.

The women appear to be content with being women, the children happy and beloved. Poverty, unbelievable poverty, and squalor are rampant, which makes these qualities even more remarkable.

This does not mean that all the people of the East are virtuous. There are crimes and cruelties. But on the whole they appear to be co-operative in their attitude and remarkably honest. Several times when overtired or confused at a new currency I have overpaid for things and been given back the change. Almost everywhere, even in the most frightful slums, there were well-cared-for pot plants in the window or by the door. This to me seems significant. There is in the East a love of beauty for its own sake, divorced from the intrinsic money value of the object.

What is the value of a pot plant, of a many-tailed goldfish? Of a Pekinese dog? Of eggshell china so thin you can see through it? Why spend days making a lacquer tray or carving a comb?

Personally I have a passion for handmade things. In each the love of the craftsman is apparent, though such things may not be as good, that is to say, as useful or as strong, as a machine-made object. But machines do not love the things they make. The most complex things, even when assembled by hand, lack this quality. Love and respect as I see them can be spread very widely to cover not only all living things but everything that is beautiful. But both love and respect are archaic today.

APRIL 2, EASTER SUNDAY

We have been at sea for Christmas, New Year, and now Easter. The Bay of Bengal is calm, a smooth blue. Today we saw more flying fish than we have ever seen before, coveys of five hundred or more out of the water at one time, all of medium size.

TUESDAY

We enter the bay at Point de Galle, or Galle, as bad an anchorage as there is anywhere and as pretty a bay as could be found. Great rocks jut out of the water and many more lie lurking beneath the surface. We use both anchors and have four lines fastened to buoys astern. Four hundred yards away are the old walls of the fortress built in 1643. Black and green with age, they defended the red-roofed town behind them. Above the roofs, palms and shade trees rise, a dark frill against the sky.

There were a few black-headed gulls, the first we have seen for some time, flying around the ship as we went ashore in the agent's launch, leaving the ship to load chests of tea (each weighing from 100 to 115 pounds) from the lighters that had been towed out to her.

From the tumble-down quay we walked through an old gate set in the forty-foot-thick walls. The gates were immense, made of heavy wooden planks, iron-reinforced. On one side the arch was ornamented with the arms of England in the time of George III; on the other those of the old Dutch United East India Company, with the date 1669. In A.D. 413, Galle was the chief port of Ceylon. But its importance goes back much further, probably as far as that of Malacca, since it was also a trading center where ships from Egypt, Persia, and Arabia in the west met those of India in the north and China and Java in the east. The Portuguese took it in 1505. It was taken from them by the Dutch in 1640, and later passed into the hands of the English. A great deal of its importance was due to "the watering point," where fresh water was easily obtained. To the Chinese it was known as Lo-Le, to the Arabs as Kahlah, their pronunciation of the Sinhalese name Galah. As it was a headland the Portuguese called it Punto Galle, and the British Point de Galle.

It is famous now for its tortoise-shell, lacework, and sea food, lobsters (really crawfish) and prawns. Its glory, like that of Malacca, has departed from it. But there has been glory here and death and horror. It hangs over the place, a sinister miasma in the steam-silent heat, like an ancient flag that once knew the fury of battle and the shouting of the captains.

The enormous ramparts, clothed in short, very green grass that is kept cropped by starving cows, are shaded by great trees. There are Ceylon house crows, rather small with brownish hoods, excessively tame and impertinent, everywhere. There are cars—great red busses that charge down the streets—bullock carts with matting roofs and sides, little wood-wheeled cabs pulled by little bulls the size of ponies, rickshaws, man-drawn—the first I have seen since Durban—and people: men in white, women in bright silk saris, beggars. We saw few children. The banks were closed, due to a strike. Since 1956, I was told, there have been 411 strikes of one kind or another. We had a beer in the Oriental Hotel and then walked through another immense arch under the crumbling defensive walls into the town. Beyond the short-cropped grass where more thin cows were grazing and eating garbage, we saw a number of red hundred-gallon tanks, mounted on bullock carts and fitted with a tap astern, selling oil, used, I assume, for illumination and cooking. I noticed no street lights. Recently the town had been without water for three days. We visited the Catholic cathedral that dominated the town from the top of its only hill. We went through the market, where nothing of interest or value was being sold—cheap enamelware, empty bottles, rubbishy clothes—looked at the food stalls that compared in no way with the delicacies offered by Chinese itinerant cooks. These people in the town are even more unbelievably poor than most others we have seen and, reasonably enough, communistically inclined. What have they to lose? There seems to be no industry here and the harbor is moribund.

Near the great gateway through the wall at the dock is a remarkable fig tree—enormous—its aerial roots dripping like rain, its shadow a sepia lake in the burning brightness of the sunlight. The heat here is intolerable, or is heat cumulative? Does one's resistance to it, one's tolerance of it, weaken as hot day is added to hot day—as gallons of acrid sweat are added to gallons, burning the skin as it pours out, stinging the eyes, and melting the character of the Western man—sweating out virtue as if it were tallow? It is easy to understand the acts of certain white men in the tropics, mad with prickly heat, weakened by fever, unbearably homesick. The dates in the graveyards show how young many of them died, furious, hopeless, utterly lost. Doomed. This is the only explanation of some of their actions. News from home took months to come, their clothes, books, and papers deteriorated in the damp heat of the climate, the food strange and hot, the water bad. The mosquitoes and other insects a plague. What escapes had they? Drink, gambling, and native women —beautiful nightmares to a Victorian puritan. The life of the old colonials scarcely corresponds to the popular picture of luxury and decadence.

The Oriental Hotel—this is the third we have stopped at in the East—was built in 1865, when the colonial policies of the great nations were still one of expansion. Dark red in color with high gloomy rooms and wide verandas, one has a feeling of macabre history here, of illness and disillusion, of drinking parties, of new brides wondering if this was the glamour of the East as they rested here before going up-country.

Nothing was bad here. The drinks were good, the lunch

good value, but the place was as impersonal as a barracks. Great fans painted different colors—red, yellow, green, and blue—revolved slowly at the end of colored pipes that carried electric wires so that beneath each fan there was an electric bulb. The walls were a neutral grayish yellow, the paint work a neutral brown, the floor neutral, faded tiles that had once been red and blue. There were some faded water colors of flowers—never good, now blotched with damp and foxed with spots. Bedrooms like loose boxes opened off each side of a central passage. The walls were partitions that climbed up nine feet toward the high ceiling and then abandoned the effort, coolness being more important than privacy. The rooms were bare of all but the most essential furniture—empty and cool. The beds, large and mosquito-netted, stood in the center of each room. There were strips of matting on the floor. These rooms, like most others in the Far East, were utterly without any comfort beyond utility. These were even less aesthetic, since they were without either anteroom or bathroom. Such rooms emanate a kind of bleak unhappiness that must induce despair. As they were keyed down for coolness, big and empty, one experienced a sense of loss in them, a curious aloneness, a feeling of being alien and far away.

The rooms we had had at the Rama, Caravelle, and Merlin were so beautiful and modern that we might have been in America. The best and gayest rooms that still had atmosphere were at the Oriental in Bangkok. The Raffles room had atmosphere—of the Somerset Maugham kind—comfort, and gave onto the garden but was not gay. The Oriental in Penang was good too, especially with its view of the ocean and garden. But in all these old hotels there is a sadness, perhaps of vanished glories, of better days. Like old women in dresses that were once in the height of fashion, old women with memories of dance cards and dead lovers.

At the back of this hotel, through a passage past an empty bar and empty storeroom, past boys gossiping idly, was a small compound or garden that also made us think of the past, of pretty girls led out to be kissed beneath the trees. In the good old vanished days. From here one looked into other compounds, back yards where tumbling-down roofs were half hidden by the great green flags of banana leaves. Deterioration is the feeling we had—of buildings and people, of starving cattle that looked like crossbred Jerseys and Frieslands, starving dogs, some pink with mange and too dejected to move; only the crows were lively and numerous, for they profit by disaster. Crows and kites are the undertakers of the animal world. The kite one sees here, the Brahmany kite, is dark brown when young, and the adults are chestnut red with white heads and chests.

On the wide veranda where we had a beer a woman squatted making lace on a small cushion. Did lacemaking come from the East too? The fan must have, and the silken Spanish shawls with their embroidered chrysanthemums. Beyond the woman was a jewelry display. The jeweler showed us the signatures of Prince Philip and Lady Mountbatten. He had some beautiful things, very reasonably priced according to our standards. He showed us blue moonstones that I have never seen before, and fine star sapphires. We bought a small scorpion pin of moonstones and silver, and a little tortoise-shell box. We try to buy some small thing everywhere—so that by holding it in our hands when we get home we can bring it all back by a kind of psychometrizing act of memory. For what is a souvenir but a magic carpet? Something, not to impress others, but to delight us with the memories that might otherwise escape.

We went on board by launch at three and sailed next day at dawn. There were twenty-two crows on deck visible from our window, scavenging for scraps of food left by the longshoremen as we sailed.

The captain was glad to get out. He has on occasion, he said, sailed before the lighter had finished offloading, so dangerous is this anchorage.

We got two new passengers here, ladies whose ship had

been wrecked on a reef off Colombo and who were returning home. Their ship had also had two fires before she was wrecked. They were never in any danger but suffered some discomfort and their trip was spoiled.

WEDNESDAY, APRIL 5

We anchored outside Colombo, the capital of Ceylon, at midday. The city, a modern one, lay spread out before us a mile or more away. In the afternoon, since no anchorage was available, we sailed for the "Horn of Africa" in a calm sea followed by a single gull.

THURSDAY, APRIL 6

In the morning we saw some big flights of flying fish and a small whale in the distance, later a shark that actually showed its dorsal fin as it cruised near us and in the evening a school of enormous, rather sluggish porpoises that I took to be Indian pilot whales—a large porpoise often up to sixteen feet long with a wide range in the Indian Ocean.

The marine life in these tropical seas seems to be very rich in large and curious animals—sharks, the manta, or giant ray, giant turtles, and the great squids, or krakans. Some of these deep-sea squid are gigantic, as much as forty-five feet long including the tentacles. We are now just south of the Arabian Sea.

Our visit to the Far East, which we approached by going West, a reflection that always intrigued us, is over. Columbus, going west, thought he had discovered the Spice Islands, or East Indies, when he reached the Bahamas, never even suspecting the existence of America. And now, having left these same islands and still proceeding west, we return to the eastern shores of the United States, our minds and hearts filled with wonder at what we have seen.

Three great facts stand out. The people, their races and cultures, all set against the immense historical background of these waters, for it was the waters—the seas and the rivers —that were important. It was along them that every town or village was built and even today water—sea or rivers—carries most of the goods and people that move from one part of Southeast Asia to another. Roads are an innovation and subject to being swallowed by the jungle in the twinkling of an eye if neglected.

The jungle is the third fact of the tropics—the outstanding master fact—that has already swallowed cities like the Angkor Wat in Cambodia, and others in India and East Africa. For the jungle is the great enemy of man on the equator.

Behind everything in East Asia lies the jungle. Vast areas in Malaya, Borneo, Sumatra, Burma, Laos, Cambodia, and Vietnam are either completely unknown or only partially explored. Rain forest, tree-girt mountains, and vast swamps still lie virgin. But in order to grasp the forest at all it must be seen as an entity—a savage, living thing, controlled by great trees that have succeeded in establishing themselves like kings in the forest. These great trees form an interlocking canopy of leaves and cast a green shadow over everything below them, each thrusting its trunk upward a hundred feet or more before branching. Many have white bark and are buttressed like churches. The shorter trees, less powerful, form a second canopy of interlocking crowns here. They live and die with no chance of reaching the sunlight unless one of the giants falls.

Then on the floor of the jungle in the damp shade are the fan palms and gingers, the ferns, smaller herbaceous plants, and the roots of the climbers, the plants which, though rooted in the ground, cannot support themselves. These are the only plants other than the tallest trees that reach the sunlight and the upper air. A single climber may have as many leaves as the tree itself. Having reached its goal, the crown of its host, it does not stop growing, and the older part, the bottom, slips downward to rest in great snakelike coils on the forest floor. It is an interesting fact that because these creepers need no support their stems, lacking in the woody cells of a tree, are little more than tubes conveying water from the subsoil to the leaves in the upper sunlight. This has saved many a traveler lost in the jungle who, by cutting the creeper and collecting the water as it drips has saved himself from death. This water is always pure, since the vessels through which it has passed are devoid of living substance.

The idea that the soil of the jungle anywhere is rich is an illusion. The appearance of fecundity is due to the rapid turning of the wheel of life in which things grow on other things before they have even begun to decompose. If the trees are felled and the floor of the jungle exposed to the drying winds, the heat of the sun, and the full impact of heavy rains, it rapidly decomposes and washes away since there is nothing left to renew it. This great mulch of leaf mold that has taken hundreds of years to accumulate is the capital of the forest, the richness upon which it lives.

This is why jungle cannot suddenly, by means of bulldozers and machines, be turned into agricultural land, why the rich rice paddies have taken years to build up. Rubber will grow, since tree replaces tree and a plantation is merely a controlled forest of only one variety of tree. Cocoa will grow, since it is grown in the shade of the primeval giants that are allowed to stand. Crops might be grown in narrow strips running north and south so that, except at midday, they would be partially shaded.

The jungle remains, and the waterways: they are the corridors and walls of history.

At the present time, in Asia as in Africa, we are tricked by maps, by arbitrary lines. These continents consist of peoples and tribes joined and divided by mountain ranges, rivers, straits, and seas. The interest of the Western world in the East and Africa was due to their products—spices, silks, and ceramics, gold, jewels, and ivory. The bond that joined these worlds of the East and West, the muscles, as it were, that

controlled the movement of these goods, were the traders—
Phoenicians, Arabs, Moors, Romans, and later the Portuguese, Dutch, French, and British. The Chinese, Burmese,
Indians, Cambodians, and Thais swept over Southeast Asia,
each in turn, each seeking power, but in the end product of
power was trade. In those days manufactured goods came
from the East. It was the West that imported the textiles
and works of art.

As early as A.D. 150 Hanoi was the terminus of the ancient
sea route from the Red Sea. And already, even then, the
Straits of Malacca were a great highway. But the pearl of the
East was the Moluccas with their treasures of clove and nutmeg. It is odd to look at these spices on a shelf in the kitchen
and think of the adventures and wars they have caused.

In addition, gold, which was very scarce then, was found
in Malaya, Burma, Sumatra, and Borneo, and tin and tung-
sten were plentiful in the mountains of Malaya. Beyond this
were the luxury goods of China—silks, lacquer work and
porcelains—which, to reach Europe, had to pass through the
narrow gut of the Malacca Straits. This was one of the muscles or routes. The other was the overland route, the caravan
route across Central Asia, sometimes called the "silk route."

For many years before this was opened, as early as 3000
B.C., Eastern merchants had sailed around the Indian coast
from the Persian Gulf. They sold their goods in Mesopotamia,
and from there they went overland to the great port of Tyre
and the delta of the Nile. In 332 B.C. Alexander founded the
city of Alexandria, and here Greek and Egyptian merchants
met those of India and exchanged their goods.

About 100 B.C. a Roman captain sailed to India on the
monsoon. This was after the Romans had conquered Egypt.
A ship could now leave Egypt in July and reach the Gulf of
Aden in time to catch the southwest monsoon that would
bring it to India by September, where it would pick up a
cargo—pearls, beryls, diamonds, spices, cottons, tortoise
shell, rice, pepper, and silks—some of which had come over-

land from China. The Romans even had a settlement, between 23 B.C. and A.D. 200 near Pondicherry. They sailed to Klang, on the site of the present Port Swettenham, and up to Kattegara in Tonkin.

So that our route, that of a modern freighter, follows sea trails blazed by ancient seamen in search, as we are, of trade. Rome was the first European power to reach the Far East. But the East then had no desire for any Western product except gold, glassware, and glass beads. When the Roman gold ran out the trade ended and the sea route became a legend, lost in the past with the final fall of Rome. It was this legend that inspired both Columbus and Marco Polo. When the old overland silk route was blocked by rapacious nomads, the sea route cut by the rise of Islam, a new way to reach the Indies had to be discovered—across the Atlantic, around the Horn, or the Cape of Storms.

Between these two periods immigrants from Yunan, beginning about 300 B.C., armed with iron weapons, took over Malaya, conquered the natives, who had only stone weapons, and married into them, so that over the last two thousand years millions of Chinese, Indians, Arabs, Persians, and Thais have merged to form a race that is even today far from homogeneous. Despite Indian influence during most of this time the Chinese emperor was tacitly looked upon as the final authority by all states in the Far East. Both China and India were the major sources of outside culture, but neither succeeded in completely swamping the native arts and customs. It seems important here to note that Chinese political power (if the future, as is likely, is only an extension of the past) will probably regain what it lost so long ago.

About A.D. 300 the Persians made a comeback and the trade with China was revived; pearls and spices were exchanged for Chinese silk, iron, and porcelain. Chinese iron had been much valued centuries earlier by the Romans. Ivory from Africa, musk from Thibet, amber from the Indian Ocean, glassware from Syria, slaves from Africa, spices, tin,

and scented woods all changed hands in the trading centers
of the Near and Far East.

The importance of spices before refrigeration, both for the
preservation of food and to make food that had begun to
go off palatable, cannot be overestimated. Camphor, aloes,
cloves, nutmeg, sandalwood, and cardamon were more than
luxuries. They were essentials.

Tortoise shell, gharu wood, pearls, frankincense, rose water, gardenia flowers, myrrh, aloes, asafetida, putchuk, elephant tusks, sword blades, cotton stuffs, gold, silver, porce-
lainware, silk brocades, skeins of silk, silk gauzes, sugar,
camphor, rhinoceros horn, bezoars, pepper, pearl shell, all
were carried on Chinese junks and Arab dhows over the
routes we sailed, to the ports we visited. This continuity hit
us harder every day.

By 1498 Malacca had succeeded Palembang as the greatest port in Southeast Asia with ships of all nations lying in
its harbor. At one time eighty-four languages were heard
spoken here. Again one reads with astonishment the list of
trade goods that changed hands here. Arms, colored woolen
cloths, and golden glassware from Venice, opium from
Mecca, thirty kinds of cloths and merchandise from Canboy
and Aden, silver from Pegu, silks and porcelains from China,
jewels from Ceylon, pepper and gold from Sumatra, rice,
beef, swine, onions and garlic from Java, cloves and nutmegs from the Moluccas. The list is endless and endlessly
romantic.

The work was all done by slaves who were abominably
treated. Beauty and horror, poverty and wealth merged into
a pattern in this port where the variety of race, costume, and
types of vessel has probably never been equaled. It is curious
to remember this when one sees this sleepy backwater now
sunk in lethargy.

In the sixteenth century the control of all the Far Eastern
trade was in Moslem hands. The Arabs and Persians traded
from Arabia and the East African coast with India and
China. The Turks controlled the Mediterranean and allowed
only Venice and Genoa to trade with Alexandria, which was

the doorway to the East. They had to pay for the privilege, of course.

This monopoly was broken by the Portuguese when they defeated the combined Egyptian and Indian fleets in the Indian Ocean in 1509. They took Ceylon and Malacca. They took Mombasa and the other Arab cities on the east coast of Africa, and Goa in India.

Since that time the West has dominated the East—the Portuguese, English, Dutch, and Spaniards all had their turn. Only today is East Asia gaining an independence it never knew before. But today, as it did two thousand years ago, the shadow of the Chinese dragon lies over these green and golden lands. The traders and artisans and businessmen are Chinese in the Malayan countries—or Indians. The Thais and Vietnamese are Chinese in blood and culture. China presses down on India. The poor and starving often seem to see their only hope in China and in Chinafication. True or false, this seems to be the way their eyes are turning. We of the West, and our culture, are so distant from theirs as to be irrelevant. Our tastes, our manners, our tempers, our disrespect for age or beauty, our morals—even our appearance—appalls them. The West is now meeting the East with patronizing equality, but the emulsion of love, the only thing that could blend the oil and water of our separate psyches, is not apparent.

I am not sure that the Western tourists are good ambassadors, or that the dollars they spend compensate for their patronage. We do not understand the Asian's sense of time, of family and paternity, or his love of the abstract. We cannot see how a few potted plants in a window may make him happier than a refrigerator, or why, had he to choose, he might prefer a radio to a refrigerator. We have lost our hope that happiness is the aim of man, our belief in contentment and the will of God.

We have seen elephants working in the jungle beside bulldozers, and women with flat, two-handed baskets filling in roads that were then leveled with giant scrapers. I don't remember seeing a single wheelbarrow in the Orient.

There is no blend of values here—just mechanical vehicles

coexisting and working with the hand labor of the distant past. The same is probably true psychologically. The girl in Western dress with a permanent wave may be nearer to her lotus-footed grandmother than the typist she emulates so successfully.

How sure are we that we are right? And how often do we remember what we owe to the East and Near East, or realize the high style in which they lived when our ancestors were still savages?

Steel, bronze, ceramics, enamel, gunpowder, paper, printing, painting, silk, lacquer, bells, kites, umbrellas, carpets, and topiary all came from the East. So did spices, rice, garlic, onions, oranges, and peaches. And such arts as astronomy, chess, navigation, algebra, and even the figures we use. Our poultry, both ducks and hens, is of Eastern origin—so are peacocks and pheasants. Our race horses are Arabian. Polo, football, and basketball all come from the East. So do the fan and the Spanish shawl. The Western saddle is Moorish. Cooking stoves, ivory, pearls, and jewels, gold, tea, coffee, sugar, bananas are all of Asiatic origin and all in use thousands of years ago. Goldfish, Pekinese dogs, tailless cats and flowers of all kinds existed in the Orient while we lived in a state of barbarism.

Most of these wonders have one thing in common. They have been brought about by people who thought in terms of beauty and comfort rather than what might be described as material practicality. I can only answer the man who says, "What use is a goldfish, a rose, or an ivory carving?" by saying, "What is the good of a bomb?"

One can go very far and fast in a car or plane, but they will not lengthen a man's days, and may even end his life abruptly. They are not the measuring stick of civilization.

As to slums and squalor, we have them too, but we do not have many slum dwellers who will cherish a rose or embroider a cloth.

It is an emotional and psychic gap that separates us. It is based on our different concepts of time, money, happiness, honor, and love.

COFFEE AND
STOWAWAYS

Twenty-four

THE RED SEA—A LONG-TAILED GULL—THE HILLS
OF AFRICA—SLAVES—MEN, GOATS, AND CAMELS—
DHOWS—ASSAB—PILES OF COFFEE—STOWAWAYS
—A TOWN IN DISREPAIR—ELVIS IN AFRICA—A
GOOD DINNER—ISRAELI ORANGES—PORPOISES—
PETUNIA-COLORED JELLYFISH—SUICIDES AT SEA—
THE END OF AN ERA

SUNDAY

We saw a few gulls, and a line of big fish a hundred yards long being pursued by something bigger. They broke water, never actually coming out of it, but churning the calm sea into a reef of foam.

After dinner we sat on deck in the dark, and a gull, evidently disturbed as it slept on the water by our ship, bewildered by our lights, banged down on the boat deck below us. I went down to find it surrounded by some of the officers and crew. It sat quite still, frozen by fear. I got someone to find a box and a bit of tarpaulin. I popped it inside and covered it over. It was, I think, a biggish tern, fine-billed, because when it bit me it hardly broke the skin. It was amazingly light, weighing less than a pound, mottled black and white with black beak, eyes, and black webs to its feet. Above the webs the skin was white. It had a beautiful tail —a serrated fan with a single long feather in the middle. Having caught it, we took it down to our cabin for the night. It never moved or uttered a sound.

When we woke we were in sight of Africa and saw the bare mountains of Somalia ten miles or so away. The sun was just rising and the sea milk blue. We took the box with the bird up on deck and when I put my hand in under the canvas to get hold of it, it offered no resistance. It neither screamed as it did when I first caught it, nor did it bite. I held it a moment or two to let it get used to the light. Its eyes were bright, like black buttons. Then I threw it up into the air and, without a moment's hesitation, as if it knew exactly where it was going, it flew East toward Arabia. One day I hope to find out what this long-tailed gull was. The only others we have seen are the tropic birds that nest on Little Tobago. But they have two long feathers like a swallow's on the outer edges of their tails.

MONDAY

Today we saw several porpoises swimming in an undulating fashion, one behind the other. They were close, less than fifty yards away, and it is easy to see how the stories of sea serpents came to be believed. They looked exactly like a great snake. But even so the existence of sea serpents has not actually been disproved.

The winds here are very strong and many land birds are blown out to sea, swallows, hawks, and other birds. They must all drown eventually as they tire and begin to feel the effects of hunger and thirst, for none can fight these fierce gusty winds for long.

Tomorrow we shall be in the Red Sea. It is strange to think of all the traffic there has been in these waters—of trading ships, dhows, and junks, of British ships patrolling here less than a hundred years ago looking for Arab slavers. There are still slaves here by the hundred thousand in both Saudi Arabia and Ethiopia. Soon we shall pass close to Mecca, crossing the invisible track of the Moslem pilgrims to the Holy City. For 1300-odd years they have been coming here from all over Africa and Asia. We have now been to the two boundaries of the Moslem religion, having seen them in Nigeria on the Atlantic and in Indonesia on the Java Sea. This bond of religion and dark skin cannot be ignored as a political and social factor.

We got a note from the captain as we were having breakfast. "Passing the Gate of Hell"—the entrance to the Red Sea. There are the bare hills of French Somaliland on one side and the equally stark hills of Saudi Arabia on the other, with the installations on the British island of Perim, deserted apparently and falling into disrepair.

We are now in the Near East, the worn-out cradle of another culture. These waters have been sailed by man for four thousand years and tied by the string of the monsoons to the Orient, equally old or older, for two thousand years at least. Historical geography in terms of spheres of influence assumes a new significance for me. Perhaps one really has to see to understand.

First the lush green world of Southeast Asia dominated by China and India. Next this dry Semitic and Moslem world dominated in the past by Persia and Egypt and now by the Arab republics. Next, and still to come, the classical world of Greece and Rome—the Mediterranean world bounded by the Pillars of Hercules. Then the European world, now called the West, which for a time controlled all trade and governed most of Africa and Asia. And finally, the New World, and how new it is, as one looks back into history.

Historically, neither Africa, except the north, nor Australia has ever existed.

These arid Near Eastern and North African lands are worn out and overpopulated, their vegetal fertility gone—only that of mankind continuing to perpetuate disaster in their fecundity. Mankind with their goats, donkeys, and camels have suicidally destroyed the green earth skin that supported them in these parts, eating it away as moths eat a garment. Only water, the sea atomically cleaned of salt, can save them. But the sea we sail remains the same—unchanged.

Contrary to what we expected the Red Sea is cool, with a strong wind and quite choppy. Some medium-sized dark gulls with white bellies are following the ship, several porpoises, more active and less snakelike in the cooler water, play around us. We are heading for the port of Assab, in what used to be Eritrea—Italian Somaliland—and is now part of Ethiopia, to pick up coffee brought down by truck on roads the Italians built from Addis Ababa.

More and more I see history as commerce, as man's search for trade outlets and raw materials. This is real history. Kings and battles are only incidental. Even political explosions and revolutions can, in the end, be traced to such material causes, with the possible exception of religious wars, and even they were often not entirely divorced from the commercial rewards that went to the victor.

About lunch time we came into a bay and saw a couple of small fishing dhows. The shore is golden sand, the sea turquoise, the hills the usual dark African khaki. Some building is going on—more warehouses. There is a big mosque with a shiny, tiled, onion roof. There are hundreds of pigeons that must live on coffee. A lot of coffee is stacked, bagged, on the dock, marked "Hand Picked Coffee—Product of Ethiopia." More coffee arrives in trucks. Coffee originated here and was probably first used as a medicine—a laxative. The stevedores are African—black, with a few Somalis in gay turbans. The whole effect is Beau Gestish. A small dirty white town set against the blue sea with a backdrop of stark hills and sand. The port officials come on board to collect our passports. Landing cards will be issued at 4 P.M. In the meantime we wait.

It is curious to be back in Africa. We could be nowhere else. This continent has an atmosphere of its own—stark, brutal, and loveless, grown old without ever having been young, vigorous, or progressive. Progress may be coming to Africa now—with mechanization grafted onto an early Iron

Age scion. It also may not be coming. It all depends on how much help the Africans receive.

At 5 P.M. we went ashore, past the mountains of coffee and great bales of sun-dried hides that were being loaded onto the ship next to ours. Later, on our return, we found that two stowaways had been caught hiding behind the bulkhead of the swimming pool and handed over to the police. Stowaways present a serious problem, since, if they succeed in getting away from their home port, no country will accept them because they have no papers, and their own countries sometimes refuse to have them back.

Assab has two main streets, both unpaved. The houses, whitewashed and thick walled, are Near Eastern, arched, single- and two-storied, the people a mixed lot—African, Negro, Somali, and Semitic with hooked Arab noses. Many men walked hand in hand. There were quite a lot of prick-eared dogs all lying asleep as if dead, and a number of cats, some with strong Egyptian characteristics. Mice must be a problem here. Behind old tumble-down walls there were groups of date palms. Other palms, twisted by sun and drought, gnarled, distorted, and dusty, gave the impression of being survivors. The soil was volcanic and we picked up a number of pieces of lava. There is no real drinking water here. It comes down in tanks. This may be why there was no big Arab port here, although we did see a few traces of buildings that might predate the Italian colonization. There are now four hundred Europeans here. At one time there were five thousand Italians and the town was much larger. The exports seem to consist of coffee, hides, lentils, and of salt, which is evaporated from the sea here in pans. The lentils account for the large pigeon population, and also for the many cats who must feed on the mice. Rain falls about twice a year. The heat in July and August is intolerable, reaching 125°.

A great deal of the town has fallen into disrepair. The Italian houses are in ruins. Behind the streets are the shacks in which the natives live, some five thousand of them, only seven hundred of whom have jobs. There were quite a number of police and soldiers, in khaki with berets or slouch hats, walking the streets. We were reminded of Kano, Nigeria, and the Sudan. The people seemed friendly enough but savage in expression. Many of them have longish fuzzy hair and some of the men remarkably hairy legs. When we had explored the town we went to the hotel and had a Cinzano while the juke box blared Elvis Presley songs. I wonder if he knows how popular he is in the Far and Near East? If he did a good-will tour for us he would probably have a much better effect than any member of the Government. Below the hotel there was a plantation of palms—a kind of park. The water table must be higher here and the palms able to survive on brackish water. Next to the courtyard, enclosed by Moorish-looking arches and paved with terrazzo tiles, there was a dry fountain built by the Italians. They must have had some method of getting water which has fallen into disrepair.

Dinner was simple and excellent. Minestrone, spaghetti, and fruit—big, sweet, thick-skinned navel oranges from Israel —coffee, and a bottle of chianti. Several dogs came into the dining room and were fed scraps impaled on toothpicks, each dog confining himself to a certain area. The dining room was full of Italian men and, at separate tables, Ethiopians—grouped in natural selective segregation, each preferring his own kind. After dinner we walked back through the velvety night to the ship.

One incident was particularly moving. Before dinner as we sat outside an African carried in a little white girl of three and handed her to her father. He held her on his lap and kissed her. Then she was passed around like a cake and a dozen of his friends must have kissed her and dandled her on their laps. She laughed all the time. These were her friends and her father's friends. I believe in demonstrative love. I think that little girl probably has a better chance of happiness than children who are never kissed by friends and seldom fussed over by their parents.

WEDNESDAY, APRIL 12

We should have been going to Djibouti, but instead sailed for America, which we regretted, but which the other passengers seem pleased about. To us a trip is a trip and the more we see the better. To them it was something that was over.

The sea is smooth, bright blue, and streaky. A lot of white jellyfish that look like mushrooms float by. A fine marlin broke water near us as we passed through isolated rock islands, streaked with guano, rising like mirages out of the sea. A possible explanation of the increase of gulls in Africa may be such nesting places, the lack of typhoons, and fewer enemies—which include man. In the East the Chinese fishermen would rob the nests if they found them, and there is certainly a scarcity of cliffs.

The costumes in Assab were drab white nightshirt-like garments known as *khanzos,* except for an occasional outbreak of Somali sartorial gaiety. Many of the women wore white trailing scarves over their heads and shoulders. None were veiled. Some of the men wore similar scarves in an almost toga-like fashion. The town, such as it was, seemed geared to seamen—wineshops everywhere and women who looked more than accommodating. There must be thousands of such towns in North Africa, Egypt, and the Holy Land, Jordan, Syria, Iran, Iraq, and Saudi Arabia. Thousands, rooted in sand and squalor, burning under the sun—ancient in vice. The cause of their existence a desert crossroads, a well, an oasis, or an anchorage. Assab may have been an Arab slave port, or on the other hand it may be relatively modern—born of the Italian occupation. No one seemed to know much about it.

One curious feature is the lack of fishermen. We saw only two fishing dhows in waters that abound in fish.

The towns of the Holy Land in the time of the Romans and our Lord must have looked very like Assab, and the people, particularly the women, have dressed in a similar fashion. How is the unchanging changed? How is progress, in the sense of an attitude of mind, brought to people like this? Juke boxes, bicycles, canned food, and bottled beer are not progress. Would literacy help them? Their needs are more basic. Fresh water to drink (and they may get a pipe line soon) and food, such as fish from the sea. These people are hungry, but seem unwilling to fish or work. I have seen a few stout shopkeepers, and the harlots are well covered. The rest are skin and bone. We saw no livestock. Only one young, yellow, fat-tailed Roman-nosed sheep of the usual Sudanese type.

The arches of the cloister-like streets are nicked at the top, almost elliptical, and represent the female principle, as the minarets and pillars do the male. The phallic cult persists vestigially all over the world, from the pedi in Thailand to the Maypole of Europe.

On the walls of the restaurant at Assab we saw two of the biggest geckos we have ever seen. They came out of hiding as soon as the neon lights went on. These little semitransparent lizards always fascinate us.

THURSDAY, APRIL 13

Bathing in the pool today while the decks were being washed, I was astonished at the fishy smell of the water and its buoyancy. The water in the Red Sea must be very salt. We have passed a great number of ships, sometimes four being in view at one time. The Suez Canal, like the Panama Canal and the Straits of Gibraltar, is a great bottleneck through which the world's shipping must pass—the alternative being the Strait of Magellan or the Cape of Good Hope. This sea was once known as the Arabian Gulf, which seems a better and more descriptive name. We are always surprised at the way ships pass each other without greetings. I thought ships spoke to each other, giving their names and destinations. But they go by without even saying hello.

More and more I reflect about different people and races —their desires and aspirations. I find that all men have the same needs—food, sexual gratification, shelter, and the respect of their fellows. But they are not equal, either as individuals or races. Any difference at all prevents equality. Taking a watch as a simile, races, and people within the races, differ as a cheap five-dollar timepiece differs from a Swiss watch that tells not only the time but also the day and the month. All watches operate on the same principle (excepting certain new kinds), but the manner in which they work and their precision differs a great deal.

Food, sex, and shelter, taking the basic necessities, vary from boiled yams, a naked lady, and a grass hut to a five-course dinner at the Ritz, a beautiful and educated woman in a Dior dress, and a Park Avenue apartment. In both cases the primary needs are satisfied. Both a camel and a Rolls-Royce are means of transport. Both palm wine and champagne are means of obtaining alcoholic pleasure. But when one is subtracted from the other the resulting answer is what we describe as civilization.

A head-hunter obtains the respect of his fellow by the number of heads in his collection. A civilized American by the importance of his business and the value of his possessions. These are simply heads in a different form and his business or professional skills an exact parallel with the skills of the head-hunter who succeeds in taking heads without losing his own. Both will fight to the death to protect these possessions, for in losing them they would both lose "face," face being simply a word that expresses a man's place in society, a measure of the respect accorded to him by his peers.

It is here that the importance of politeness in strange places comes in. By rudeness of any kind to a non-European we cause him to lose face, and face is more important than money. The primary object of money or its equivalent in material possessions is to gain face. This is the object of all spending that goes beyond that of actual necessities. I fail to understand people who are so arrogant that they will not shake the hand of or sit down to eat with the people in whose land they find themselves.

The Red Sea, or Arabian Gulf, was one of the great slave routes. It was from here, and the East Coast towns of Africa that the great slave caravans penetrated the interior as far as the Congo River, almost reaching the Atlantic coast. For some reason the Arab slavers have been forgotten. This ancient and horrible trade is attributed to the white man, who never captured a slave. Slavery on the West Coast of Africa began in the fifteenth century and ended in the nineteenth. Here on the East Coast it began 4000 or 5000 B.C. and is not ended yet. The whole question of slavery has never been fully explored, being so emotionally charged. Since the beginning of time man has been a commercial product—an export or an import. The slave was the first laborsaving device and, taking Russia and China into consideration, there are probably more slaves in the world today than there have ever been, and more have died or been liquidated than were ever lost in the middle passage between West Africa and the Americas.

An interesting cultural point occurs when comparing the civilization of the underdeveloped countries and that of the West—that is the level of contentment. It is probably lowest in the African and highest in the American. Many, if not most, Africans will cease to work when their simplest and most basic needs are satisfied, whereas no American is ever fully content. He has no plateau that satisfies him. There is always more ahead and the best can always be improved upon. This factor of a low contentment level will always act as a brake and check the full development of any people who are easily satisfied and refuse to exert themselves fully, not feeling that the game is worth the candle. Our problem is, of course, that they may be right.

STILL THURSDAY, APRIL 13

In the afternoon there was a school of small porpoises playing around the ship, and the blue oily sea, smooth as bottle glass, was flecked with thousands of small petunia-colored jellyfish floating vertically, just submerged, swaying so that they looked like amputated fingers. All jellyfish except the complex, deceptive, and beautiful sky-blue Portuguese man-of-war are hideous. They look like contraceptives, like tripe, or bowels.

Looking into these smooth oily seas, one can easily see how a suicide is tempted to leap into the soft green curling breast of the ocean when it looks like a satin sheet, white-frilled with lace, turned back on a bed of water by the sliding hand of the ship. It could be done almost absent-mindedly as a bed calls to a tired man, as if the sea called to him to rest, as if he could hear the voices and the music of the mermaids rising out of the deep. It might under certain conditions require a conscious effort of will to resist and this may be the explanation of some suicides that have no apparent cause. They generally occur in smooth oily waters such as these, or those off Cape Verde.

Before dinner a young eagle landed on the mast, exhausted, swaying. His talons, designed for the branches of a tree, failed him on painted steel. He will not last till we reach land, I am afraid.

And, as if to end a day filled with signs and portents, the news comes over the radio that the Russians have a man in space.

As I lie in my bed looking at the stars I know a man to be up there among them, a man in the firmament, where only the gods belong. This is another wonder, another terrible

thing that I have lived to see or hear about. I saw Blériot fly
the Channel, I fought on the Somme with the first tanks, I
saw Sputnik. The German concentration camps were in my
time and the atomic bombs that fell upon Japan. I have lived
to see great empires wither away—and now this.

APRIL 14

In the night it grew cold and the temperature dropped to
78°. It has been 86°, still cool for the Red Sea, but we felt
the heat less, as there is no humidity. In the high eighties a
drop or gain of two degrees seems to have a much greater
effect than it does in the cold of the forties. Most heat, if it
is not too humid, is bearable up to 90°. At 90° a candle
bends over into a reversed U in its stick. In Malaya the temperature was never much over 90°, but the humidity was
very high, the air too full of water to drink up the sweat.

The eagle has gone, drowned without a doubt. We went
to look for him at dawn. The visibility is low, the sky and sea
are dull. We are now in the Gulf of Suez—with Egypt on one
side of us beyond the horizon, and Sinai, also Egypt but
separate in one's mind from it, invisible but there, on the
other.

But all this is nothing. The new era of space has begun.
It began with the atomic bomb. But this is in some ways
even more dramatic. The fifty-thousand-year period that has
elapsed since man discovered fire has ended. The new and
final phase of man's existence has begun. One wonders how
long it will last. We are the last primitive men, the last bead
on the string! The next generations will be irrelevant to us.

THE CITY
OF THE DEAD

Twenty-five

APRIL 15, SUEZ

We go ashore about midday, having secured visas and arranged for a tour to Cairo by land, passing the entrance to the canal and a new monument, presumably to the Egyptian victory over the Israeli, British, and French in 1956. They are now convinced that this was a victory. At the base of the monolith are four really splendid lionesses derivative of Rodin but streamlined and modern. The town of Suez is much larger than I thought it would be. In fact I did not think there would be a modern town here at all. Yet Suez has a long history, being another link in the Far East and European trade—the place where camel caravans met the ships from the Orient and transported the goods they brought to Alexandria and Cairo.

Driving north, we crossed a causeway that had the Red Sea on one side and the Mediterranean—an arm of the canal —on the other. We were surprised at the mountainous character of the landscape. Flat bare sand, backed by steep bare hills like those of South-West Africa. We had first seen the mountains from the ship when we anchored, but now we drove parallel to them along a military road that was being improved and widened. We were checked twice by military posts and passed an immense convoy of army vehicles—none of them recognizable and all, by the cut of their jib, Russian. The troops, a division, I should think, were all well armed with automatic weapons. Their uniforms and their cars and trucks were a yellowish ocher—the exact color of the desert. Our guide said that Egypt had a million men under arms, with a population of just over thirty million. This seems a high proportion. The distance between Suez and Cairo is seventy miles of sand and rough dunes. They were covered with the car tracks of military maneuvers along the way.

There are odd patches of green succulent bushes, presumably inedible, or they would not be there, some small dry scrub, and a few typical African thorns. Every depression and dry watercourse was marked by this kind of desert vegetation. We saw mirages of great bodies of water, lagoons and cliffs in the distance that faded into nothing as we approached. In several places there were patches of surface water that was probably brackish. In one, near Suez, there were some coots swimming. In another a big hawk, or small eagle, was bathing. The only other birds we saw were crows. We passed two ruins, old mud castles set on hilltops, and a group of grazing camels, almost invisible in the scrub and sand, and that was all.

This is an empty world except for the soldiers and working parties of laborers dressed in dirty nightshirt *khanzos* widening the road. The only trees we saw later in the day were casuarinas, blue gums, tamarisks, and date palms. The only flowers were occasional sunflowers, geraniums, and petunias, the hardiest of the hardy.

Cairo was another surprise—a great modern city. We passed Nasser's house, where he was born and still lives, ex-

King Farouk's palace, and, because the museum closes at
four, made straight for it, its wonders somewhat clouded
by our hunger. Nevertheless, even though we were hungry,
the magnificence of the statuary and the sophistication of
the jewelry, paintings, and artifacts, some executed three
thousand years before the birth of Christ, left one aghast.
Boats five thousand years old, like many of those in use in
Asia today. Paintings on papyrus and linen, all in perfect
condition. Enamel and gold necklaces, earrings, jewels, and
daggers—all were beautiful in design and craftsmanship. The
golden chariots fascinated me. We thought of the chariot-
wheel ruts in the streets of Pompeii, and how odd it was that
horses were used this way as draft animals thousands of
years before the employment of cavalry. Who invented cavalry? Perhaps it was due to some soldiers watching children
galloping about. We looked at outer coffins, sarcophagi, cut
of solid granite. Inner coffins, or mummy cases, of gold.
Golden rooms, golden beds, all gave some idea of what the
life of the rich and royal must have been. There were elaborate jars in which the entrails were interred in fitted golden
boxes, mummified flesh, fruits and delicacies entombed for
the dead when they reached the other world. On the inside
of the granite lids of some coffins there was a beautiful
woman sculptured in bas-relief—so nothing was forgotten.

But an hour, and hungry at that, is no way to see all the
wonders removed from Tutankhamen's tomb or the other
splendors of a past to which we owe so much.

We had an Arab lunch that was excellent. Shish-kebab,
small sausages, vine leaves, unleavened bread that we dipped
in a pickle sauce, and an Egyptian sweet. We drank a good
Algerian wine and ended with Egyptian coffee. We ate off
low brass trays, sitting on leather poufs. The waiters were
dressed in baggy trousers and wore little embroidered waist-
coats. The walls and low ceiling were covered with Egyptian appliqué designs on faded purple and red cotton that

gave one the impression of being in a great tent. This was a perfect meal in a perfect atmosphere.

After lunch we were taken to the citadel of Saladin, built in 1166, and visited the mosque of Mahommed Ali, the biggest mosque in the world, with alabaster walls and pillars. Our guide, a tall Arab, had blue eyes and the manners of a king. He might have stepped out of a picture book of Bible stories. We did not take off our shoes to go into the mosque; instead we put on canvas overshoes designed for Donald Duck—they had great heaps of them in assorted sizes—to pad over the great carpets that covered the floor. From the terrace here we looked down over the roofs of the city and at the Pyramids on the horizon. How many men for how many thousand years have done the same?

Leaving the mosque, we drove down through a city of the dead, an immense cemetery of roofless houses in which the graves were dug in rooms open to the sky. The houses had doors and shuttered windows. Except for the lack of roofs and living inhabitants they were like any other Eastern houses. I have no idea how old this cemetery was, but certainly the earliest graves were hundreds if not thousands of years old.

We now visited the Omar Khayyam Bazaar—a perfume shop that sold only essential oils, mainly to the French manufacturers who add spirit to them and blend them into such scents as Arpège, Cobra, and My Sin. After this we went on to another store, a small bazaar that catered exclusively to tourists and was without much interest. They sold leatherwork, appliqué, brassware, silver, jewels, but all of it junky.

It was dark when we set off for the Pyramids across the Nile. This, something we had looked forward to all our lives, was a great disappointment. In the last few years the town has crept up to their feet and, in a way that must make every pharaoh turn in his museum, this resting place of kings who were half gods has been thoroughly commercialized. We had to buy tickets to approach and were herded into an open-air auditorium to witness, to my mind, the last word in pseudoartistic vulgarity. The Pyramids and Sphinx were floodlit in color—white, fading to blue, changing to green that merged into red and rose white. Over loud-speakers several invisible men and women declaimed in impeccable and academic French the glories of the Egypt of the Pharaohs, to a crowd of two hundred or three hundred people sitting in hard chairs facing these wonders of the world that had been reduced in stature to the backdrop of a theater. This was the last thing we should see on our voyage around the world, the last time we should go ashore till we reached American soil again, and to me it epitomized the way the world has changed. The graves of men who were man-gods turned into a peep show, minimized into a vulgar spectacle for people insensitive to grandeur. As if the silence of the desert stars was not enough. This was no embellishment, no gilding of the lily. The lily was a paper flower, not even made by hand. It bore the same relation to reality that a silver-sprayed nylon Christmas tree does to a forest giant. Like Christmas, the Pyramids have been embellished into non-existence. Childishly unable to bear our disappointment, we crept away from this chef-d'oeuvre of the Ministère de la Culture et de l'Orientation Nationale and dropped his ticket marked *"Son et Lumière"* into the desert sand. Sound and light indeed!

We dined at a smart restaurant that might have been anywhere in the world and ate mediocre occidental food. Tomato soup, a tasteless fish, tough, overcooked beef with French beans and potatoes. The meal ended with ice cream —what else? We did not even wait for coffee. But had the meal been the best Paris could offer I could not have eaten it, for, as the French say, I should not have had the liver to do so. Tired and heartsore, at once excited by what we had seen and the implications of history, and upset at what had been done to history, we drove south to Suez again, after a day we shall never forget.

In the morning, Sunday, we started up the canal, passing

a couple of ships sunk in the Israeli war of '56. On each side of us the desert lay pancake flat, pale-ocher-colored and bordered by distant lavender hills and dunes. To our right the foothills of Sinai—to our left the mountains we drove past yesterday on the way to Cairo. We saw three camels, descendants of those that had carried the trade of the past across this unchanged desert.

It was extraordinarily cold with a bitter wind. We came to strips of irrigated farmland, a patchwork of various greens split with ditches. Flat-topped hovels like mud boxes housed the peasants. There were more groups of camels grazing, one with a foal at foot. Big palm plantations, olive gray and dusty, appeared and were left behind. We saw men plowing with oxen. The plows were wood, antique as the Pyramids. From the look of the trees the prevailing wind is from the east. The ships proceeded in convoy, one behind the other, spaced well apart. All along the canal there are bollards set in concrete so that the ships may be tied up in the event of an accident or sudden sandstorm. As well as the pilot we carried two manned boats, one forward and one aft, attached to booms so that they could be dropped quickly to tie the mooring lines.

The view was at once monotonous and exciting. We passed flocks of sheep and goats—the regular-desert type animals of the Sahara and Sudan—more camels and more people dressed in their nondescript nightshirts. We were back in biblical times. In one place the canal was being widened, and a thousand men worked, carrying the sandy soil in baskets up the great heaps they had made—climbing steps dug into the bank and weaving like ants along the little paths that snaked up these artificial dunes. There were heaps of baskets to replace those that were worn out. The diggers on the bank slashed at the ground with the heavy hoes that are used as spades in so large a part of the world. In the canal, on floats, were tanks of drinking water. We saw one man baling some out with a small can. It was very low and he had to lie on his belly to reach the water. How hot and stinking this water must become in summer. How strange to see this gut through which so much of the world's trade passes being enlarged by hand, with baskets. This was the way they built the Pyramids.

We passed a splendid monument—two pillars side by side—in memory of the dead of '14-'18 War. Trains and automobiles passed us along the road running parallel to the canal.

Suddenly, in the evening, we dropped anchor and the two boats we carried were lowered to tie us up. A Russian tanker, seven ships ahead of us, had gone aground. Her steering gear had failed. The danger here is from the wind and current once a ship loses way. Behind us, a Japanese ship went aground, having swung right across the canal, but she got off by herself. Tugs from Port Said pulled the Russian clear and by ten o'clock we were moving again. We woke in the Mediterranean—a calm sea and much warmer. We had not even seen the lights of Port Said. We had been too exhausted to stay up or awake.

Looking back at what we had seen—digesting it as if it was a meal—we recalled some of our impressions of Cairo, this great city where the West and the Near East meet.

The black-veiled women who looked like nuns. People in their nightdress-like clothes and pajamas who look as if they had just got out of bed. The horses almost all had their tails set on slightly sideways, a sign of Arab blood. We saw some white donkeys and one of broken color, gray and white. I have seen only one other like it. Much of the brasswork on the harness was clean and bright, but all the animals, except one gray horse, were ill kept. The shops were full of oranges and onions. Other vegetables seemed scarce.

We passed street bookstalls that reminded us of those in Paris on the banks of the Seine, while the men, dressed in their white garments, made us think of the Hausa traders we had seen in West Africa and the Congo. From the Nile westward along the southern border of the Sahara it is these men who do the trading.

The citadel was decorated with monoliths set like teeth along the tops of the walls and resembled those of Kano and Zimbabwe; the stone birds in the museum too were like the ones found in Zimbabwe. All these resemblances seem to be more than accidental and we probably still have a lot to learn about the early travels of man.

Arab writing looks like shorthand and Mr. Pitman may have got his ideas from a visit to the Near East. Everyone looked like Nasser. He is a typical Egyptian and his smiling picture was hanging everywhere. This country is rich in oil, cotton, and the possession of the canal. But nowhere is there more poverty. One of the passengers visited a new agricultural settlement for veterans where contraception is insisted upon and no mothers-in-law are allowed. An interesting combination that might make for happiness. Around the railway station thousands of people were sleeping on the ground waiting for trains. In front of the station, a fine modern building, was an immense granite statue of one of the ancient Pharaohs. Everywhere there were flags, red, white, and blue in horizontal stripes with two blue stars on the white. French, even more than English, seems to be the second language.

As usual, we were shown no slums, the beggars have been driven from the streets, and police and soldiers were in evidence everywhere. We saw two men being arrested very roughly as we drove out of town.

In a day it is hard to get an impression, but the impression that we did get was one of modernity superimposed on a Bible book picture of poverty. How deep the modernity goes, how long these new roots will take to penetrate the great mass of fellaheen, remains to be seen. Pride and militarism are apparent everywhere, and, again, these are unproven. The best military equipment is only as good as the man behind the gun. We saw few fully veiled women, few men in tarbooshes. Most of the young men and women wore Western clothes in the better parts of the city. But the biblical robes, the donkeys, horses, mules, camels, and oxen are still here, with the spade hoes and the wooden plows. The kites still sail, circling the air. The crows still perch on mud walls. The desert still extends from the Nile to the Atlantic.

It is still difficult for me to realize that, to the vast majority of the world's population, the hundreds of millions of Asia and Africa, one of our city garbage dumps would be a gold mine—the waste food a meal for the gods, the broken furniture, worn-out rugs, handleless cups, and discarded refrigerators all objects to be treasured. This emphasizes the gap between the have and have-not nations. What we throw away is to them the riches of Croesus. A bottle is a valuable possession. Broken umbrellas and old medicine jars are exposed for sale and the coinage reduced to tenths of one of our pennies or less. In many places, most perhaps, subsistence farming, which was at least subsistence, has broken down through the increased pressure of population on an already-worn-out and eroded soil. Industrialization may come, may be on its way, but what happens in the time lag, in the time space where the earth will no longer give up its fruits, and the wages of industry are still so far in the future that the factories that would pay them are not even planned?

To succeed, they must have foreign capital and foreign know-how, but added to their xenophobia and hatred of all but their own race is the fear of foreign industrial domination and economic imperialism—while capitalists fear the nationalization of their plants should they invest in these still politically unstable areas. They have reason for their fears.

Even when industry does come, the answer will not be complete. Vast slums will spring up. There will be insufficient guarantees against exploitation, with an immense labor pool fighting for work at any price.

We forget that the mass of the world, the people, whom we never see as men and women but only as world statistics, are still peasant farmers. That, except for North America and Northern Europe, very few parts of the world are industrialized or even mechanized.

What are the immediate needs of these undeveloped lands? Some education, particularly in agriculture suited to their specific area. Some knowledge of hygiene and a great number of small village projects rather than impressive works —small dams, small weirs, small hospitals, small schools, and small agricultural demonstration plants.

They do not require electric light or water-borne sewage. They need help in treating human refuse, which is their only fertilizer. They need forest reserves to be planted for fuel. They need co-operatives to help them market their produce. They need water.

They could do with thousands of old discarded refrigerators, not to keep their food cool but to keep their food and papers, their schoolbooks, bills, and receipts from being destroyed by termites and other insects.

A thousand small hospitals with even half-trained doctors who can give first aid and treat simple disease are worth more than one big hospital with every facility in the capital. If the few who need serious surgical attention die through failure to get it, the thousands who need much less will live.

Water, fuel, and the preservation of sewage by some form of composting are vital necessities, plus the prevention of erosion and overstocking. Livestock improvement can be brought about only by education—by demonstrations proving that ten good beasts are worth one hundred scrubs.

Basically, there is only one need—to fill bellies. This is the test of any project. Will it help to do this or will it not? Neither freedom nor education is edible.

More fruit- and nut-bearing trees can be introduced from one part of the tropics to another. Women can be taught to cultivate and cook them. Where there is water, fish farming can be encouraged. Talapia will give up to four and one-half tons of protein per acre per year.

But the other problems are immense. In Ruanda-Urundi men starve before they will kill cattle. The Hindus will eat no meat. The Moslems and Jews no pork. The success of the

Chinese may be in part due to the fact that they are omivorous and will eat anything from a snake to a dog.

Finally, the problem is simply that man is destroying his own environment—and the solutions are those which lead to a decrease in population and an increase in food supply. These again can be broken down to massive and universal birth-control measures and the application of desalted sea water to the deserts of the world. As long as men are hungry there can be no peace. As long as men are satisfied there can be no war.

If the scientific brains that are now applied to space travel and new devices of destruction were switched to these basic necessities the world situation might be changed.

What we have seen has done nothing to change my opinions of mankind. I do not believe that all men are brothers or equal. My belief in man's inhumanity to man is confirmed on every side. Man is a savage and gregarious animal—a savagely gregarious animal, fighting always for his own interests and those of his group. I do not see more freedom, but less. I do not see more love or more integrity. I do not see less fear. There is more hypocrisy, more living by slogans and platitudes and less thought than there used to be.

The factors that have brought this about are Darwinism, which destroyed our belief in God, Henry Fordism, which, in breaking down the distance barrier, has widened human contacts but in doing so has weakened all natural ties and morals. (In this I include all transportation and communication that goes beyond rail and sea transport. Radio and telephonic communication has done little to increase the sum of human happiness.) And finally, Freudianism, which has changed our attitude toward sin, enabling us to blame society instead of ourselves for our errors, and has even turned love into a question of chemical glandular reaction.

The most important loss has been the loss of God and the Christian ethic. For this is the key to our Western culture. Having lost it, how can we expect others to open the door?

Today we saw warships between Sicily and Malta. A newscast from Moscow spoke of the American imperialists who are attacking Cuba. How many feathers has the dove of peace left today? How firmly are they attached? What is driving the world mad?

When does a rebellion turn into a revolution? At what point do rebels become freedom fighters? When do brigands become partisans? When does murder turn into war? And nationalization and expropriation cease to be theft? When and how is national repudiation justified? How can individual honesty be reconciled to public theft? If treaties and solemn promises are no more than bits of paper.

In mid-Mediterranean. The air is good, sharp, brisk, and worth breathing for the first time since we left the China Seas. With the high humidity of Indo-China and Malaya the air appears to lack oxygen and to be dead and flat. This air is strong and sleep-inducing, as full of bubbles as champagne.

THE PILLARS
OF HERCULES

Twenty-
six

THE FARMS OF ALGERIA—THE ROCK—THE AZORES
—THE CAPTAIN'S DINNER—HURRICANE—THE GREAT
BLACK WAVE — A SUNSET LIKE A FLAG — HOME
AGAIN

APRIL 19

We have been listening to Radio Moscow. Both Moscow and Peking come in very clearly and talk beautiful English. The Voice of America speaks slowly and distinctly in an almost infantile manner that must annoy educated listeners.

THURSDAY, APRIL 20

In the night we saw lights on the African coast and in the early morning were buzzed by a French army plane from Algeria. They fly over all ships, looking for contraband carriers taking arms to the rebels. Still another facet of the turmoil in which we live, the uncertainty that makes all plans for the future a matter of optimism rather than relative certainty.

The mountains of the North African coast resemble those of Eritrea and Egypt; bare rolling hills, part of the Atlas chain guarding the deserts that were once the granary of Rome. This is one terminal of the old slave routes that ran across the Sahara from Kano and the Sudan, and the hangout of the Barbary pirates. Beneath this blue, calm sea the bottom must be strewn with skeletons of men and ships from thousands of years of history—Greece, Rome, Egypt, France, Venice, Italy, and Great Britain have all fought and traded here.

Soon we shall go through the Straits of Gibraltar—the pillars of Hercules, the very end of the ancient world. And the first to cross it were the Phoenicians, as brave as the space men of today, or braver, since they went into a world utterly unknown and peopled, they believed, by strange sea gods and monsters. Yet they reached England to trade for tin and West Africa for gold.

It is interesting to think of the advances we have made. The Civil War cannon of a hundred years ago were muzzle-loaders, dragged by horses.

Still the coast of North Africa; still the mountains, now pale gray, drop into a purple sea. We hug the coast because the current is weaker here. Porpoises play about our bow. There are a few gulls swinging in the wind.

At midnight we pass Algiers, a blaze of light, a golden stripe on a black horizon that rises a little to a small hill and falls again like a golden bow on the black of the African night. Algeria, the pride of France—its creation—now one of the world's great headaches, another symptom of the disease of unrest and boredom that disfigures the face of our century. Another city on the water, as all cities, with only few exceptions, are on the waters of the sea or up rivers.

FRIDAY, APRIL 21

At lunch time we are out of sight of land, heading for Spain. Tomorrow we shall be back in the Atlantic and we shall have completed our trip around the world, because we have been to the Rock before. No great achievement, but one that has changed our lives. We can never be quite the same again. Our horizons are wider, vastly wider, illuminated by experience. Everything is now richer. The fabric of our lives is shot with the gold of distant travels. Names that six months ago were no more than words now ring bells that chime in the wind of memory.

At 4 A.M. we pass the Rock, its black mass a pyramid crowned with a gray cloud against a night-blue sky. There is a small light like a star on its tip, a flashing lighthouse at its foot. Across the straits are the last lights of Ceuta. Beyond us to the west in the darkness of the Atlantic lie the Azores.

APRIL 25

Tuesday at dawn we arrived at the Azores. Dark gray island peaks sticking up out of the sea like the limbs of a drowned continent. With daylight they took form. Ruled along the hillsides, sculptured green terraces showed up. White, red-roofed villages, waterfalls brown with erosion from recent rains poured ribbons of water over the cliffs into the sea. We saw gulls again, herring gulls and terns.

I thought of the lines I had learned at school: "At Flores in the Azores Sir Richard Grenville lay." That was fifty years ago. All the time, right through the trip, this turning of known names into real places has been like a kind of miracle, like meeting famous people one has read about "in the flesh" as the term is—places on the earth instead of names on maps and in books.

On the last island two volcanic peaks have recently sprung up, leaving the lighthouse grounded with two humps like those of a camel between it and the sea. Perhaps Atlantis was stirring.

This is somewhere we must come one day, for, except as a landing field for transatlantic planes, time seems to have stood still here. How many of us are there who, like Canute and the waves, would like to pause, to stop the clock, so that we might have time to think?

SATURDAY, APRIL 29

Tonight we had the Captain's Dinner, a farewell party, with chicken, schnapps, beer, and speeches. Brought together fortuitously, we would now all separate again. There was no element of sadness. No great friendships had been made. Everyone was tired of the ship and tired of each other. A group of young people can get on well just because they are young and as yet undifferentiated; with older people the opposite is true. However, in the glow of the candlelight, and schnapps, a feeling of well being and good will settled like a hen upon us. The day after tomorrow we would be home, free of this steel, water-borne nest, and have hatched out on our own.

That was what we thought when we went on deck to look at the full moon casting a silver track over the sea. Everything was calm, the sea smooth. There was little wind, but high in the sky big black clouds were racing over the moon, covering it like blankets frilled with silver, and then racing on.

At midnight the sea became rough. At dawn we were in a hurricane. Hardly moving, we headed into it, just riding the waves. Looking out of the porthole, we saw only a wild waste of water, an ocher-colored desert dotted with the white-flowered shrubs of the breaking waves, their blooms tossed like a gift to the hands of the whipping wind, which seized them, smashed them into nothing, and flung them down— shards—into the marbled foam that curded the dark valleys of the rolling ocean.

Clouds, shapeless, disordered as plucked feathers, scudded over a livid, citron-tinted sky. The gray horizon was jagged with great hard-edged dunes of water that grew in size as they rolled toward us in serried hills, one behind the other, like lines of charging cavalry, each divided by a wide valley streaked with sweatlike veins that ran upward to meet the white mane crests of the stallion sea.

In the glass-smooth troughs there were small smoking fires whose plumes, caught by the wind, were extinguished, but, refusing to die, burned up again in dandelion puffs. The seas were dark gun metal, the dull olive of dying, trampled leaves, but at the crests, before they broke, caught at an angle against the sky, they were jeweled—aquamarine, turquoise, set in steel and diamond white.

We stared out, frightened. Anyone but a fool is frightened at the majesty of such phenomena—at the power of the waves and the wind and the anger of God. The steel skin of the ship shivered beneath the blows of the squalls like the hide of a nervous horse. There was no vibration from the engine. We were only just ticking over, only using enough power to keep us facing the tremendous seas that roared down upon us.

Everything in the cabin was adrift. Everything that had been up was down and everything that had been in was out. The sofa mattress had left the springs and lay like something dead on the floor. The drawers had come out, distributed their contents, and then quietly slid to rest. Two plates voyaged from one side of the cabin to the other with every roll. We saved the whiskey bottle that had become hysterical and was rolling madly. We opened it and had a good drink, and we had not had breakfast yet. This Dutch courage made us feel better. We became heroic and decided that if we were going down at least we should die together. We also decided that from all we had read drowning was not a too unpleasant way of ending one's life. And if we saw our whole life in review, as was reported, we should repeat some quite interesting experiences.

Of course there was no real danger, but it's quite easy to be frightened by something you do not understand.

In the saloon things were adrift too. But more or less under control. Our friend Ole, the third officer, stood with his legs apart, leaning and swaying with the movement of the ship, like a cowboy on a bucking horse. We should be delayed, he said. We had guessed that. If you stand still you are delayed.

The waves averaged thirty feet in height, he said. He was enjoying it because not much happened to break the monotony at sea. There was nothing to worry about. We had a fine captain, a fine crew, and a fine ship with a seven-thousand-horsepower motor. With that he left us, and we tried to eat, holding onto the table with one hand, eating with the other and trying to save some of the food on the table and the crockery as best we could.

One objection to a storm is the discomfort. It's hard to eat, sit, sleep, read, or move. There was, too, a sense of anti-climax. We had all said good-by, had all parted spiritually from each other, and now we were back together again, being flung into each other's arms, like peas in a saucepan, by the rolling seas.

Twenty-four hours later we were out of it. We had done eighty miles instead of the usual three hundred plus. But the storm, with winds of sixty miles an hour or more, had gone past us and was roaring off toward Europe.

The passengers in their shore-going clothes looked odd. None of us appeared to recognize each other in suits, hats, and caps. Some of the women had on high heels. Some of them had their hair curled, their nails painted. We were not going to be too late after all—just one day. And then another storm hit us.

In an hour, from a calm sea, we were in another hurricane or a piece of the same one—a kind of second installment. This time we were much braver and Tiny was back at her post by the forward window. I do not know how many hours she has spent in the last few months just staring out to sea. She must have some seagoing blood somewhere way back. She also has some laundryman blood in her because she cannot see a faucet without beginning to wash something. These appear to be her two main bloodlines.

The seas were enormous, but much the same in form and color to those of the storm we had just gone through. Tiny was staring out at it and I was lying in my bunk trying to read when Tiny shouted, "Look out!"

The cabin was suddenly darkened as the green water cut off all light. It came in a kind of slow motion. First Tiny's cry and then I saw the wave, a monster, a mountain, among the hills. It grew higher, turned from green to black as it reared up—black as the belly of a black horse plunging over us. Then Tiny screamed as if she was hurt. When I got to her she was on her knees with water sloshing all around her.

In spite of the port having a rubber flange and being screwed up, the pressure of the wave, running into hundreds of tons, had forced the water into the cabin with such force that it had knocked Tiny down. She was soaked to the skin.

It took the stewardesses a couple of hours to mop the water up. Captain Bergan said that the wave had reached the bridge and it must have been sixty feet high. He said sometimes waves like that stove in the whole window, not breaking the glass but smashing the bolts that hold the frame to the hull. So we were lucky.

That one wave tore a big chest bolted to the foredeck from its seating. It smashed a mahogany seat amidships and twisted one of the davits. We spent the rest of the day imagining what would happen to a ship if her engines failed, and picturing a sailing ship wallowing about with her masts gone. How near we were to the truth. When we did get ashore a couple of days later we heard that the training schooner *Albatross* had gone down in the same storm, with much loss of life—perhaps while we were talking about it.

But no one is on board any more. We are all projected into the future. All back in America. These last days a limbo, an anticlimax before our dispersal. Even the ship's company feels it. Most of them are being paid off. But the ship itself will continue in orbit round and round the world.

Tonight, the last night at sea, the sun went down symbolically in a bright red ball like a Japanese flag—sinking into America. Still going West, still pursuing this blood-red sun, we are headed for New York, where we began, and the circle will be complete.

SOME POLITICAL
IMPLICATIONS

Appendix One

In June of this year, 1961, a letter of mine to the *New York Times* was printed:

Soviet Gains in Far East

Basic Gap in West's Understanding Is Emphasized

The writer of the following letter, a South African, is the author of "Watch for the Dawn," "Congo Song," and "The African Giant," among other books.

To the Editor of The New York Times:

Having just returned from the Far East, where we spent several months, going from port to port in a freighter, the situation that has arisen there is no surprise. The only surprise is that it can have surprised anyone.

There are millions of people there who do not even have "chains to lose." People with no homes, no clothes and no food. Nothing could be worse than what they endure now. Any change might be for the better.

This does not apply to Hong Kong, where the refugees from Red China accept hardship as the price of freedom with unbelievable good nature, but they were peasants robbed of their land.

It is here that the immense gap between the East and West is most apparent, for here we are confronted by people with no material possessions whatsoever. This is the river we have failed to bridge. What is the good of talking about refrigerators or hygiene or the American way of life to men who sleep in the open and grub in rotting garbage for food? What do they know of million-dollar dams, of new roads?

Present Needs

What they need is something here and now, that they can see and use, such as some single-furrow plows, some small weirs and dams, a few thousand Rhode Island cocks; little things, cheap things, but things they would know came from us.

If we build a road, how is a peasant a hundred miles away or even ten miles away to know we did it when he is told it is a gift from the Russians? Even bags of rice from the United States have been marked as gifts from the U.S.S.R.

Every technician the Russians send to any country is first taught the language, so each artisan is an agent extolling the virtues of Communists and a spy reporting on the internal situation. Compare this with our diplomatic corps who, with few exceptions, can only operate through interpreters, never mix with people, consorting only with their peers from other embassies.

The Communist aims are simple. They are after the rubber, tin and other riches of Southeast Asia. There is the beginning of a pincer movement already with Vietnam and Laos in the north and Indonesia in the south. We had trouble picking up rubber in Java though the godowns were full of it. It was earmarked for Russia.

In Jakarta the bookstores were full of well-produced, illustrated books and magazines at very low prices with such titles as Red China, The New China, U.S.S.R. Today, The Five-Year Plan. These were all subsidized, all propaganda. The books in English were ten times the price. What choice has a young literate man? He wants to read and he reads what he can afford to buy.

Role for Peace Corps

What is the answer to all this? Perhaps the Peace Corps may be an answer, though there seems to me some danger of its backfiring and even being infiltrated by Communists.

But basically the problem is one of human relations and understanding, of ceasing to think we can buy love with dollars, or that our materialistic culture is the only possible way of life.

I have heard people asking the price of things in Bangkok, getting the quotation in bahts and saying "What is that in real money?" I have seen women wearing white cotton gloves because they were afraid of contamination. I saw them hold their noses in the streets of Saigon because of the smell.

There may be other keys to the door of Asia, but perhaps Orientals are just like us in that they like to be liked.

STUART CLOETE

New York, June 12, 1961

The situation in Southeast Asia grows worse day by day. The communists hold North Vietnam and most of Laos. There are still pockets of communist guerrillas in Burma, Malaya, and the Philippines. Indonesia is committed to Russia. The only anti-communists in the republic are the rebels. China, having absorbed Thibet, presses down on India, where there is a strong Communist party.

The prizes are magnificent. The tin and rubber of Malaya. The rice bowl of Thailand and Cambodia. The unbelievable and undeveloped riches of Indonesia.

None of these are countries we can fight in even if we are prepared to do so. Not only are the climate and terrains unsuited to mechanized warfare (there are few roads and no good ones), but, and this is the crux of the question, there is no enemy. We should find ourselves, as the Foreign Legion did in Indo-China, with no one to fight. No fixed lines, no definite objectives, no front, no rear. In front of us, all around us, and behind us would be a mixture of guerrillas, bandits, Chinese, and Vietnamese— regulars, criminals, peasants seeking revenge, blackmail gangs, patriots, traitors, and spies all blending into each other and out again, each being one thing today and something else tomorrow.

Secrecy, vital in all military and political operations, is impossible to maintain, since interpreters must be used to convey all orders or receive information. We have few nationals who can speak oriental languages. In this we differ from the Russians, whose whole staff from ambassador to chauffeur has to be a linguist.

Nor can SEATO act unless called upon to do so by the government of a country that is being attacked. But countries are not being attacked. South Vietnam is not being attacked, but averages a hundred political murders and other outrages directed against well known anti-communists a week.

We can count on no love. The billions we have spent have not reached the people for whom they were intended. In Korea, Taipan, and South Vietnam we have supported rulers merely because they were anti-communist. They were and are anti-communist, but spread their net wide enough to include those who were not communists but against their regime. In Peru it is estimated that only 5 per cent of the aid sent there reached the people. The rest stuck to the fingers of the ruling classes. There seems to be no reason to suppose that things in Southeast Asia are much better.

This is the crux of the question. The problem is far more economic than political. The masses want political change only because they think, or have been conned into thinking, that the change will better their economic position.

We have to change our whole outlook on the underdeveloped nations. It is not education they need—not yet. They need food. Not handouts, but assistance in growing food. Know-how, plows, dams, and roads to move food to markets.

Our problem, in the mechanized West, is that we are moving into a period of automation and unemployment due to prosperity with leisure, and what to do with it is a major problem.

The great masses of Asia, Africa, and South America seldom get a square meal. Some live and die without once in their lives getting enough to eat. This gap between us, the haves, and the have-nots is increasing every day, and the greater the distance between us the less chance we have of understanding each other.

Literacy is splendid, but food is better. A man can be perfectly happy who cannot read, provided his belly is full. This is the basic truth.

There is a war going on in South Vietnam, an almost invisible civil war. It is in a sense the same war that the French fought and lost. They were military imperialists and were defeated. Ngo Dinh Diem is a ruthless dictator whom we are backing because he is anti-communist.

The communists are winning this war by killing a hundred or so civilians a week, and by so doing intimidating a thousand. What are the Vietnamese to resist? These communists are their own people. How are they to resist them?

The key to all warfare is physical geography. In this case the three great river systems of Indo-China. The Red River, with its fertile delta, is already in communist hands. The Mekong River, running along the Thailand border, may fall into their hands. The remaining river is the Mae Nam in Thailand.

We, with our road and railroad systems, do not realize the importance of rivers in these Eastern countries. They are the only means of transportation and run through the most fertile, alluvial rice-producing valleys.

The picture is simple, which may be why we do not see it. With the explosion of the atomic bomb the immensely long period of history and prehistory that began with the discovery of fire has ended.

Almost simultaneously there has been a population explosion and the outbreak of a religious war (because communism is a religion in the sense that it is a belief) that has split the world down the middle, with both sides playing for the uncommitted nations. The vast Moslem, Buddhist, Hindu, and animist masses, who are at once undeveloped and immensely rich in natural resources.

In all these countries the young men are on the rampage, preaching violence and nationalism, the old leaders and chiefs in retreat, and the moderate, go-slow majority intimidated into submission.

To add to the confusion, there is the certainty that within a decade almost every nation will have an atomic bomb of one sort or another.

War, politics, and religion have always been different facets of the same national ambition—cross or crescent, hammer or sickle —always objects of both terror and veneration.

We tend to see every revolution, every uprising of angry young men, as communist inspired. Some are and some are not, but all are grist to the communist mill, and, where possible, assisted by communist technicians and arms.

With our views, our short-term policies of expediency, we fail to understand the long historic view of such nations as Russia and China. Since Peter the Great, Russian policies have remained the same, while those of China have scarcely changed in forty centuries.

Russia wants to move South toward Constantinople, Turkey, Iran and Iraq, Afghanistan and India. There is nothing new about this.

The Chinese intend to regain their ancient powers in Southeast Asia.

Both are very thorough. Both began looking ahead and training men years ago to go into these countries they are after, teaching them their language, their customs, and their history.

They are doing with men what we are trying to do with money —and what we used to do in the good old days with gunboats. People always take money, but no one likes being a debtor. There is no better way to lose a friend, especially if the money has strings on it, still more if it supports a corrupt and tyrannous government.

Whereas men are always welcome. If I meet a foreigner who talks English, I am impressed that he took the pains to learn, even though I know he did it only because such knowledge would benefit him. Other people are no different. And apart from this, how, without knowing the language, can we communicate? Through signs? Through interpreters who lie?

Nor when we do go abroad do we behave with either dignity or even common sense. We consort only with other Americans and we pay our foreign service hardship pay for living abroad, something that cannot endear us to our hosts. We talk about real money, meaning U.S. dollars. We complain about food and toilet facilities. We are noisy. We get drunk. We make crude passes at their girls. And then we are surprised that we are neither respected nor loved.

This is where we stand today. This is our jumping-off point. For we have about reached the point of no return. We can face the truth about ourselves, change our approach and win—because no country really wants to go communist if it can get a better deal —or we can go down. Not today or tomorrow—but in X number of years.

This has been the story of a journey with observations on what we saw, and the thoughts that occurred to us as we traveled. Other things would occur to other people, since each man sees everything with different eyes. The businessman and the artist see different worlds. Some people even succeed in seeing nothing at all in spite of every explosion being supposed to produce a recoil of equal strength. The result of a blow is a bruise, the result of an emotional impact an impression. Here, as far as we are concerned, are the blows and the bruises, the impacts and the impressions, none necessarily correct, since experiences of this nature are very personal and each man a mirror who reflects a different image. Even a five-month trip is superficial. The skin of the orange, to which the world is so often compared, remains unbroken, its heart untouched. But at least we have become aware of its pulsing heart, of humanity—of men—an unbelievable number of men striving for unknown goals. Of the past, trying in one great effort to enter a present that is already the future. Time has become so vastly accelerated that even highly developed nations find that they must run if they wish to remain in the same position. How, then, are the underdeveloped countries that have not yet learned to walk going to catch up? How are they to gain the concepts of justice, honor, and individual liberty, which are assumed to be the basis of our culture?

How are they free if they produce no finished goods and depend on the industrialized nations for every cup, saucepan, and automobile? What is this new freedom? Is it something to offer on the market place of commerce—dickering with both the West and the East for the best terms on which to sell their birthright?

No one can reasonably uphold colonialism. No one can reasonably condone it indefinitely. But it is possible to say that this intermediate stage, in the progress of many nations, has been passed too swiftly. The chick hatched under the maternal hen of great metropolitan nations has been abandoned before it was fully fledged—that these are chicks that peep rather than young cocks who crow. Our only aim can be to prevent the communist housewives from wringing their necks and popping them into the Marxist pot before they grow their spurs.

What we have seen, and sailed past, from the Philippines to Gibraltar—except for Thailand—are the old colonial empires. The Philippines, Hong Kong, Indo-China, Indonesia, Malaya, Ceylon, India, Eritrea, Ethiopia, Egypt, Kenya, Tunisia, Algeria, and Morocco, all are in a state of flux and political ferment. Our problem is to discover the emulsion that will blend these different cultures—to deal with time in two opposite ways: to slow up the nationalist forces that will lead to economic disintegration, while at the same time accelerating the development of each area. But the problems are Hydra-headed. How are improved health services reconciled with populations that have already outrun their food supply? How does one deal with a starving India that has a cattle population of twenty million useless but sacred cattle? How does one solve the question of the Tamils in Ceylon? Of the Chinese in Malaya? How is hatred turned into love? How is the xenophobia once directed against the white man to be prevented from becoming tribal and breaking out into civil war? How do we prevent the Chinese from wanting sons to pray for them when they die? Or the Moslems' acceptance of their fate—rich or poor— as the will of Allah?

It is we of the West, with our Industrial Revolution, with our ideas of freedom, with our rapid communications, and our insatiable greed for raw materials, who have upset the relative stability of the world. This is our baby. How right have we been? Were some of these people better off before we disturbed them —before we gave them automatic weapons to replace their bows and spears? Are we convinced in our hearts that all this is progress? That happiness and stability cannot exist without affluence? May we not by reducing infant mortality upset the law of survival and produce still further misery by bringing to maturity individuals incapable of living fully in an environment we are incapable of improving?

Only one thing can bring peace anywhere, and that is a full belly. But I do not see the key to this lock. There are few full bellies in East Asia and every minute hundreds of new babies are being born.

Freedom, Uhuru, Liberté are magnificent, but they are only words—

Here are the answers:

Food, love, understanding, and contraception—all on a scale that defies the imagination.

GENERAL ADVICE, EXPENSES, CLOTHES, LUGGAGE

Appendix Two

Do not eat raw vegetables, as most of them are fertilized with night soil. There is no better fertilizer, but it can carry various diseases, so leave the salad alone except in the best hotels. Here are some dos and don'ts from the Hong Kong guidebook which seemed superfluous to me.

Don't carry on your person or in your luggage any gold bullion to or from Hong Kong. Don't carry or use drugs. Tourists who carry or use opium, heroin, morphine, or other drugs are subject to imprisonment. Don't carry firearms and/or dangerous weapons, including flick knives. The offender is subject to prosecution.

Any person found guilty of cruelty to animals, such as keeping them in an overcrowded cage, or carrying them upside down, is liable to prosecution. It is illegal to remove young birds from their nest.

It is illegal to carry, buy, or sell obscene pictures and films. The maximum penalty for the offense is a fine of $5000 or six months' imprisonment. It is illegal to play mahjong or any other card game for cash stakes. No spitting. The offender is liable to pay a fine of not more than $500. Loafing in the street late at night is prohibited. Unbuttoned trousers may cause the wearer to be fined.

The following seem to be a more useful selection:

Upon landing from a ship or a plane, be sure to check your luggage before leaving them with the porter; ascertain the porter's fee beforehand; do not let any porter handle your luggage who does not wear the proper uniform.

Be sure to have adequate clothing at hand to cope with Hong Kong's fickle weather.

Leave your valuables in the custody of your hostess or the management of your hotel when you go out.

Always carry your passport and other documents with you, but beware of pickpockets.

Don't carry large amounts of cash in your wallet. Use traveler's checks. A letter of credit is useful on an extended trip.

Be sure to have adequate small-denomination bank notes in your wallet for paying taxi drivers, sampan girls, etc., who are unable to change large-denomination notes.

Always patronize reputable shops and be sure to get an *invoice and certificate of origin* for whatever you may buy.

At the money exchanger's counter, make sure that the amount you get is correct.

It is always preferable to receive callers in the parlor of your hotel, not in your room.

On the principles of hygiene, it is safer to patronize the first-class restaurants, particularly those recommended by the Hong Kong Tourist Association or the Hong Kong handbook.

They also suggest that you:

Don't get drunk.

Be sure to get enough sleep.

Keep to the left of the road, whether you are walking or driving a car, in accordance with the local traffic regulations.

Don't go to a first-class restaurant or night club in your shirt sleeves.

Don't swim at any beach not recommended by the guidebooks, or where sharks have just been sighted.

Beware of unexpected onrush of flood waters, when you swim in a stream or pool near the hills in the rainy season.

Don't venture into prohibited areas or out-of-the-way places.

If you have any knotty problem, consult your consulate, trade commissioner, or other diplomatic representative of your country.

Be tolerant and try your best to avoid quarreling or coming to blows with anyone.

If you intend to stay at your hotel longer than the period

booked for, be sure to notify the hotel management as early as possible.

If you intend to stay in Hong Kong longer than the period specified in your visa, be sure to make application to the immigration office well ahead of time for an extension.

ADDITIONAL HINTS

1. Drink bottled water except where it is known to be safe, such as Singapore and Penang.

2. Don't touch ices or drink even bottled water to which ice has been added except in first-class hotels.

3. Don't eat fruit that has been peeled or that has no peel.

4. Don't catch cold in air-conditioned bars and restaurants. Take a coat or scarf with you.

5. Don't get overtired.

6. Attend to any cuts at once.

7. Don't spend all your money in Hong Kong if you go there first.

TAKE WITH YOU

flashlight
duplicate keys to suitcases
checkbook
credit card(s)
American Express checks
a letter of credit
toilet paper
spare socks
Kleenex
safety razor and blades
nail scissors
pocketknife
Scotch Tape
2 spare ball-point pens
sunglasses
1 extra pair reading glasses
  (and prescription)
6 spare passport photos
alarm clock

Paste a card with your name and address inside each piece of luggage.
Take suitcases, not trunks.
Mark all luggage with a colored stripe.

field glasses
sewing kit
books—paperbacks. At least twelve for each month at sea.

CLOTHES

WOMEN

1 tweed suit
1 dark suit
1 wool dress
4 blouses (nylon)
1 afternoon dress
1 cocktail dress
2 sweaters
1 set wool undies
2 silk dresses
4 washable cotton dresses
1 medium-weight coat
1 raincoat (light plastic)
2 scarves
1 bathing suit and cap
1 dressing gown
1 bed jacket
stockings
3 sets underclothes
2 pairs walking shoes
2 pairs street shoes
2 pairs dress shoes
1 large pocketbook
1 hat for sun
2 pairs pajamas

MEN

2 suits (1 dark)
sports jackets (1 thick, 1 thin)
6 cotton or drip-dry shirts
6 sets underclothes
handkerchiefs
2 scarves
3 ties
raincoat
overcoat
2 pairs walking shoes
1 pair dress shoes
2 sweaters
1 hat for sun
bathing suit
slippers
2 pairs pajamas

MEDICINES

Entero Vioform (for diarrhea)

Dr. Whitfield Ointment (for prickly heat). This can be bought anywhere in the East.

Johnson's prickly-heat powder

Any ointment for athlete's foot (for between toes and on folds of toes) and powder (put in shoes and socks)

Tiger Balm (for headaches and strains). Buy this anywhere in the East.

eye wash
eye bath
eye drops
ear drops
aspirin
sleeping pills
Dramamine
embrocation (Elliman's or Sloane's Linament)
iodine
laxative
thermometer
Band-Aids
bandages
Alka-Seltzer
corn plasters
adhesive tape
enema
ice bag

EXPENSES

The best hotels all run about $12 to $17 a day for a double air-conditioned room and bath.

The best meals, with wine, cost about $10 for two.

Tours run from $20 to $60 for two people.

Tips 15 per cent.

These figures are maximum de luxe costs. They could be cut by staying on the ship, by eating more cheaply and taking fewer tours, by having rooms with just a fan instead of air-conditioning.

The whole world, East and West, is now geared to the American tourist and prices are based on the assumption that we are all rich—which we are compared to them. Still, on the whole, everything is much cheaper than in the U.S.A.

Chinese meals are cheaper and often better and safer than European, and it does not take long to learn to eat with chopsticks, and in most places knives and forks are available.

Ashore $40 per day should be ample for hotels, food, and taxis. Allow another $30 for tours as an average. Both these quotations for two people are on the high side.

Here are some sample figures:

Double Room	*U.S. Currency*
Royal Orleans	$15.45
Bel Air, Los Angeles	25.50
Manila Hotel	11.00
Hong Kong	16.00
Saigon	13.00
Bangkok	17.00
Singapore	12.00
Kuala Lumpur	12.00
Penang	12.00

A long tour from Suez to Cairo and back, including lunch and dinner for two   60.00

A tour around Penang without lunch, for two   20.00

THINGS TO BUY

MANILA

Carvings, lace, and local fabrics.

HONG KONG (Free Port)

Clothes, field glasses, cameras, etc. (We bought sports jackets for $24 U.S., two-piece dresses—raw silk—made to order in twenty-four hours for $42, silk dressing gown for $10, and field glasses at $8.00.)

SAIGON

Paintings on silk, lacquer trays, ivory.

BANGKOK

Thai silk, silver, gold, jewels, brass, bronze, temple rubbings.

SINGAPORE (Free Port)

Batik from Java, carvings, Indian silk, cameras, etc.

CEYLON

Jewels, carvings, lace, tortoise shell.

CAIRO

North African leatherwork, Egyptian appliqué hangings, silver, jewelry, perfume.

EXPENSES AND ADVICE

These are our expenses. For others they might come to less or more. There is no reason to spend the night ashore in the best hotel or eat expensive meals. One can generally sleep on board if one wishes. There is no need to buy clothes or souvenirs.

Because I am not a first-class mathematician I always get taken with the rates of exchange. A smarter man can save money.

One thing is certain—however much money you bring, it will not be enough to do everything you want to do. On the other hand, you are not likely, or we at any rate are not likely, to pass this way again, and it's no good saying six months later, "I wish we had done that."

My figures are approximate. They are as close as I can come, and give a rough idea of the expenses incurred on the trip.

Before you buy anything, think where you will put it, wear it, to whom you will give it, and how it will pack.

The $300 in traveler's checks you may carry on you is more than many a man here may make in two years.

When buying your ticket specify a front cabin. Every ship has two of them. They are generally bigger and have more windows.

IN ROUND FIGURES

We spent between December 14, 1960, and May 1, 1961:
Fares for two people $2600
Expenses on the trip other than purchases 3000
Purchases 500
                                        Total $6100

We scrimped on nothing and bought what we fancied in the way of clothes and small portable objects, carvings, pictures, lacquer, and odd bits of cheap jewelry and brass. We took every available tour, even one into the jungle in Bangkok.

These expenses could therefore be cut in half at least, though a great deal of pleasure and excitement would be lost. What is not seen this time is not likely to be seen at all.

MONEY

American Express checks in $10, $20, and $100 denominations.
A letter of credit would be a good idea too. I wish I had had one.

EXCHANGE RATES IN ROUGH FIGURES:

Manila: 3.25 pesos, call it 3 .... $1.00 U.S.
Hong Kong: 5.67 dollars, call it 5 .... $1.00 U.S.
South Vietnam: 82 piasters, call it 100 .... $1.00 U.S.
Thailand: 20.78 ticals (baht), call it 20 ... $1.00 U.S.
Indonesia: 45-300 rupiahs .... $1.00 U.S.
Singapore: 3.03 dollars, call it 3 .... $1.00 U.S.
Ethiopia: 2.50 dollars .... $1.00 U.S.
Ceylon: 4.77 rupees, call it 5 .... $1.00 U.S.
Egypt: 2.88 piasters, call it 3 .... $1.00 U.S.

These round figures are good enough to check the approximate value of any goods.

Do not change too much anywhere, though. There are always money-changers at the next place you reach who will change the balance left over without too much loss.